American Druidry

American Druidry

Crafting the Wild Soul

KIMBERLY D. KIRNER

BLOOMSBURY ACADEMIC
LONDON • NEW YORK • OXFORD • NEW DELHI • SYDNEY

BLOOMSBURY ACADEMIC
Bloomsbury Publishing Plc
50 Bedford Square, London, WC1B 3DP, UK
1385 Broadway, New York, NY 10018, USA
29 Earlsfort Terrace, Dublin 2, Ireland

BLOOMSBURY, BLOOMSBURY ACADEMIC and the Diana logo are trademarks of
Bloomsbury Publishing Plc

First published in Great Britain 2024

A catalogue record for this book is available from the British Library.

A catalog record for this book is available from the Library of Congress.

ISBN: HB: 978-1350-26411-3
PB: 978-1350-26412-0
ePDF: 978-1350-26413-7
eBook: 978-1350-26414-4

Typeset by Deanta Global Publishing Services, Chennai, India
Printed and bound in Great Britain

To find out more about our authors and books visit www.bloomsbury.com and
sign up for our newsletters

For All Existences—My Teachers and Kin

CONTENTS

List of Illustrations viii
Acknowledgments ix

Introduction: The Why, What, and How of This Book 1

The First Triad—All as Sacred: Place, Time, and the Body 15

1 Claimed by Place 17
2 Echoes through Time 28
3 Becoming a Body 39
4 The First Spiral: Recognizing a Participatory World 50

The Second Triad—All as Conscious: Relational Spirituality 81

5 A Congregation of Nature Spirits 83
6 A Community of Ancestors 95
7 A Covenant with the Shining Ones 106
8 The Second Spiral: An Ecocentric Community 118

The Third Triad—All as Worthy: Living Druidry 145

9 The Foundation of Right Action: Knowledge 147
10 The Foundation for Peace: Justice 158
11 The Foundation for Divine Connection: Loving Others 170
12 The Third Spiral: The Druid in the World 182

Bibliography 207
Index 222

ILLUSTRATIONS

1   The personhood of place 17

2   The web of time 28

3   The cauldrons of the body 39

4   Communion with horse 83

5   The ancestral tree 95

6   The Morrigan 106

7   Learning 147

8   Peace-making 158

9   Loving 170

ACKNOWLEDGMENTS

This book is the result of so many years of conversations with other Druids and Pagans, all of which were formative for this work. I would like to particularly thank, however, fifteen Druids who were interviewed for this book and who encouraged me as I wrote it (in no particular order): Joseph, Reverend Kirk Thomas, Elizabeth Boerner, Dana O'Driscoll, Siobhan, Murtagh anDoile, Reverend Monika Kojote, Fiona McMillan, Rory Harper, Kat Reeves, Dawn, Maggie, John Beckett, and those who wished to remain anonymous. Without their participation and insights, this book would not be possible. I would also like to thank those whose mentoring over the years shaped my professional work: Gene (E. N.) Anderson, David Kronenfeld, and Sabina Magliocco. Last, but certainly not least, I must thank my parents, Jan Mills and Mark Kirner, for all of the time we spent in nature, for demonstrating how to build a personally meaningful spiritual life, and for loving me as the weird child I was (and am).

Introduction

The Why, What, and How of This Book

When I was approached about writing an autoethnography on American Druidry, I found the idea exciting but also a bit nerve-wracking. While I have increasingly moved into research in Pagan studies, and therefore into a role as an insider-researcher, my primary training has been in environmental and medical anthropology—and secondarily in religious studies and the anthropology of religion. It is at times uncomfortable to feel as vulnerable as I do when I am writing about my own community. Autoethnography was another giant leap forward into leaning into this discomfort and newness because I was not only writing about my community but also writing about myself.

However, I think it was worthwhile to meet the invitation I had offered to me in this book. My purposes behind this book are threefold. First, I wanted to provide the reader with an accessible and detailed account of what a practicing Druid experiences—explored through themes relevant to this spiritual movement. Druidry, as you will learn, is a spirituality (and I argue a religion—but more on that later) that is neither orthodoxic nor orthopraxic, and that has no authoritative text or leadership. My work focuses on three dimensions of Druidry as it is practiced and experienced: the ways that Druidry shapes our orientations to reality (to place, time, and the body); the ways that Druidry connects us in relationship to other-than-living-humans (to nature spirits, ancestors, and gods); and the ways that Druidry informs our actions in the world (through core values and our struggles to enact them).

My second purpose was to describe how the Druidic experience can be understood through psychological and cognitive processes that guide both the ways individuals come to have spiritual experiences—particularly the ways in which people come to have personal experiences that are mystical or magical in nature—and the ways in which Druids come to have a religious culture without any authoritative body or text and indeed, despite often practicing Druidry as solitary practitioners. In essence, the second purpose of the book is to bring an analytical framework to my own (and others') experiences and practices as Druids, to explore how our considerable commonalities of Druidic practice and experience can arise in the fertile ground where our brains and bodies meet the natural world around us.

Finally, because Druidry is organized and functions differently than many world religions (though it has spread globally), it is a useful new religious movement to explore how scholars might expand the boundaries many have set around the concept of religion. Druids themselves disagree on whether Druidry is a religion in the way they understand the term from an American overcultural perspective, and the reasons for their hesitation are instructive for scholars trying to define religion in ways that remove Christo-centrism (the way that Christianities permeate American overculture, including academic religious studies). Understanding how Druidry works can help us understand how decentralized new religious movements operate in a globalized world in which people can, for the first time in human history, seek out spiritualities that speak to who they are rather than fitting themselves (or not) into a limited range of localized options. Druidry offers an invitation to the scholar to consider their definition of religion and what fits into it, and to wrestle with what we consider essential to religion and why.

These purposes were informed by what other recent extensive academic works on contemporary Druids have not covered, and a few of these are worth briefly discussing up front, particularly so that the reader understands what has been left out of this book and where to locate such information. I do not discuss ancient Druids and I only tangentially refer to the Revival Druids, who were Druids practicing esoteric traditions from the mid-1600s to early 1900s. Contemporary Druidry has been informed to varying degrees (depending on the individual Druid and Druidic organization) by both scholarship on ancient Druids and by imagined pasts, and to a greater degree by the Revival Druids. Ronald Hutton's *Blood and Mistletoe* (2009) provides an excellent, detailed history of the Druids—both in what we can know and in what we cannot know (and there is much we cannot know due to the Druids having been from a pre-literate society, so the scant sources on them are from outsiders—frequently enemies or from a time after their societies had been converted to Catholicism and colonized).

Michael Cooper's ethnography on contemporary Druids, *Contemporary Druidry* (2011), focuses primarily on linking these historical sources to the ways Druids (both in the United States and in England, in three particular Druidic organizations) imagine their connections to the past through the process of ancientization, of pushing backward the origins of a new religious movement into an ancient past. Additionally, he addresses the diversity of beliefs Druids have about such matters as the afterlife. While he is a Christian, Cooper's work was considered balanced and fair by Druids, and provided a valuable discussion on the ways some Druids relate to their imagined past in ways I will not duplicate in this work. Rather, I focus on contemporary Druids' practices and experiences, and particularly how these are developed in and give rise to a Druidic religious culture and community—even among Druids unaffiliated with one of the larger Druid organizations.

"Belief" is a tricky term in Druidry, as it is often associated with Christian conceptualizations of it: of holding tightly to one or more doctrines held in common with a religious community and often considered necessary by the community or a religious authority to maintain group recognition of one's religious identity. This does not exist in Druidry, so Druids often dislike the term "belief." Instead, I speak of my own and other Druids' current understandings, working hypotheses, or ideas. For Druids, these are often tied either to their own experiences or to the way they have worked through ideas drawn from many sources—and they are nearly always viewed as subject to change. "Ask three Druids a question and you'll get four answers" is a saying Druids often provide when asked belief-related questions, because Druidry is less about certitude and more about developing a comfort with exploring the unknown, with listening to diverse sources of wisdom, and with change. The saying refers to this openness to revision over time—drawing from new experiences and learning from conversations with diverse others to probe and refine one's own ideas rather than to shore them up.

This internal diversity in Druidry happens for several reasons. Druidry is not a mutually exclusive religion or spiritual path. Druids can be other religions simultaneously with being Druids. While this is unusual for Abrahamic religions (most Jews, Muslims, and Christians—though not all—believe in exclusivity of their religious identity, so you can only be one in religion at a time), it is common in indigenous religions and in Asian religions. Druids can freely choose to practice other religions alongside their Druidry, though some religions are more difficult to square to Druidic practices than others. Furthermore, Druidry has no doctrine. No one has the authority to reject you from Druidic identity because you do not conform, and there is little that demands conformity anyway. As I will explore in this book, this does not mean that Druidry has no religious culture. However, there is no doctrine—no explicit set of beliefs—to which any Druid must adhere to be recognized by other Druids as a Druid. Instead, Druidry is a constellation of more common and less common practices and ideas. Finally, Druidry is generally viewed as first and foremost an individual spiritual journey, and as such, subject to change as the person has new experiences and ideas. Rather than viewing stasis in spiritual experience and interpretation as desirable, it is viewed as improbable and unimportant. The journey, not the destination, is the primary purpose of Druidic spirituality, and this means people not only have diverse experiences and understandings as Druids but also they view it as likely that their spirituality will change over the course of their lives.

The full breadth of this diversity, along with a detailed description of the demographics of contemporary Druidry, was recently published in Larisa White's *World Druidry* (White 2021). The book explores many dimensions of contemporary Druidry across the world in detail using data generated by a large sample of Druids who took a mixed methods survey. While White's work does not theorize the results, it is a valuable description of contemporary Druids both as a global new religious movement and in the differences that exist between Druid orders and between nations. I was incredibly grateful and relieved to see this work emerge during the time I was working on this book, because it provided a much more robust dataset about Druids as a whole than my own limited survey data (n=135) that I used to inform the choices of themes to discuss in my book. The publication of the book also meant that I could focus more narrowly on select topics in depth, and particularly topics that would afford me the opportunity to explore how scholars can understand the ways decentralized new religious movements work at individual and community levels.

In summary, *Crafting the Wild Soul* describes the Druidic spiritual journey in depth and then offers analysis on how we can understand such a journey through the lens of psychosocial processes that shape the Druid's individual learning and experience, the way that Druidic culture and community forms, and the successes and challenges that Druids experience as they attempt to live out a worldview that is very different from the overculture of the United States.

The What: Druidry and Druidism

If you are new to Druidry, you might have very little idea of what it entails, though you may imagine white-robed figures at Stonehenge. It has been my experience that Americans have few, if any, associations attached to the word "Druid"—in contrast to the ways in which Americans have a very rich set of associations (often negative) attached to the word "witch." Because Druids are highly diverse and without an onus to come to consensus, we also find that while Druids have a conceptualization of their own Druidry, there is no one way that they define the term. Suffice it to say that while I will provide an overarching definition here to orient the reader, this is standing in as a placeholder for a much more nuanced conversation—one worth having, as it illuminates not only how Druids think of themselves but also interesting processes at work in Druidry as a spiritual movement. For now, I will offer that Druidry is generally categorized as a "Pagan tradition" (an umbrella term for new religious movements in the Western world that integrate magic, center nature, and focus extensively on individual development). Druidry is a nature-centered new religious movement inspired by pre-Christian European cultures—and in particular (though not exclusively), the folklore, mythology, and religious traditions of Ireland, Scotland, Wales, and England.

Druids practice in a variety of different orders and as solitary practitioners, sometimes calling themselves Hedge Druids. While there are many small Druid orders, three of the largest and most influential (particularly over the popular literature available on Druidry) are Ár nDraíocht Féin (ADF), the Ancient Order of Druids in America (AODA), and the Order of Bards, Ovates, and Druids (OBOD). ADF and AODA originated in the United States, whereas OBOD originated in England. You may have noticed that I use the term "Druidry," not Druidism. This is deliberate. "Druidism" is a term primarily used by ADF, which is structured and functions differently than AODA or OBOD. This distinction is therefore significant for a study of this type. ADF is structured as a religious organization in the United States, and it self-avowedly leans both toward polytheism (a belief in many gods) and reconstructionism (the attempt to use scholarly works on ancient pre-Christian Europe to develop contemporary religious practice). Additionally, ADF has supported a clergy-laity model of organization (ordaining leaders).

Druidry, as it is formulated by both AODA and OBOD, and as many solitary practitioners engage in it, lacks these elements. Neither AODA nor OBOD operates in a clergy-laity model, and in fact have deliberately avoided this in favor of a model we might instead consider a gathering of equals (or a gathering of priests). Neither AODA nor OBOD has a singular theology (each individual Druid is encouraged to develop their own, and no consensus is expected in either group). Neither is reconstructionist. AODA draws extensively from Revival Druidry, and OBOD takes inspiration from the folklore and mythology of Ireland, Wales, and England—but both orders now recognize that there are no direct or clear ties to an ancient past. This supports an extremely individualist and highly diverse Druidic community in both orders, and both orders place individual spiritual development and the sacredness of the earth at the center of Druidic spiritual practice.

This book primarily investigates American Druidry, not American Druidism. I include in this book interviews with several people who have, for varying lengths of time, been members of ADF—including at leadership levels. Members of ADF also contributed to the survey data from which I draw in order to occasionally demonstrate points in the analytical essays. However, I do not attempt to fully describe Druidism, in part because I could not do so in an autoethnographic fashion. My own Druidic journey has been shaped primarily by OBOD, and to a lesser, but still significant, extent, by AODA. Yet within the larger umbrella of Druids, like others in these orders, I both recognize ADF Druids as equally Druid and I have had extensive conversations and ritual practice with them, which has also been a force in the ways I have come to understand Druidic community writ large.

The How: Autoethnography as a Bridge between Selves

The opportunity to write this book arose in a moment of synchronicity, one of many that has shaped its eventual development. Synchronicity is a common experience in Druidry and is a basic tenet of magical work—work in which our will is made manifest in the world in ways that are only partially directly caused by clearly connected actions. After tenure, I had been giving much thought to reorienting my academic research toward more vulnerable and personal topics and exploring autoethnography as an approach to writing more engaging, meaningful work. It had always stuck with me that, early in my teaching career, a student had approached me after class and, looking a bit deflated and forlorn, held aloft the book I had assigned and asked me: "Anthropologists always tell the best stories in class. So why are their books so boring?" Years later, Michael Billig (2013) would write about the problem of the academic dialect that limited our reach into a more engaged and public audience. I believed that we had the power to tell stories that could help people empathize with one another, understand themselves better, and become inspired to think more deeply about the human experience. But I was not sure how to get there from where I stood. The opportunity to write this book came at a moment in which I was committing myself to a shift in my research agenda and the ways in which I attempted to communicate with readers, but before I had extensively planned my next steps. Such is the magical life.

Synchronicity, while always feeling like the "yes" from the universe I need to embrace an opportunity, does not make any of the work easy. This has been true of being an anthropologist, of being a Druid, and of writing this book integrating the two selves. Looking back over my life, never so systematically as I had to in order to write this book, I could see that my neuroatypicality led me to a fascination with the human experience and human problems—which drove me to cultural anthropology from the "hard" sciences as an undergraduate. Studying ethnoecology and religious studies as a student led me on an initial dark night of the soul as I searched for a spiritual life and community that fit with my own mystical experiences. Eventually, while in my doctoral program and teaching my first class independently, I had to do some research on new religious movements to develop a lecture. I stumbled onto Druidry through that research and recognized its fit with my own values and experiences. It would be nearly another decade before I began doing research on Druids as an anthropologist and the two communities that had provided me a home began to be integrated rather than existing as two parallel identities.

Yet it was this current research opportunity—this book—that was offered to me like a beautiful piece of fruit from Faery: a gift, but with consequences. A gift that bound me to a process from which I cannot ever return. In saying yes to this integration, I committed myself to two very difficult processes: to work through emotionally charged memories to offer meaningful insights about spiritual experience and religious culture and to face the anxiety I felt as an introverted mystic to be so fully exposed in a public academic light. As Ursula Le Guin said, "People crave objectivity because to be subjective is to be embodied, to be a body, vulnerable, violable" (1985: 151). I spent much of my career to this point as an applied anthropologist grounded in supposed objectivity, and as this eroded over the course of the last decade, with each step of being more firmly an insider-researcher, I had to wrestle with the voluntary erosion of the privilege of distance that protected me from criticism that mattered. Criticism of ideas, even of professional work, is still only criticism of a role I currently occupy. But criticism of my experience, especially for a person who had frequently been odd, queer, different, eccentric—and had experienced the loneliness of feeling continually misplaced—this was a vulnerability that was sometimes nearly incapacitating. But such is the work of autoethnography, and I devoured books like Ruth Behar's *The Vulnerable Observer* (1997) that encouraged, through demonstration more than instruction, the integration of all the parts of ourselves—personal and academic—so that our writing could be intimate and deeply human, offering relationship to the reader rather than mere explanation.

Autoethnography is a methodological approach in the social sciences that combines systematic inquiry into sociocultural phenomena based on participant observation (ethnography) with extensive reflection on the researcher's personal lived experience (autobiography) (Bochner and Ellis 1992; Denzin 1989). Its role has often been to represent marginalized groups or to describe complex experiences (Ellis et al. 2011). While earlier social science methodologies have generally maintained distance between a subject-researcher and object-the studied, conflating distance with objectivity and value-neutrality with accuracy, various theorists in the latter part of the twentieth century increasingly challenged those assumptions, which silenced dimensions of power and positionality that influenced the researcher, the research, and the final product of research (see, for example, Bochner and Ellis 2016; Conquergood 1991; Ellis 2007; and Lyotard 1984). In fact, conventional empirical social science masked the ways that professional academia had been shaped by only certain social groups and reinforced the marginalization of others. What was supposedly value-neutral was, in fact, latent support of only some people's values and not others. Academic research had been shaped by those in power—white, male, straight, middle-class, Christian—and the distance between researcher and researched is a continuity of the privilege that those in power have historically enjoyed vis-à-vis marginalized others.

In response, some theorists offered that it was more meaningful to create a methodological approach that focused on the usefulness of narrative—of stories—rather than on objective theory (Rorty 1982). After all, we are inherently storytelling beings—it is central to how humans understand themselves, others, and the world around them (Fisher 1985). As philosophers and social theorists deconstructed the purpose and process of conventional academic work, it was increasingly impossible to consider research in the social sciences as impersonal and objective, when we came to understand that each of us are social agents with our own assumptions, experiences, limitations, and relationships that shape both our data and our analyses. This brought new and exciting directions for anthropological work, offering opportunities for rewarding innovative and personally risky research—work that makes us vulnerable (Geertz 1988; Marcus and Fisher 1986; Rosaldo 1989). One of these new directions was autoethnography, which offered that an engaged researcher's insights were valuable, in part because of their honest subjectivity (Poulos 2021: 29).

Contemporary autoethnography takes many forms, but along the poles of the spectrum are evocative autoethnography (Bochner and Ellis 2016) and analytic ethnography (Anderson 2006). Evocative autoethnography is "both transgressive and critical," rejecting many social science conventions in order to emphasize the aesthetics of written work and the emotional connection between the researcher and the reader—making the work fundamentally about accessibility, engagement, and art (Bochner and Ellis 2016: 60). Its unique offering is engaging a public audience emotionally. In the author's vulnerability, the reader has a chance to respond in kind—to do the difficult and often messy work of self-examination, relationship, and ultimately, of transformation through personal connection. Evocative autoethnography is revolutionary—in both how it upends conventional research processes and products and in its potential for leading the reader to changes in emotion and relationship rather than merely in thought.

The criticism of this approach has been precisely what its developers and advocates most value—its lack of orientation to the scholarly community. In contrast, analytic autoethnography prioritizes being "committed to developing theoretical understandings of broader social phenomena" (Anderson 2006: 373) and pairing analytic reflexivity with other qualitative data collected from the social group or community under study. Arising from a recognition of two levels of understanding one's own experiences—a practical level for oneself and a more abstract one inherent in scholarly analysis (developed from Shutz 1962)—analytic autoethnography is defined by moving between these two levels of understanding (Anderson 2006: 381). In doing so, one finds that variation within practical understandings or interpretations of experiences within the community or social group can pose problems for the accuracy of autoethnography resting solely on the researcher's own experience and interpretation to represent the community or social group as a whole. Analytic autoethnography, then, is a way of both addressing perceived methodological weaknesses and reorienting the works away from public engagement and toward scholarly merit.

I could not help but see value in both forms of autoethnography for the current work, not only in fulfilling the purposes I had for the book but perhaps more important in capturing my two selves as methodological approaches and writing styles. As a Druid and a mystic, my sense of self is fundamentally relational. My interest is in engaging an audience with new ways of feeling, perceiving, and understanding. I have a desire to create more than a well-reasoned and interesting text. I want to create something beautiful out of my life, something that matters to more people than a handful of scholars or coerced-into-reading students. But I am also an analytical person. I was primarily trained in methods useful in environmental and cognitive anthropology—methods that are very concerned with generalizability and actionability in solving practical problems. This is also an authentic self. The challenge was how to unite these two selves and these two forms of autoethnography—to balance integration and fracturing, art and science, self and broader implications (Chang 2016: 128–9).

Evoking the Druid in the Work

Autoethnography is uniquely suitable for a work on American Druidry not only because it offers a meaningful container for the phenomenological dimensions that are necessary to fully explore a relational spirituality that emphasizes personal experience but also because storytelling is a foundational part of Druidic learning, teaching, and expression. Druidry is inclusive of the bardic arts, most notably the performance of poetry and stories—including original pieces and interpretations of folklore and mythology. Inspired by a pre-literate society before the Roman invasion of the insular Celtic world, many contemporary Druids seek to build skills in performing expressive pieces that are meant to engage the audience and lead them into their own spiritual experiences. Stories are at the heart of Druidic practice and so autoethnography is a uniquely suitable approach to interweave Druidic and anthropological methods and communications.

There are other qualities of autoethnography that have mirrors in Druidic practice as well. Druidry draws from several forms of meditation, including visualization and discursive forms. In meditative practice, Druids journey inwardly to the past and the future, to other realms, to other perspectives. In both AODA and OBOD, these experiences are recorded in journals and later processed in summative essays or letters that are reviewed by tutors or mentors. There is a common structure of recording spiritual experience, reflecting on it over time, and interpreting it in the present moment. Discursive meditation brings the Druid into conversation with written and other texts; the Druid contemplates such texts in multiple ways, both analytically and in seeking spiritual insight. These processes of layering consciousness and reflection over time, generating increased self-awareness, are similar to the autoethnographic process (Bochner and Ellis 2016: 66).

Autoethnography, then, not only collapses the distance between me as a researcher and me as a Druid but also provides a useful and reasonable bridge between two different approaches to experience and knowledge. In both autoethnography and Druidry, intimate relational engagement is centered in a process of charting one's own life journey, which provides bountiful opportunities for self-reflection, empathy, examination of ethics, and trying on new perspectives (Bochner 2001; Ellis and Bochner 2000; Fisher 1984).

I wanted to provide the reader opportunities to engage in Druidic experience—in the spiral of the Druidic journey—without the intrusion of scholarly analysis. I also wanted to allow myself to use Druidic methods for developing narratives about my own spiritual experience. While intuition has been acknowledged to be a part of some qualitative research traditions (Creswell 1998), and memoir as a significant form of self-narrative influencing autoethnography (Chang 2016), neither of these fully captures Druidic methods of memory work, insight, and synthesis. The idea of spiritual inspiration—to spark creative expression, guide action, understand the self, and gain new perspectives—is central to the Druidic journey. Called *awen*, it is understood to be the same process that inspired the great bardic poets of the past. Awen is a meeting of human consciousness and the wisdom and beauty held by the other-than-human, and it can come as flashes of insight, images, and symbols, and in dream.

The initial themes of the book emerged as a combination of awen and analytical reflection on mixed methods survey data from 135 US Druids, drawn from a larger dataset I had produced in 2014. In writing the book proposal, I allowed myself to move back and forth between data analysis and spiritual contemplation, and the book's themes and structure emerged from this liminal place. To offer that first-order practical level of understanding— the Druid understanding of my own spiritual experience—unencumbered by the second-order theorizing I do as an anthropologist, I conceptualized a book that was memoir punctuated by analysis, allowing readers to join me in both my spiritual experiences and in the ways that I currently interpret my experiences as an anthropologist. Memoir was written using primarily Druidic methods for memory work and synthesis; analytical essays were developed using multiple qualitative methods of inquiry (including analysis of texts, interview, and survey data) and interpreted using theory drawn from multiple disciplines, but particularly from cognitive and psychological anthropological approaches. I thought of the work as a type of layered account, as a conversation between selves (Ronai 1995).

I had never written a memoir before, so my first step was to take a short course by memoirist Edvige Giunta in the art of doing so. I conceptualized a mutual emergence of an academic work on Druidry and new Druidic experiences resulting from academic inquiry. Druids frequently engage in concentrated efforts to improve their creative skills, and so rather than viewing the endeavor of writing this book as a purely professional one,

I utilized it as a process to integrate Druidic and anthropologist selves in one effort of learning, self-discovery, and engagement of an audience. I am often a visual thinker, particularly in my spiritual experience, and I wanted to capture the multisensorial nature of Druidic practice. Free drawing as part of the process of autoethnography (Chang 2016) allowed me to engage my spiritual experiences more authentically and fully, and resulted in a series of prints that are included in the book as a means of illustrating how inspiration and expression can take myriad forms in Druidry.

The themes for each of the chapters of memoir were used as topics for discursive meditation. Rather than systematically reviewing my memories—which I could have done through analyzing some 500 pages of Druidic journals I had written over the last twenty years—I approached the selection of memories by engaging what Druids sometimes call the deep or wild self. I had developed an intuitive self in relationship to the spirit world as a Druid, and now I asked this intuitive self to provide guidance for what moments of my life provided the most useful, meaningful, and engaging doorways to the themes of the Druidic journey my work would describe. The insights came at times as a flood I could scarcely capture, at times as a trickle as I pleaded with Brigid—an Irish goddess of poetry and inspiration—to help me. As memories came and I received insights into their initial synthesis, I would then locate them in my personal journals—reflecting on how I had once experienced and interpreted them, how I understood them now, and why that memory had been sparked by the theme. The work was emotionally demanding, involving reliving memories that brought me intense joy and pain. My evening spiritual practice, which is focused on time spent in solitude and silence, became elongated to accommodate more extensive writing and the time I needed to process the emotions associated with the work.

To maintain the integrity of this work and allow myself to accurately write what I experienced my memory to be (which is never exactly what happened, but instead is its own meaning-making process), I wrote the entirety of the memoir first—before engaging in collecting or analyzing other, external data and before analyzing the self-narratives. It was important to me that this autoethnography reflect more than anthropological analysis of Druidic experience. I wanted the reader to have a sense of two different ways of knowing and experiencing: the Druidic and the anthropological. In marking boundaries around two different genres of writing that represented the two selves in communication, the reader could choose to move through the work in any number of ways that met their interests, allowing them to co-create their path of discovery.

Through it all, writing was a constant companion. Writing is an integral part of Druidic synthesis. Druids are encouraged by various books and training materials to maintain journals that document their spiritual experiences and interpretations, and both OBOD and AODA include both journaling and writing essays that synthesize one's spiritual experience as part of the process of moving through the various levels of curricula.

Writing is not merely a description of the spiritual experience but part of the experience itself. Writing is opening to awen and it is also a process of discovery as one attempts to put the numinous into words. Likewise, writing in autoethnography is part of the research practice itself, rather than a report on the research (Ellis et al. 2011; Pouos 2021; Richardson 2005). Regular writing practice as one sifts through memory and emotion is key to discovering what is worth offering to an audience and interpreting why it is of value. Writing one's own self-narratives is the foundation, though arguably not enough in and of itself.

The Bridge to the Analyst in the Work

One significant criticism of autoethnography is its limitations for representing a community or social group. While particularly apt at connecting to the reader and bringing them into relationship with the author, the author's life experiences are those of only one individual and cannot be taken as an accurate, full representation of the aspects of identity, processes, or phenomena under study (Anderson 2006). Considering how others in the same group or circumstances experience and interpret their lives is critical for bridging the author's self-narratives with broader representation and theorizing, which can be accomplished through combining one's own life history with other qualitative data and review of peer-reviewed literature (Ellis and Bochner 2011). Likewise, such work can limit imbalance in the final product, ensuring that the author adequately addresses sociocultural issues rather than losing sight of the analysis in the self-narrative (Chang 2016).

Balancing self-narrative with other forms of qualitative inquiry is particularly important in studying Druids, because Druids as a social group are much more openly diverse than many other religions. Because it is neither orthodoxic nor orthopraxic, Druids have a wide range of spiritual experiences and interpretations of those experiences. Druidry self-consciously affirms diversity—biological and cultural—as a worthwhile, valuable, and healthy state. The variable experiences, practices, and ideas Druids hold are viewed within the Druidic community as a feature, not a bug—that is, as useful characteristics of Druidry itself, not a problem of its recent development. Likewise, autoethnography (when offered in dialogue with others' voices and critical self-reflection of one's own experiences) brings the reader into intimate relationship with similarity and difference, resonance and challenge (Derrida 1978; Ellis et al. 2011).

As I will discuss in my first analytical chapter on the individual person in Druidry, my spiritual experience is somewhat unusual for being an American that grew up in the United States, and it is even a bit unusual (though less so) in Druidry. I have had mystical experiences my entire life and was raised in a form of mystical Christianity that was highly supportive of personal gnosis—of experiences in which one directly experiences the divine and learns from it, rather than believing in something because of what you are told by others. Both being raised in an environment that supports mysticism and having many mystical experiences is statistically unusual, and it colors Druidry as I practice it. Because of this, and because Druidry is highly diverse, the autoethnographic stories are paired with other forms of data that are inclusive of other Druidic voices, gathered through interviews, a survey, and analysis of texts Druids are likely to encounter in their explorations of Druidry.

As I described previously, this work really began in 2014 with analysis of mixed methods survey data. The survey was taken by 799 Pagans of various traditions and was focused on many facets of their spiritual practices, beliefs, and experiences, as well as their household choices related to sustainability. Of these participants, 135 of them were Druids from the United States. Their responses, combined with my own Druidry and the purposes I had for this book, informed the themes I selected for structuring the memoir portion of the autoethnography. Additionally, I used cultural modeling and grounded theory to analyze qualitative data related to spiritual experiences and beliefs to better understand the similarities and differences among Druids. This work informed the analytical essay on Druid community and religious culture.

Likewise, to understand what Druids—even solitary Druids outside of Druid order (organization) membership—might access that shapes their Druidry, I conducted content analysis on eighty-two popular texts on Druidry. Texts were selected based on a number of criteria (of which the text only had to meet one): that the text came up in an Amazon search for "Druid" (and variants on that word); that it was linked to another text in an Amazon search; that it was directly suggested by a Druid order or a Druid on social media (which I particularly used to note suggestions by and for "Hedge Druids", or those who view themselves as solitary and outside any of the major Druid orders); or that the book was written by a prominent Druid author, order founder, or order leader. I did not differentiate between works I found personally valuable or even accurate, and works I did not. The purpose of the text analysis was to understand how people in the contemporary Druid community may explore Druidry through published works, and how this might generate common religious culture. While White's work (2021) had established that it was unlikely that Druids were reading the same books to explore Druidry, I suspected based on my personal reading over the years that they were encountering similar ideas and suggested practices that might inform religious culture across Druidic community. This, too, is discussed in depth in the analytical essay on Druid community and religious culture.

Though the survey data included qualitative remarks, they were relatively short for each of the topics, and since the themes emerged from that earlier work rather than prior to it, the data did not provide adequate material for comparison to my own experiences. At the same time, I wanted all the data collection done specifically for this book to center on Druid community as an individual Druid (me) experiences it. As a consequence, and with the purpose of focusing the interviews on phenomenological aspects of Druidry, I selected Druids within my own close social network. I interviewed fifteen Druids who I have known personally for several years or more—people with whom I have had deep discussions about spiritual experience and practice and with whom I have practiced ritual. Some are those with whom I have practiced alongside for years in what we call a grove or seed group, a small local group. Others I met at larger gatherings of Druids and maintained contact with over the years. All have influenced my own spiritual journey, and in interviewing them, I found that likewise, I had influenced many of their journeys.

At the same time, they were as diverse as the survey data—something I suspected I would find, but only confirmed during the interview process. Some were relatively agnostic; others were mystical polytheists. Some were members of OBOD, some of AODA, some of ADF, and some of other smaller orders. Some worked as religious leaders in interfaith settings, others in nonreligious jobs. Some were prominent Druid order leaders and authors, while others were primarily engaged in personal, solitary practice or participating as members of a small local grove. Some practiced a Druidry that was heavily psychological; others described their practices as shamanic or mystical. These differences and similarities informed all three analytical essays, but they also informed my Druidry. I gleaned bits and pieces from the interviews that became sources of further discursive meditation in my own spiritual practice. In this way, my journey through crafting this book has mirrored crafting my own wild soul in Druidry—which for me has uniquely been a process of discovering Druidry through anthropology, and in turn, personalizing my exploration of the human experience through delving deeper into my own consciousness.

The First Triad—
All as Sacred

Place, Time, and
the Body

Three things can be sacred to the Druid: all places,
all time, and all bodies.

CHAPTER 1

Claimed by Place

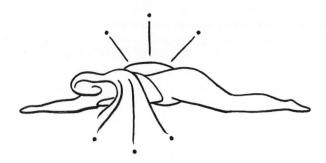

FIGURE 1 *The personhood of place.*

I was touched by your fierce love for me, even though I scraped your knees, made you ache with bitter cold, and splashed you with snowmelt when it was inconvenient. When you first had to leave me, and your tears fed my dusty skin, I wished there was a way to tell you how much I would miss you too. But I knew that one day, you would come home to me. Your three-year-old voice sobbed that you didn't want to leave "the wilderness." I lodged a piece of my wildness in your heart, so you would know how to return.

When I was three years old, I lived in a tiny mountain cabin with my mama. Despite my mother's hard work, we prayed for miracles while we rolled loose change to make our rent and buy food. It was winter and we had no hot water, no heat at all. The cabin would dip near freezing indoors during the night, so my mama piled on the quilts—a dizzying array of colors, patterns, and textures—draped one after the other on my small form before she huddled with me in bed. Despite my discomfort, I dearly loved the place with all its adventures. I would put my little plastic tugboat in the stream and send it whirling and spinning down to my mother waiting to catch it. I traipsed up and down the hills, caked in dust, holding a helping hand on the steep parts. In spring, deep purple lupines and crimson Indian paintbrush popped up through the snow-fed soil. I watched, fascinated, as thousands of ladybugs swarmed tree stumps, covering them in a constantly shifting painting of red and black.

When my mother finally acknowledged we could not afford to live there and had to return to the city, I found the loss nearly unbearable. Regardless of how hard it was, the mountains were—from the moment I had a sense of place—my home. I could not know then that I would return, again and again, to this place. I could not know that it would become a central character in my spiritual journey. I only knew that this place loved me, and I loved it. When we returned to the city, I would stubbornly insist, pointing to a barren lot of weeds: "Look! Wilderness!" Even then, I sought the spirits of place. Under the concrete and trash, behind the chained link fences and strip malls, the earth's wildness still called to me.

Druidry is a nature-centered spiritual movement, fundamentally rooted in the earth, both conceptually and literally. For many of us, long before we found Druidry, we were claimed by the earth, by the spirits of places. Places are persons in Druidry, with spirits, memories, and wisdom to share. One of the first things we do in ritual in the Order of Bards, Ovates, and Druids is to honor the spirits of place, where ever we are, and to connect our breath with the earth, sea, and sky—the three realms of the natural world. "Together, with the earth beneath us . . ." Deep breath in, slow breath out. My feet grow roots into the soil. "Together, with the sky above us . . ." Deep breath in, slow breath out. My face tilts up to feel the warm sun. "Together, with the sea around us . . ." Deep breath in, slow breath out. Even when distant, I can hear the roar of the ocean waves. "Let our ceremony begin."

Place and the natural world is at the beginning and ending of the Druid's journey: it is what calls to us, and it is in giving to places and the natural world—through planting trees, picking up trash, and protesting harmful policies—that we express our love for this complex network of geographic beings. Druids are encouraged to develop a Druidry that reflects the land they are on. If the essence of Druidry is an elixir, every Druid is encouraged to mold a different vessel to contain it. That vessel should reflect the place in which the Druid lives and practices. We are encouraged to learn all we can about our local ecology and their history, in order to develop a relationship with *this particular place*, not merely a general concept of "earth" or "land." Because of this, Druids vary considerably in the ways they honor, connect to, and are shaped by place—both within the United States and globally.

For urban Druids, they may be drawn to a particular tree, the wide expanse of a park, a small garden, or the river that cuts through the city center. For me, it was the California mountains who called to me. The relationships I have with mountain places have never been easy or comfortable, but they have always been fulfilling and helped me feel deeply alive—bringing me to a greater and greater awareness of the interconnected nature of myself and place. The mountains have demanded everything from me at one point or another—focused awareness, pain, fortitude, and time—and they have given everything to me as well. This is the nature of the Druidic relationship with place: lifelong reciprocity.

While I always knew that the wilderness of the California mountains had touched me, it was not until I flew across the Atlantic in search of my ancestors' homelands that I realized how much its wildness had stamped itself on my soul. In one campfire conversation, one British Druid described his trip to California: "I went hiking. I mean, as a Druid, it's how to connect to place—to walk the land. I got a few miles out and then realized this was nothing like my walks in England. This was frightening. I was totally alone; I could die out there, and no one would even know. There were bears and cougars." He swept his hand in a gesture toward the wooded hedgerow between the farms that surrounded our camp: "This. This is what I was used to. You can never get lost. There is always another small village close by, a farm you can walk to. The Sierra Nevada was something else entirely. It was still wild."

It was only then that I realized how much these differences in place shaped our Druidry. The materials that formed my training in the Order were developed with the understanding that walking into the woods was a safe thing to do—a nice jaunt on a soft grassy path cutting through some hawthorns and sycamores and oaks. For me, a child raised rock climbing hundreds of feet up granite walls in Yosemite and backpacking the high country above the tree line, instructions to take a walk in the woods meant hiking out alone for miles—swinging a staff to make noise to scare rattlesnakes, picking up the bones left from cougar kills, picking my way through overgrown, barely visible trails. My Druidry was shaped by knowing I could get lost. I could die. I was small in the face of the expanse of the West Coast wildlands.

This sense of Druidry-as-wildness was imprinted on me from the very beginning of my journey, informed not only by my childhood and early adulthood spent in the California mountains but also by my fieldwork as an environmental anthropologist. I discovered Druidry in the same year I spent my second summer in the field doing ethnographic research with cowboys and cattle ranchers. The Owens Valley is an impressive high desert landscape, encompassing valley pastures at 5,000 feet elevation and the surrounding summits of the Eastern Sierra Nevada and White Mountains, which contain the highest peaks in the contiguous United States (over 14,000 feet). Over the course of years in my field site, I developed an even greater appreciation and respect for the vastness of the deserts and mountains of the Western United States, where cowboys still lived in 100-year-old rustic cabins through the summer in high pasture country and sometimes risked their lives in the sudden inclement weather on the steep, long trails back to the valley floor.

Early in 2006, still in the depths of winter, my aunt and I packed up snowshoes and cameras, and headed out for a several-mile hike into Bodie Ghost Town, a once gold-mining boomtown, now state historic park. We parked at the edge of the road where the plows had ceased clearing the snow, strapped on our snowshoes, and set out across the desert. The air was beautifully crisp and clear, a blue dome atop white drifts as far as I could see. Hiking atop the snow was hard work, but eventually we reached the town's cemetery and dilapidated buildings. The place rewarded us richly for our efforts. Crawling with tourists in the summer, we were alone among the silent and windswept snow drifts. The scenes were phenomenal for photography: sharp contrasts of eroding umber wood against grey shadows. A white marble angel gravestone with boundaries barely discernable from the alabaster snow. Only the crunch of our footsteps disturbed our solitude.

The only other living human in the place was a park ranger, who greeted us and offered us a brief warm-up in his cabin, then encouraged us to leave soon as a storm was expected to roll in. We had checked weather reports before we had embarked on our hike, but Eastern Sierra Nevada weather is known for its impulsive nature. Slightly alarmed, we headed back toward the car. Being trapped between the ghost town and the car could be fatal, a warning I had heard often from cattle ranchers I interviewed, who had occasionally been caught in tumble-down abandoned historic shepherds' cabins and makeshift tent shelters in unanticipated blizzards. As we walked ever faster, the sky darkened with clouds. Equally stunning and frightening, the layers deepened to a dark steel, choking out the afternoon sunlight. As we neared the car, I snapped one last photo: a teeming vortex of charcoal, its center a single small patch of light.

Much later, alone with my field notes and thoughts, I wondered what I would have—what I could have—done if the mountains had chosen to betray my trust. Love does not mean safety when it comes to the land, especially if we love places that are wild. Sometimes, we love places that claim us, both body and soul. There was something exhilarating about loving these wild places I was born into—these places where the earth moved, the fires regenerated life, and the rivers cut new and unexpected paths toward the ocean. The relationships I forged with the spirits of place challenged me and asked me to grow beyond my fear, to listen for their wisdom, to ask for their mercy. Inevitably, this forged a vessel for my Druidry that was different than if I had lived somewhere tamer—not better nor worse, but different.

Belonging

Druid magic is a magic that harnesses the forces of the human body and brain, and the connection between humanity and the earth. It is a magic that demands more than it defers: a force of its own, woven into relationships, not to be used so much as served. Druidic practice both taught me how to become more mindful of the guidance and wisdom the seen and unseen worlds and also demanded that I serve these worlds in return. In opening to the spirits of place and their long-held memories of and sometimes pain from change, I came to know myself better.

As a child, I longed to belong to somewhere, but I knew I did not. It was not the many times we moved as we struggled with poverty. I was raised by a socially conscious mother, who from a tender age, ensured I understood the sufferings of the indigenous peoples who our ancestors had forcibly displaced. Eager to break the assumptions my mother knew society inculcated, she kept me isolated throughout my early development. She taught me in the private school at which she worked as a Kindergarten teacher. I watched very little television; instead, she read to me at night, beginning with challenging literature from a young age. We openly identified and discussed racism, colonialism, xenophobia, and misogyny.

By the time I wandered alone through Yosemite Valley at age nine, turned loose for four-hour blocks while my father worked, I knew this land did not belong to me. I was a child from nowhere, a long string of wandering ancestors trailing behind me, some forced from their native homes long ago, some more recently by war or economy—conquered, defeated, starved, persecuted. They had carried their wounds with them wherever they went, and as is the cycle common in abuse without healing, they turned from victim to oppressor. Many years later, I would read the will of the ancestors who came first to this continent, fleeing religious persecution as French Huguenots in the late 1600s. After arrival in the Dutch colony, they set up house with slaves and went to war against nearby native tribes.

Nearly 400 years later, I wandered through the demonstration Paiute village in Yosemite, sitting in a small bark shelter, snow all around, until I ached from the winter cold—in desperate attempt to connect to something that felt more *right* to me than the confusing and overwhelming modern world. I look back now and wonder what the Paiute basketry artists thought as I silently watched them work for an hour at a time, warming up in the cozy museum until my cheeks held color again. I sometimes heard the steady drumming from the ceremonial lodge, into which I could never enter, and I ached with longing I could not understand. And then I roamed out to one of the many trails and walked away from the world of museums and human complexity into the world of granite domes and tall trees, where the land—despite my ancestors' many wounds, those they caused and those they carried—welcomed me.

Sitting with British Druids around the campfire, they posed a question to me: "How does it feel to try to connect to land that has so recently been forcibly taken from others?" *Where do I belong? When my spirituality is a spirituality of the land, but the land doesn't belong to me?* I had no easy answer, and it is different for every American Druid. I had had a complex and painfully close relationship with the beloved mountains of California my entire life. The spirits of these places featured prominently in my spiritual journey from my earliest memories. Some places were more welcoming than others; some held more pain than others. Some Druids were more acutely aware of the pain that places held than others.

Many, though not all, American Druids are white and, as such, must come to terms with how they live out a spirituality that is fundamentally connected to place in a nation that was built through the genocide of other peoples. For many American Druids, including me, there is a longing to return to ancestral homelands and at times, a fixation on iconic places associated with an amorphous ancient past. Stonehenge, Avebury, Brigid's Well in Kildare, Greek temples, Norwegian fjords . . . for many of us, a motley assortment of European languages, cultures, and ancestors crowd our imagination with the promise of belonging at last.

In October of 2013, I found myself on a flight to attend Druid camp for nearly two weeks. When I arrived on the organic farm outside a quaint village in Southern England, one of many of my ancestors' homelands, my heart searched for a sense of belonging. I found welcoming people, soft gentle rolling hills, and charming stacked stone walls. I curled up on cushions in a large communal yurt, feeling as if the land was a pair of worn slippers into which my tired feet gratefully came to rest. Though the place felt familiar and kind, I did not fit. My wild soul was shaped by California earthquakes and wildfires, granite cliffs and high country glaciers, lumbering bears and singing coyotes, and the kind of darkness you can only see when there is nothing for miles but stars. I breathed into an understanding and a pain: I could not go back to being my ancestors any more than I could claim the land they had stolen. I was irrevocably betwixt and between.

Druidic magic transformed this pain into reconciliation, and it did so through the land. Places invited me in, not always nicely and not always gently. The land I was born to is prickly and bristles with raw power, as if to say, "How dare you think I could ever be owned or controlled?" The spirits of place in America always remind me that they had their own peoples who understood them better, who they still love, who they still mourn. And yet, this land claimed me for its own, this child from nowhere, landless but willing to open to its pain. This land does not belong to me; nowhere belongs to me. I am caught between the past and the future, too many strands of transience and suffering to have a homeland. But I belong to California. The realization of this, borne of the relational magic that comes with listening to the memories of places, was a gift beyond measure. It was also a gift that demanded repayment. The reciprocity Druids have with the spirits of place is a lifelong obligation.

During the Christian Holy Week in 2010, I walked across the desert in Nevada with a small group of Catholic monks and nuns, Catholic Workers, and Pagans. It was a 65-mile trek from Las Vegas to the Nuclear Test Site in protest of nuclear war and the testing that had defiled the ancestral burial grounds of the Western Shoshone (or Newe) people. I trudged along resolutely, my duct-taped feet aching from blisters, my face chapped from the dry desert wind. While the Christians perhaps contemplated Christ's journey to the cross, I meditated on a different history of pain. This land had cared for its people for thousands of years, first tenderly sheltering them in caves, still reaching out to those who had foraged and cared for the desert in mutual relationship up to this present moment. Their ancestors were buried here, peacefully resting until the United States seized this sacred land to bomb with nuclear weapons and store nuclear waste. All those thousands of years of providing for its people, now bearing the pain of its ultimate sacrifice—poisoning that would last as many generations into the future as it had sheltered in the past.

On the last day, close to our final destination, I trailed off from the roadside into the desert, allowing myself to fully open to the spirits of the place. A wave of grief washed over me, welling up from my feet and crashing over my head. I touched the tips of brush as I walked by, a loving and silent apology. Tears created tiny rivers through the dust on my face, dripping from my chin onto the sand at my feet. I let them come, the smallest of gifts in the face of the land's suffering, but all I could give. I held the grief as long as I could bear it, then walled off my heart.

Druidry is about joy as much as it is about pain, but most of all it is about relationship, about empathy. The land I was born to and live on has given me food, shelter, peace, and great joy. It has given me everything; my very life is dependent on this land. In turn, I offer my empathy, making space in my heart for its grief. This reciprocity is no more and no less than I would give any of my closest friends and family. When they are hurting, I open my heart and my arms to embrace them. I cry as I wipe their tears. I can give no less to the spirits of place. It is the least I can do when they have given me so much.

Transformation

In 1999, I was a young bride, twenty years old, renting my in-laws' cabin. I had returned to the same small mountain town that had embedded itself in my heart as a toddler. Forest Falls is as dangerous as it is beautiful, a mile high in elevation nestled in a V-canyon with only one way in and out. Beneath peaks soaring to 11,000 feet, its center is Mill Creek, a vast riverbed of large boulders that holds a trickle of water most of the year. That riverbed speaks to the place's history of being shaped by water, and not in gentle, predictable ebbs and flows. It is a landscape of flood.

One July day, the sky fomented an enormous thunderstorm, and rain fell in a great torrent of quarter-sized drops. And then came the sound: a freight train. Rain had poured across the high peaks so quickly that it brought with them, in a great crashing wave, boulders the size of houses and entire trees. The river swelled to many times its size, brown with mud, rolling over the bridges. My then-husband and I were working at a conference center lower in the canyon and were required to stay at work to keep the many guests safe. I went through the motions of my work numb, terrified that my babies, my dog and cat, were buried or drowned. I neither knew that the river had not taken this from me, nor that the river had taken so much from others.

Before nightfall and shift-end, we stood on break at the edge of the river, watching it angrily pour over the bridges. Eventually the water slowed and began to lower, but it still carried a terrifying assortment of debris. The entire canyon was without electricity and phone service. The roads were closed, covered in deep layers of mud. A police officer stood at the road closure to ensure no one would take the risk of traversing the treacherous and shifting ground above it. We took flashlights, locked up our car, pulled on hiking boots, and started walking. It was unthinkable to leave my pets on their own.

My husband had spent his entire life in this little canyon. He knew it inside and out. I followed him, cutting through the woods between the embankment leading to the swollen river and the road. In the utter darkness, we plodded forward through the mud that sucked at our ankles. Once safely past the police officer, a single flashlight beam guided our narrow path forward, circumventing large rocks and downed pines. Slowly, we went deeper and deeper, seemingly without end. I became more and more anxious. I was thigh deep in thick mud, rocks and debris bruising my legs. Each step became harder, and I knew I was not hitting the ground, even as deep as I was sinking. It was a strange, spongy feeling, much like stepping on a very deep mattress. I sunk in and then was only just able to extricate myself on the rebound, but there was no solidity. Exhausted and frightened, like some wounded animal, I stopped. Sinking, bit by bit a little deeper, the mud pushed past my thighs toward my hips. Tears coursed down my cheeks.

My husband barked at me to keep going. Roughly holding out his hand, I grabbed hold of him and he pulled me forward. Like a drill sergeant, he firmly told me to keep moving, that there was no other option. He was right. Like being in the middle of a climb as a child, hundreds of feet in the air, there was no other option than through. This nightmare could only end if I persevered. I forced my rubbery legs forward another step, and then another, until, miraculously, we slowly felt a more solid foundation return, and we were on pavement. The sheer relief sent me into another wave of tears. I crouched a moment, touching the rough, firm pavement ecstatically with my hands. He flitted the beam of light back where we came. The light illuminated a thin slice of a veritable wall of mud and debris. We had been hiking across the road for quite some time. The mud was some twelve feet deep.

After catching our breath a moment, we began the mile long walk home up the road. As we walked, a different anxiety built. The damage to our town was incalculable. My mind struggled to comprehend what I hiked past. A piano. A stove on its side. An overturned car. An entire wall of a house, with the garden house still dangling attached to the siding and spigot, ripped from its foundation. Walking became harder and harder at this point because I feared we would return to death—to total destruction of our home. And then, at long last, we came up the last stretch, and looked up to see our home still standing on the uphill side of the road. Our entire apartment was covered in an inch of standing water and silt. But we had all survived.

After any flood, snowstorm, or fire threat, there was always an exodus from that little mountain town. Those who had fancied a less extreme confrontation with nature, an easier relationship with place, fled to the safety of the suburbs. I was never one of them. There were times I left, but never because of its wildness. The thunderstorm that year—that claimed eighteen houses and one life—was the same thunderstorm in which I felt sheer exhilaration. I could not have the powerful sense of inspiration I felt when I saw lightening and heard thunder, or the lovely scent of rain pelting the forest floor, without risk. Mill Creek's capricious ways were also its gift: the gift of change, of transformation.

Place is more than location; place holds memories and places have their own interests. Place is interactive historically, ecologically, and spiritually, existing in both the embodied, incarnate world we see around us and in an inward world—the world of imagination, dream, and inspired art. We engage with place through learning about our local ecology and history, as well as through developing an inner grove, an imagined place to which we can go at any time. This inner grove is different for every Druid, but for each of us, it is a place to which we can retreat for spiritual renewal and guidance. I was unsurprised to find, when I held my first Druid meditative ritual to enter my inner grove, that I was in the mountains. After all, since my childhood, this was where I felt most at home and most connected to an abiding divine peace. All that I need from the apparent world, and so often do not have—silence, simplicity, solitude—is ever present in my inner grove. The mountains of the apparent world teach me about the transformative power of nature; the mountains of the inner grove teach me about the transformative power of my mind.

Visualizing images in my mind has always come easily to me. When I first created—discovered?—my inner grove, it did not look exactly like any of the mountain places I held so dear. But it was everything I loved about all of them. I leave the world my body lives in, riding a pale grey horse quickly through the woods away from my body, galloping along a winding stream through a forest of mixed pines and white oaks. The horse stops at the edge of a great meadow that stretches to a distant line where it meets the slope of the mountains, sweeping sharply upward to where snowy summits touch the sky. Here my spirit sits, stilling my waking thoughts, absorbing the peace and power of the place.

Shortly after beginning my training as a Druid, I quickly learned that when physical or emotional pain pummeled me and I felt battered and worn, I could retreat to the inner grove. In the apparent world, I sat or lay in meditative repose, slowing my breathing to four deep breaths per minute. My mind relaxed, unraveling the incalcitrant knot of physical or emotional pain, escaping for a while the complex challenges and sufferings of the embodied life. I always returned from this inward landscape refreshed. The inner grove cannot entirely heal the pain of the outward world, but in this Druidic practice I found the first very real uses of magic. Magic was the power to transform my consciousness, and in so doing, reshape my life.

The inner grove creates a liminal space between any place our body exists and a magical landscape within us. The world around us also contains liminal places, places that invite us to a deeper connection, to wisdom, to the extraordinary. Some of these, such as megalithic and rock art sites, were built by humans. Others are given, like invitations to a party, by the earth herself. So-called "fairy rings" of mushrooms, hollowed-out trees, branches fallen into the shape of an open doorway . . . the earth provides us with thin places, narrow slices of space where the spirit world touches our embodied, waking one.

The Ancient Bristlecone Pine Forest marks the borderlands between California and Nevada. Toward the top of the White Mountains, some of the oldest trees in the world—more than 4,000 years old—carry on with their meager existence. In a land of extremes—little rain, high winds, hot summers, and cold winters—these trees grow slowly, spartan and seemingly dead but for the tufts of life peeping through as needles. The first time I hiked through the groves, I was entranced by the myriad of time-worn shapes the wizened trunks took. I came upon a venerable tree, still reaching its crooked arms skyward as its roots arched, as if in sympathy, away from the ground. The small, dark space invited me—a whisper on the breeze: "Come. Come. I have stories to tell." I shed my backpack and camera and eased my way into the tomb-like opening just big enough for my body. I wriggled a bit, trying to get comfortable despite the small rocks digging into my ribs and thighs. Finally, I was still.

I closed my eyes and images intruded in my mind. I reached upward, through the branches of the tree, toward a star-filled sky. The tremendous vastness of the Milky Way stretched out before me as it had for thousands of years. I had seen so many, many years: a slow, steady march of seasons across time. I was staid and generous, providing shelter for small creatures. My breath became their breath, and their breath, mine. The enormity of a life so long, so patiently and quietly lived as everything around me lived, died, and was reborn again, was breathtakingly beautiful and lonely. My fellow trees were the only companions who remained with me, century after century, in my unique existence. And then, my eyes opened to the rough bark. Covered in dust, I shimmied out of the little cave and sat next to the tree, my hand resting on a root. My eyes slowly adjusted to the bright sun and azure sky, and when I felt the tree was satisfied, I swung my backpack on again and went on my way.

Thin places, whether built by us or the natural world, generate a shift in us, producing new insights and perspectives. Such places are not always comfortable; in fact, they often produce a sense of the uncanny.

Old cemeteries at dusk, tombstones overshadowed by large oak trees. The early morning fog at the edge of the ocean. The weak light at sunset filtered through dense forest. Abandoned houses with creaking garden gates. They are places that embody the liminality of worlds touching—the living and the dead, the mythic and the ordinary, the past and the present.

Over time, keening our awareness to the spirits of place, Druids become mindful of thin places and as we do so, we also come to create thin places of our own. Like the inner grove, these outer expressions of relationship to place demonstrate both our reciprocity with place and our connection to it. In my home, my office is also my shrine room, containing two cabinets that honor the relationships I have with deities, my ancestors, and the nature spirits. The shrines honor these beings and provide space for me to enact reciprocity symbolically through offerings of candles, incense, water, grain, and alcohol. These symbolic acts are affirmative of a deeper commitment: my time, my energy, my attention, my service. The shrines also provide a thin place, an epicenter of spirituality in my home and life, an open doorway to the worlds of the disincarnate beings with whom I work.

Each evening, I light the central flame of the shrine and then sit before the gods. While I sometimes engage in a full cycle of prayers, lighting each of the altars individually and pouring offerings, even the minimum of the single flame is a magical act that helps me shift from waking consciousness to a meditative state. I sit and watch the flame flicker against the labradorite pillar, the icons of the gods, the symbolic miscellany of small stones, leaves, feathers, and animal bones. Like a raucous crowd exiting the room, the chatter of my thoughts fades away until I am left with inner silence. Into this emptiness, this void, the spirits can speak. To each of these beings, from the old gods to the youngest nature spirits, I commit my life to honor their lives. Through them, I am connected to something more. I am transformed. Together, in one ecological and spiritual whole, we are complete: one process, one integrated state of Being Itself. This is the power of a thin place, consciously created and consistently cared for. It holds the magic we enact in it, day after day, until all we must do is to spark a small flame and open to its light.

CHAPTER 2

Echoes through Time

FIGURE 2 *The web of time.*

The liquid world in which I tumbled, grabbed and tossed by some unseen powerful force, was punctuated by a confusing but beautiful interplay of flashes of light. Sunlight arced through the Aegean water, reflected off foam, cradled my body through its erratic movements as if it spun a map to guide me to the surface. I was ten years old, caught in a riptide in the Pacific Ocean off a sunny summer beach in Southern California, where my best friend's parents rested blissfully unaware on the shore. It was the third time I had attempted to swim back to shore, and this time, as the current dragged me back toward the deep sea, I panicked and began to feel exhausted. It dawned on me that I might drown. As I was pulled, twisting and turning, all directions blurred and blended in a whirlwind of vertigo.

Suddenly, total calm washed over me. I no longer felt fear. The sea held me in her fluid embrace, merging with the light above. A knowing entered me from the sea, still and quiet and clear: "Do not struggle. Do not swim. Just. Let. Go." I listened and floated up to the surface, far from shore. An image entered my mind of swimming sideways; I followed this idea without question. I flipped into a sidestroke, the easiest for me, and I began to swim parallel to the shore with smooth, long strokes. When I began to feel the ocean tell me I was free, I followed the diagonal line I saw in my mind until, gasping and so relieved I was nearly crying, I came through the breaker with surfers, feet gratefully touching the rough bits of shell, dragging my heavy legs through the last of the water to dry sand.

Water is one of the great elemental forces that never failed to pull me—so often unwillingly—from my solid practicality into its chaotic ever-changing nature. This ancient force's indelible power shaped the land of my beloved West Coast for millennia, and no less it shaped me. I couldn't know as a child, first facing water's destructive potential, how it would go on to sculpt my sense of self. In Druidry, the elemental forces—Earth, Air, Fire, and Water— are tied to forces in the universe and in human nature. They flow through our physical manifestation, intellect, passion, emotions, and subconscious. They are archetypes that bind together all beings in the universe. They are representations of and bound to the gods, and they are strange, inhuman ancient gods themselves—unnamed, unfathomable, and untamable.

In the central myth of my first degree of training in the Order of Bards, Ovates, and Druids, the witch-goddess Ceridwen furiously chases Gwion Bach, a boy she hires to tend a cauldron as she works magic on her son's behalf, through the elements. Ceridwen flies into a rage when the potion that contained all knowledge ended up in Gwion Bach rather than her beloved son. Frightened but now magical, Gwion Bach shape-shifts through various animal forms as he moves through the elements, with Ceridwen likewise shape-shifting in hot pursuit. At the end of this chase, Gwion Bach, now desperate, transforms himself into a single kernel of wheat, falling to a farmer's threshed pile of grain far below. Not to be outdone, Ceridwen lands in the farmyard as a plump black hen and promptly gobbles him up. Through this act, Ceridwen begins the second of Gwion Bach's three births: she becomes pregnant with Gwion Bach, who has lodged himself inside her. After his birth, loving him too much to kill him and yet still angry that her son was cheated of the potion that was to make him powerful, she sews Gwion Bach into a bag of leather skins, encapsulating him in his next womb and then setting him afloat on the ocean. It is not until he is born of the ocean, gently pushed to shore into a fishing weir and then freed from his cocoon by a lowly fisherman, that he becomes what he was destined to be—Taliesin—the world's wisest and most beautiful poet.

Gwion Bach never really has a choice—he *will* become the inspired great poet Taliesin. He *will* be initiated by the gods and nature forces. Despite his attempt to run from his fate, he goes on to his destiny. Gwion Bach spirals through time, growing more powerful with each successive rebirth, first from a human mother, then from the witch-goddess, and finally from the ocean. In each iteration, he gains wisdom and comes closer to becoming a liminal being, occupying a role that moves in the limitations of the human world, but with an unfettered capacity born of the totality of nature's wisdom. Time's linearity crystallizes into one boundless present in Taliesin.

The gods claimed Gwion Bach, and Water in its various forms claimed me, whether I liked it or not. The Pacific Ocean was my first introduction to Water's power, but not my last. Water would echo through my life again and again, leading me on a journey toward insights that required a gradual expansion, wrought through trauma as much as beauty. Danger opened spontaneous moments of liminality, in which time seemed to come close to stopping as my awareness became heightened. My chattering human mind would go silent and my animal soul would come forward with the ancient wisdom of millions of lifetimes embedded in the evolution of my body.

I survived the riptide and a flood before Water initiated me into a new relationship with the divine and myself. I was twenty-four years old and in my doctoral program when I woke up with a start. I got up and stood, mesmerized, at the side of my bed. Moonlight softly illuminated the room. My then-husband was asleep in the bed, and so was I. I looked again, confused. Both of us were asleep in the bed, but I was also standing next to the bed. Where the closet usually was, against the far wall, was an enormous birch arch supported by two large columns, elaborately carved with a language I could not read. Beyond the doorway was soft darkness. Near one column, just inside my bedroom, a woman glowed with a soft luminescence, inclining her head graciously and smiling gently. Naked, her skin was pale and her silvery golden hair fell in waves over her thin shoulders, down her long back, and over her chest. She was barefoot, standing on the velvet moss that had crept into my room. Her eyes were a very light teal and they held the depths of many lifetimes. She radiated the union of celestial and earthy energy: an embodiment of a star, an ancient and knowing being, kind and yet detached. The thought entered me from her: "If you go through, you can never go back."

My immediate assumption was that I was dying. I had been quite ill for a couple of years; though the doctors had assured me that while they did not know what was wrong, I was not in any immediate danger. I glanced back at myself, sleeping peacefully in my bed, and then eagerly looked forward to what was possible, to this alternate future and universe. I gazed with delight at the gatekeeper; she had known my decision before I had made it. I stepped through the portal into the darkness.

The forest was dark, and the last moments of daylight peeped through the dense canopy, shrouded in mist. The air felt like morning dew on grass when barefoot. I was enveloped in the sweet acidic scent of an ancient forest. The trees were supported by enormous trunks with vast exposed roots. Twinkling lights glowed in the trees, adorning them like jewelry. A gurgling, winding stream stretched through the center of the mossy floor into infinity, cutting through the thick swaths of trees and small dark meadows. I realized, in a flash of insight, that I had no physical body. There was no barrier between thought, feeling, sensory perception, or communion; there was only a focus of my awareness. Time was irrelevant, neither fast nor slow, and I had no recollection of or concern for my past. There was only an eternal present.

I walked on the stream; it was deep but my feet splashed only inches below the crystalline surface. Every so often, the stream would open into a pool that dimly reflected the far-reaching branches above it, and I would dive into the water, flipping over along the bottom of the pool to stare up at the lights far above me, dancing back and forth in the ripples of the water. The water itself was an entity, and I could feel myself become one with it and then separate once again. Another sudden awareness washed over me: everything—including myself—was sound. The trees and lights and water and moss—and me—were just sounds, an illusion arising from beautiful music that somehow was in all of us and beyond all of us. I never wanted to leave this state of being—I felt so very expansive, so whole.

Suddenly, I was slammed back into my body, my alarm clock shrieking. The sunlight streamed through my window with too bright a glare. Confused and disoriented, I shut off the alarm and struggled to get my bearings. The dream was so incredibly, viscerally real that the memory of it was as clear and present as any other memory I had. Rubbing my fingertips together to confirm that I was back in my body, as the incredulous feeling that I was still alive settled in, a wave of grief and homesickness washed over me, pulling me out to a deep sea of longing as if I were ten years old once more, caught in the ocean's grasp. I locked myself in the bathroom, turned on a hot shower, sat on the floor of the tub, and sobbed until the waterfall that pulsed over me turned cold. I had witnessed my own erasure, my own return to the primordial state of union, and indeed—I could never return to the me I was before I had walked through that gateway. I had been fluid, and the return to solidity hurt. What an initiation I was given! But it came at a steep price.

Collapse

Druidic practice led me toward an erosion of the boundaries between being and process. The elements became beings, someone in me and outside of me, both force and person. As the processes of the universe became persons with whom I had relationships, the concreteness of my own selfhood began to dissipate. The more I engaged in Druidic spiritual practice, the more my entire life became liminal time and space. Time is part of our perceptual reality and it shifts based on our consciousness. At the heart of magic is our ability to shift our consciousness, and in so doing, to alter time.

Nature initiated me into my inner wildness, and Druidry initiated me into merging that wildness with the rhythms of human life. Druidic ritual collapses mythic and ordinary time into a "thin present" in which myth, past, future, and present are brought into integrated consciousness. The Wheel of the Year, the eightfold series of seasonal holidays, offers a way to instantiate the spiral of time into our lives at will, generating reverberations of similar experiences offered to us again and again so that we can deepen in our understanding of the lessons offered by the universe. A cycle of eight holidays based on the seasons, it is grounded in the seasonal weather and related farming activities of the United Kingdom. Four of the festivals are organized around the pastoral calendar of Northern Europe, now reimagined for the modern world by tying them to psychological manifestations of the old cycle: fallow (Samhain), flowering (Imbolc), fertility (Beltane), and harvest (Lughnasadh). The other four are solar festivals, celebrating the balance of the equinoxes (Alban Eilir and Alban Elfed) and the extremes of the solstices (Alban Hefin and Alban Arthan). Together, they provide opportunities to enter liminal time that mark transition periods of our lives, moving us through grieving and letting go, dreaming and healing, planting and growth, and harvest and celebration.

Most of us begin with solitary rituals, often enacting the scripts we find in books or training materials from Druid orders. However, we are each encouraged to develop our own skills as priest, as ritualist. If we are fortunate, and live somewhere near other Druids, we might form a seed group or grove, a small gathering of Druids. In 2009, exhausted from years of spiraling through attempts to open to the deeper spiritual work I felt called to and yet feared, one night I opened my arms wide to the universe and demanded that if the spirits wanted more from me, I needed community. In response, within six months, I was at the vanguard of meetings to form a southern California Druid seed group and attending the first large US gathering of Druids. A year later, I had my first encounter with a group ritual where a god came when we called.

Several dozen of us sat on colorful cushions, backs up against the wall of a large yurt at a Tibetan Buddhist sangha center. We were collectively creating the ritual that we would engage in later that evening. It was Lughnasadh, the fire festival that celebrates the first harvest and particularly that reminds us of Tailtiu, the god Lugh's foster mother, who sacrifices her life for the harvest. T. Thorn Coyle, a Pagan author and teacher, was offering a workshop that would help us orient our consciousness toward a mythic now in which the spirits are present with us. We began with opening our awareness to the elemental forces. One by one, each element came forward through her drum beat and our chanting, until we could feel the room shift as we called on the elements.

Then, we began chanting for Lugh to come among us. *Lugh Lamhfada . . . Lugh Lamhfada . . .* The drumbeat carried us away from ordinary thoughts, building an energy among us that opened a thin time and place for Lugh to arrive. I went inward, closed my eyes, and focused on the steady rhythm of the drum, swaying slightly. I keened my awareness to the crescendo of voices, of my voice among the others, calling a god I had never met before. *Lugh Lamhfada . . . Lugh Lamhfada . . .* The air in the room was oppressive, not just hot but heavy and electric. The feeling was palpable, unique, and unmistakable: Lugh arrived. The drum stopped. Two people offered themselves up, recognizing Lugh's call, to later let the god enter them in possessory trance in the ritual. Others, inspired by Lugh's presence, began to craft bits and pieces of the rite to come. Gradually, the crackling thick quality of the room eased, and we bid Lugh farewell, formally thanking him and closing the thin time we had created. Easing back into ordinary waking consciousness, everything felt brighter and louder—so very alive. Our collective spiritual work had opened a thin time that brought the *awen*—divine inspiration—among us.

While the media often portrays magic as if it is learning spells to make someone fall in love or to bring money, at the heart of magic is gaining control over one's state of consciousness, practicing using the body and breath until it is possible to move at will between ordinary waking, light meditative, and trance states. States outside ordinary waking consciousness allow us to open to awen, the inspiration coming from nature, ancestors, gods, or our own deeper "wild" soul. From awen comes poetry, story-telling, music, and the arts, but also wisdom that seems to spring into our minds, often fully formed, as Athena was born from Zeus's forehead. Ritual is a primary spiritual technology that induces a shift in consciousness, producing a liminal time outside of ordinary time, into which we can open to knowledge that arises from the past, the future, or unseen realms.

Three years later, in 2013, I was at a ten-day Samhain Druid camp in Southern England. Living communally in wood-fire-heated yurts, without electricity, flush toilets, or showers, I found that within days, my ordinary reality had been stripped away and revealed, raw and unpracticed, a human soul from many lifetimes ago. I'd wake from under my blankets in the middle of the night, shivering. It was the job of whoever woke up cold to feed the fire, and this task often fell to me, the Californian who was unused to the late October damp chill. With sunrise came the tea kettle on the central fire, the movement meditation swishing across the wet grass, the chopping of vegetables for lunchtime stew.

The camp was organized to have open periods for several days at the beginning and ending, in which people came and went, flanking a closed camp period in which no one entered or exited camp unless it was an emergency. By the closed camp time, I had a completely transformed sense of daily reality, one unpunctuated by email, phone calls, texts, or even a clock. In between workshops, in which I split my time between immersion and writing field notes—by this point, both anthropologist and Druid—I wandered alone across the emerald fields and sat on the land, letting its damp embrace soothe the frantic pace of my pre-tenure life. Compared to the wilderness of my beloved home, I felt as if I had stumbled into Hobbiton, with charming crumbling stone walls and quaint paths through hospitable woodland.

Samhain was the New Year and the time in which the veil—the separation between the dead and the living—was thin. It was the time for grieving loss and for reminiscing about the good times, healing the wounds our ancestors caused and carried, honoring their gifts for us, and composting our own pain. At the Druid camp, the Samhain festival was a series of complex, layered rituals that took us farther and farther into an uncertain hedgerow between life and death. The spiritual work was heavy and challenging, offering several hours per day in which I would move back and forth between ordinary participant observation and trance states. My field journal became fluid, swinging from detailed notes to bits of poetry and cryptic messages that encapsulated what I learned in trance. The height of the camp was a central rite in which the May King, a man crowned by the community at Beltane, would act out his own sacrificial death and, deep in trance, carry our messages to our beloved dead in the Summerlands, the place of reunion between lives.

We stood in a silent circle several people deep in the largest yurt. The May King entered and a Druid offered him a cup. Taking the imagined poison to his lips, the May King began to retch and stagger until, after a few minutes, he dropped to the layered tapestries and furs on the ground and lay very still. Tenderly, the community wrapped him, first in a thick down sleeping bag, then in layers of furs. Carrying him lovingly, his consort the May Queen stoically by his side, we processed from the yurt up the slightly sloping field. It was dark and stormy, the roiling grey clouds offering the tears we could not yet bring forth. All morning, men had dug a grave into the hillside for this ritual burial, and we walked solemnly and slowly toward it. Laying him gently into the moist earth, his face pale and blank, the realness of his dangerous journey sank in. He would lie in trance in this narrow earth coffin for three hours, journeying through the Summerlands, facing his own mortality in order to bear the thread of loving connection between those who had moved on from the earthly plane and those who were left behind.

An older man in a kilt stepped up graveside and began to play bagpipes as the community came, one by one, to place handwritten notes to their dead in the grave and offer their handful of earth for the burial. The keening notes on the rising wind swept away the last vestige of myself as anthropologist, and indeed, of this particular lifetime. I found myself occupying a spiral of time, mourning not only my recent divorce but also the weight of countless lifetimes of loss. Tears dripping down my pale cheeks, red hair clinging soddenly to my temples, I stepped forward as the rain turned into snow. In my hand was a letter I had penned to my ex-husband. I was earthing my former marriage, and with it, a grief tied to losing someone in the distant past of my soul—a memory that lived at the edge of remembering. At the side of the grave, I looked down at the May King's face, drained of color and expression, so very still and empty. I was carried lifetimes back in an instant, resolutely placing the sword into the grave of my lover. *How many times have I mourned you, my love?*

The me from the past sliced into my heart in the present, steeling it in the face of loss. My warm tears turned to icy sleet. Across the chasm of time, I sucked in a great, heaving breath of the storm around me and gazed resolutely into the grave. The letter floated down like a flower, settling without a sound. My hands dug into the clammy clay. Above the beautifully aching song of the bagpipes, as if amplified, I heard the soft thud of earth on human body. And then it was done. We were each together and alone in the way that only death can bring.

Homecoming

How many times have I lost you, beloved? And how many times have I found you again?

I discovered Druidry in 2003 while preparing a lecture on new religious movements for a class in Magic, Witchcraft, and Religion I was teaching at a community college. Stumbling onto the website for the Order of Bards, Ovates, and Druids, I was fascinated to find a description of a spirituality that mirrored the way I had always related to the divine through the natural world. I ordered every book I could find on Druidry through the University of California library system, devouring Ross Nichols and Philip Carr-Gomm alongside my graduate school reading. While I had been raised in a highly individualist mystical Christianity that emphasized connecting to God through dreams, direct experiences, and nature, I longed for a religious community and body of teaching my highly introverted parents did not crave.

As I voraciously read, for the first time I saw myself mirrored in spiritual community. So different from the monotheism and materialism that pervaded American society, this was a contemporary spirituality built on relationships with a universe of persons. Many years later, I would finally have face-to-face conversations with fellow Druids, at first cautiously offering little bits of myself as I sipped chai latte at a coffee shop in Pasadena, until with time, I came to trust them with the inner recesses of my soul. Why had we all become Druids? What had drawn us to Druidry? In essence, we did not *become* Druids so much as we found a pathway to acknowledge what we already were. For some, clear and distinct memories of past lives led them to search for a way back to this former self. For others, a general sense of "what came before" had left its mark on their soul now. In most cases, Druids described a feeling or energy that they shared—often interpreted as arising from a common past.

The spiral of time moves us through the embodied and the disembodied planes, connected through the love and memories of the living and the dead. Being—both here and on the other side of the veil—that thin raiment between the worlds of the living and the dead—is meant to be fully and richly experienced. Whether arriving into embodiment on earth or disembodiment in the Summerlands, we are welcomed in a celebration of homecoming. We are our ancestors and will be our descendants; in many ways, our current life is a process of discovering who we already are rather than generating a new identity. The past reverberates through the present, calling us back to an older, bigger self we have largely forgotten but who reveals themselves bit by bit, unfolding into the present. I had discovered a connection to a self that had already existed, and Druidry was a vehicle to remembering it.

In 2005, I hiked down a steep, nearly overgrown trail toward a small grove of trees on a cliff overlooking Mill Creek in Forest Falls. The place had always drawn my eye from the canyon floor below it, and when I initiated myself into the Order of Bards, Oates, and Druids, I knew I would do it there. It was May and the several miles of trail I had climbed was edged by a riot of colorful wildflowers. When I reached the grove of trees, I first asked permission to enter. The place had a reputation among locals for making people feel as if they were being watched. I was visiting an acquaintance's home, and it was only polite to knock and then ensure I did not overstay my welcome. I wandered through the trees until I had a feeling of *here* that welled up as I stood in a small clearing, with pines marking East and North and live oaks marking South and West. I made a symbolic center fire of apricot rose petals, since a real flame would be a danger in the already drying meadow. I poured cold snow-melt from Mill Creek over my head and neck as a ritual bath, the warm breeze quickly drying my face and hair. As I meditated, my attention flitted from the hum of small insects going about their busy day to the smell of the warming grass. Love welled up in me: love for each of the grasses, flowers, ants, and spiders. The preciousness of life flowed through me as other thoughts faded away.

Then, quite suddenly, I felt the presence of a spirit in front of me. His wrinkled face was framed by obsidian hair and he reached out time-worn hands to grasp mine. As he did so, the earth opened up and swallowed me. Arms of earth and tree wrapped around my body and drew me into its embrace. Image after image rapidly entered my mind. I decayed into the earth, grew upwards into a tree, fell as a single leaf on the wind back to the ground and began once again the process of regeneration, pushing up through the soil as a mushroom. I padded through the forest as a coyote, hunting a rabbit and tearing it to bits. I shifted into the rabbit and felt the pain and joy of release, the rightness of the cycle of birth and death and rebirth. I was the raging river and the gentle stream, the quiet still of the ocean beyond the breaker and the wildness of the hurricane, the seeming solidity of soil and the heaving of an earthquake reconstructing the earth. The cycles of order and chaos, of creation and destruction, flowed through my mind over and over, each vision different and yet the same. As I realized how good this process was, how powerful and beautiful it was that even what appeared as suffering was only a transient gateway to the creative spark, the visions abruptly stopped. I was again in the quiet of the grove, sitting on the surface of the currents and cycles flowing beneath me. My initiation was done: I was a Druid. Or more aptly, I came to open to this Druid I already was.

The echo of the various selves I had been bounced into my current life; all I had to do was listen to them and follow their cacophonous trail. I was not living the brief linear life that appeared to be reality. Instead, I was keenly aware of the convergence of processes that generated self and other across time. Shifting my awareness to this state of being allowed a temporary transcendence of both life and death as the two united in single moments. Like living in two locations at once, bridged by memory, my Druidry now is neither what it was in lives past, nor wholly new. I am an immigrant from the past, with memory embedded in my bones, should I care to listen.

When I had my solitary initiation into the Ovate grade of the Order of Bards, Ovates, and Druids (the second of three grades or bodies of knowledge), I asked the spirit world to provide me with a guide, a spirit teacher. Climbing up into the forested hills of my inner grove, I stumbled across a small rustic cabin in the deep woods. It was quaint and small, a single room, with rough-hewn shingles and a thatched roof. On a little cobblestone patio just outside the blue front door was a wood table, set with tea for two. Little tarts, cheeses, sliced green apples, and blackberries accompanied a teapot, its steam rising into the cool forest air. It was autumn in the woods and a vase of my favorite flowers—sunflowers—graced the table. The late afternoon sun rendered everything warmly and faintly orange, dappling through the canopy.

And then, coming out of the cabin to greet me, was my guide. She had long curly silver hair, a bit wild with a few small wildflowers in it. Her face had more lines on it than mine, but her hands were sturdy and capable . . . unmistakably familiar. A bit shocked, I stepped back, the sharp crack of a broken twig marking the moment I stared into myself. The guide was me: an older and wiser me. Her lips swung upward in a gentle bemused smile. Her left eyebrow raised quizzically, just as mine did when I wondered what happened next. I began to laugh, in both my forms. Then we sat, myself and I, eating onion tarts and plump blackberries, and drinking wildflower honey-sweetened Earl Grey.

In coming to full awareness of time, including the process of selfhood, the boundaries between life and death become increasingly permeable. Over the course of my Druidic practice, this meant that I confronted the paradox that life contains death, and death, life. In life is the pointed and singular instantiation of a personality and journey, and in this process, all other potentialities of that movement through time die. In death, we are released from the limitations of our body and its limited experience of time, returning to a much greater and more expansive whole. Between life and death is Druidic practice, bringing the two together through thin times, asking us to confront our transience. Promising us that somehow, through all our many transformations, we will grow into the fullness of what we are.

To this day, I have not swum in the Pacific Ocean in water deeper than I can stand in. I respect the ocean. I dearly love her. But I don't know her intimately the way I know the woods and the mountains, so my excursions are only waist-deep. But many times, as I swim to the bottom of a pool, I flip over and watch the interplay of the light in the water. I remember her stillness entering my body, asking me to trust her, asking me to let go—her fluidity meeting my rigidity and fear. I remember what it was to be released from my body so that I could be part of that union of light and movement. While the trees are my friends and the mountains my cozy and comfortable home, in moments of grief and loss when I am entirely unmoored and shaken, I go to the edge of the Pacific Ocean. I sit and watch her furious waves. I wade into her icy tendrils. And I remember to let go. She never fails to push me to the surface.

CHAPTER 3

Becoming a Body

FIGURE 3 *The cauldrons of the body.*

The mist settled lightly onto my skin like dew, its cool touch bringing me inspiration and excitement. Looking down on Seattle from my nineteenth-floor balcony, it felt as if I could shape-shift into one of the seagulls that occasionally winged by on sunnier days, leaping from my little perch and soaring effortlessly through the seemingly endless fog. In my imagination, there was no street below and no buildings in front of me—only this softly shifting world of grey, barely illuminated by lights from other buildings. It connected to the dreams I'd had ever since my childhood—the dreams in which I looked out over vast space, traveling forever but never arriving, filled with potential but never reaching a destination. I was an observer, removed from the bustling world of people, more mist than human.

When I speak to friends about how they relate to their bodies, most of them seem to have accepted from infancy that they are in a body and that this body is them. As a neurodivergent person, that has not been my experience. In Kindergarten, like many children, I pretended to be an animal. I would follow my cat around our apartment, crawling on all fours, imagining what it was like to see the world as she did. Unlike many children, I maintained an internal resistance to being in a human body, believing that if I could find the just-right time and place, I could leave it behind like a snake shedding its too-small skin. Being in a body felt as if I were trapped in a cage, sadly consigned to a fragile and limited existence. In my dreams, I left my body behind, experiencing a diverse array of forms and perspectives: dogs, birds, adult human bodies of various sorts, fantastical beings who had no names. In my waking world—a confusing kaleidoscope of too much visual clutter and noise and emotion—I often looked at thin places in nature, little hollows or doorways, and felt sure that if I could just remember how, I could slip through to some other realm where I was no longer stuck in such a slow and dull vessel.

I was eleven when one afternoon I joyfully traipsed home in a drenching downpour. I peeled off my socks and shoes, letting the stream that had collected on the edge of the rural road rush around my toes. At home, I climbed the Redwood in our front yard to my favorite place, a perfect little seat the tree had made for me of three twisted branches. Thirty feet up, the wind buffeting my face as it pulled the fine needles here and there, with the intoxicating scent of rain on damp earth, I acutely longed to *become* the storm. I wanted to let go of feeling the rain and wind washing my skin and instead, *be* the wind and the rain. I felt I should be able to let go of this body, to dissipate into the storm and be scattered on the wind.

Of course, I could not. No amount of feeling that I ought to be able to find union with the storm could make it so. For the first time, my mind acknowledged that it was not that I had forgotten how to let go of my humanness. It was that there was no pathway back to the abyss, the nothing, from which all had come. It felt like I had been imprisoned, a literal life sentence, confined to just one very limited existence. My heart broke, and my back leaned against the solid trunk as my chest heaved with sobs. I was really and truly stuck in this body. My tears would never be the rain; my breath would never be the wind.

I suspect that for many more neurotypical Druids, Druidic practice permits transcendence of the physical form. Through ritual, journeying, and meditation, Druidry affords a toolkit for accessing altered states of consciousness beyond the waking world and provides a supportive structure and system for understanding what we find there. For me, born with a propensity for a very lively imagination and to a mother who practiced Christian mysticism, transcendence came easily. Grounding, returning to earth and my body, was much more difficult. Until I embarked on the Druid path, I often (even daily) felt a longing to escape the human life. The world of the forest, or even of my pets, was so much easier, more comprehensible, and more inviting. It did not hurt the way the world of humans did. My Christian upbringing did not help me with this, because the world in Christianity is viewed as fallen and the imperfect body as undesirable. Christians generally affirm the sentiment that what we want is divine union and perfection. Druidry, from the very beginning of my first initiation, demanded otherwise.

"Will you open yourself to this life's joy, as well as its suffering?" I paused, letting this question in my initiation sink in. I had not anticipated a request that I should find happiness in embodiment. I knelt on the forest floor, its thick carpet of pine needles both springy and prickly under my knees. "Can I let joy in?" I wondered. "I mean, really let the joy of *living in this body* in?" I had lived with chronic pain and illness for five long years, and the disconnect I felt from neurodivergence for a lifetime. All I could promise was that I would try. This simple commitment led me on a journey that has gradually, slowly brought me into new ways of experiencing my physicality and finding joy and peace in embodiment over the course of the last sixteen years.

The journey began with learning some basic forms of Druid meditation: the inner grove and the light-body. Perhaps because I had lived in chronic pain for so long, these two practices were like an immediate balm for my worn-out body and mind. I sat on the floor of my craft room and lit a lone candle on my sparse, newly created altar. I slowed my breathing, deepening it until it came into my belly. I had learned this much from my explorations in Buddhist sitting meditation. The pain nagged at me, but I told my body firmly that we were going to work on healing. I visualized the soles of my feet beginning to fill with bright blue and white light. It was as if a small star was born under them, and the light slowly swirled on my soles. I imagined this light slowly creeping through my ankles, calves, and knees, filling me with its warmth and radiance. My thighs were filled with light, and then it pooled into my pelvis, meeting my pain with warmth, vitality, and healing power. Like a bowl of light filled to overflowing, the light swept upwards through my ribs, spine, lungs, and heart. It spilled down my arms into my hands, until my fingerprints were lost to the light. Into my throat and mouth, my nose and eyes, until it poured out of my crown and down my body. . . . Everything I saw was light. Everything I heard was light. Everything I spoke was light. And somehow, the pain let go its grasp just a little.

The light-body meditation is useful to and loved by many Druids, but I suspect my immediate affirmation that Druidry was the right spiritual path for me was intimately connected to its offering of useful tools for handling pain. While the inner grove and light-body meditations were not specifically developed for coping with pain, the grim specter of my then-undiagnosed and poorly treated chronic illness was ever present for me. I had prayed—tearfully, pleadingly, and constantly—to no avail. But the inner grove and light-body meditations allowed me to use my capacity to enter trance states in ways that gave me brief respite from my body's cries for healing, while bringing me safely back again from these other states of consciousness without the threat and debilitation that pain medications caused.

Its result was that from the very beginning of my Druidic journey, I committed to finding joy in embodiment and living—and Druidry met me with tools to do so. My pain and attendant underlying illness were not healed by Druidry; they were pushed into remission over the course of years by medical diagnosis and significant changes to my life to manage them. However, Druidry gave me the tools to cope with the pain in a healthier way, and to relate to my body without viewing it as an intractably unpredictable teammate at best and an outright adversary at worst. As I occasionally lay on the uncomfortable gurney in the emergency room, frightened of what could be wrong with me, deeply frustrated the doctors could not solve the medical mystery my body presented, and waiting what felt like eons for the IV fluids and medications to dull my inner agony, I freed my mind and soul to enter the Otherworld—the realm of spirit—riding my spirit-horse away from my body and toward my inner grove as fast as I could. And once my pain had become bearable once more, I would return, filling it with light and giving it happier sensations . . . becoming mindful of the sunrise as I was driven home, rubbing a cold smooth chunk of rose quartz with my fingers, savoring a cup of hot chicken broth, and praising my body for surviving as it drifted off to sleep.

Druids honor the physical body and the earth as forms that allow for relationship, growth, and pleasure. The body, with all its imperfections and limitations, is inherently good. The body and the earth are united in their cycles of living, dying, and rebirth—the necessary and desirable progression through which all things come into being. Imperfection is perfect; it provides room for dynamism. Without imperfection, we could not have the delight we feel when we learn and grow. I came to view my body as an integral part of these cycles and processes of nature. Illness and injury, suffering and challenges, are part of living in a body. But so too are awe, excitement, pride, and profound moments of peace in which our bodies come to stillness and we become fully aware of our interconnections with the life of the earth.

Despite disabling pain in my early twenties, Druidry gave me the capacity to view my body as a constellation of beings—as its own world—in which my mind was divine. In this way, I came to understand how to enact my commitment to joy in living in my body. I was billions of cells, of little lives, just trying to do what they evolved to do. I could give this community of tiny beings who formed my body harshness and cruelty, or I could give them gratitude and kindness. In attuning myself to a reverence for the earth every day, I developed a parallel respect and love for my body, for *nature inside me*. The earth was doing her best to survive and thrive under challenging conditions—climate change, pollution and waste, overconsumption. My body was doing its best too.

Pleasure

I sat outdoors, gazing up at the clouds and tree canopy, feeling the dry soil on my fingertips, smelling the acrid scent of pine. I turned my awareness to each of my senses, cultivating gratitude for their incredible capacity to connect me to the world around me. I considered how enjoyable it can be to live in a body, how wonderful certain sensations are. The stark contrast of the moon in the night sky. The damp blanket feeling of fog rolling in over the ocean. The scent of salt. The sweet-bitter taste of a marshmallow floating in good drinking chocolate. The warm, soft coziness of curling up under a down comforter and flannel sheets. Every moment of our lives is filled with the sensuality of being.

Druidic training materials and books discuss the body as more than an imperfect vessel for the soul. The body is intimately connected to the earth, alive by eating and drinking of her, and one day returning this gift through death and decay. Neither the body nor the earth is alienated from the divine, and therefore austerity toward the body is unnecessary for spiritual growth. Both pleasure and pain teach us, and life brings us plenty of both. Unlike some of the common religious undercurrents of American society, Druidry tells us that the pleasure we feel is sacred and holy.

Because Druidry views the body—and its capacity for pleasure—as sacred, it has welcomed people of diverse sexualities and genders, and has generally espoused sex-positive values. Sexuality is an extension of the sensual experience, offering a way of connecting to ourselves and our partners. In Druidry, the naked body is redirected away from capitalism's use of it for marketing—both from sexualizing people and from inculcating shame. While I have never experienced nudity in Druidic group ritual in the United States, "going skyclad" is part of Druidic training, and Druids are encouraged to try it if it appeals to them. The idea is to reclaim our body for our own sensual pleasure and unlearn the guilt and shame we so often attach to our body's size, shape, and sexuality.

Early in my Druidic journey, I came across materials on going skyclad in nature, and paying attention to the ways our senses and awareness might change when we are naked. Miles into the national forest, I went off trail to ensure I would be safe from the prying eyes of others and spread out a blanket on the ground. Climbing out of my clothing, I pulled out a snack and a book from my day pack. I had figured that for my first experiment, I would just *be*. I laid down on the blanket, noticing how much cooler the summer air was. The breeze gave me goosebumps and ruffled my long curly hair against my shoulders. I had to push aside anxiety about some hiker stumbling on me, reasoning with myself that I was not only several miles away from the more populated areas, I was also off trail, and off a relatively unused trail at that. Still, it was interesting to observe how much being naked in this way—just being in a natural state of the human body—felt like a transgressive act.

So often, the body—especially the femme-presenting body—is disciplined and exploited for others' gain. Mainstream culture, particularly through the media, teaches us the many ways we must alter our bodies in order to be successful, desirable, or envied. We shape our brows and dye our hair. We cover our perceived blemishes, enhance our eyes with liner, lengthen our eyelashes, and paint our lips. We monitor our size and shape, trying to make it look like the bodies we see in magazines and movies, and then we carefully clothe it with whatever makes us fit in with others we want to impress. Meanwhile, our bodies are used to sell all sorts of things, but rarely depicted as being the locus of our own wisdom and sensual pleasure. We exist to meet others' desires and needs, not our own. The practice of going skyclad is one tool for sparking an inner revolution, helping us experience the body as powerful and wholly our own.

In the years that have passed, the skyclad ritual continues to a path to accessing my own power and sloughing off the ways our society degrades, abuses, and exploits bodies. During the #metoo movement, I sought a way to magically support the shift of consciousness happening in my nation—the shift toward acknowledging the individual and collective trauma women and femme-presenting persons faced in our society. Late at night, when the house was quiet, I shut my drapes. I peeled off my yoga pants and pajama top, and wrapped a soft alpaca wool cloak around me. Lighting a single candle in the darkness on the altar of the Morrigan—a prominent Irish goddess who is connected to battle, among other aspects of human life—I sat in front of the altar, watching its flame.

I shrugged out of my cloak, assessing if I could be comfortable enough in the cold room. I picked up my drum and began a shamanic beat. The quick, even, loud staccato pulsated through the deer-hide drum and outward through my body. I rocked a little as I played, feeling the lack of constriction, the deep tone reverberating through my flesh. A prayer for bodily autonomy, for safety, for respect, welled up in me and through the drum, an offering of my suffering for the goddess of sovereignty. Tears spilled down my face and dripped onto my chest, dampening the tips of my hair. Drumming, drumming, drumming, I let the beat fill my body and crash outward all around me. Generations of ancestors sang through the drum, generations of women whose bodies planted, harvested, and gave birth to life. Generations of women whose bodies were mistrusted or deemed unworthy, and those whose wisdom or power led them to abuse, torture, even death. I let go as I slid into a union of past and present, embodied wisdom and mystical ecstasy. No matter how much suffering our bodies had endured, they were sacred still.

While Druidry improved my relationship with my body, I struggled with some aspects of it. Druidry is inclusive of all genders and sexualities, but the Wheel of the Year is grounded, in part, in the pastoral cycle—which relies, of course, on heterosexual couplings to produce life. This is most prominent in the festival of Beltane, which focuses on fertility. While I completely understood its significance for an agricultural society, I found it the most challenging to make relevant to my own life as a queer child-free person. One year, we were gathered in a circle in a Druid grove member's backyard. The sun was very warm as we encircled a small altar strewn with brightly colored flowers around a central candle. It was time to crown the May Queen and May King and to watch their teasing ritual chase. A couple stepped forward; wreathes of flowers graced each of their heads, and their eyes sparkled, taking on the youth and vitality of the springtime earth. And then the chase began: the Queen laughed as she ran around the circle, diving in and out of it, hiding briefly behind each of us in turn. The King pursued her, a humorous smile on his face, dodging around us until at last, he embraced his bride. Laughingly, and lovingly, they kissed—the symbol of union of the oppositional sexual and gendered forces at work in the continuance of so many forms of life.

It was beautiful: the colors, the laughter, the love. It was also alienating. Unlike most rituals, I could not let go into its rhythm. I could not access full presence. Instead, I watched as a more distant observer, sliding into ethnographer mode as I always did when I could not relate to my immediate surroundings. Ethnographer mode provided comfort in a familiar role, allowing me to reflexively think through my feelings and thoughts, to observe, and to unpack meaning. I realized how foreign it was to me, deep down, to think of a gendered world, a world with clearly defined boundaries and categories. I was born breaking the categories, fitting nowhere. Who I loved, who I lusted after, had nothing to do with gender. I was after energy, soul, spirit—those who ignited the flame within, who catapulted me toward ecstasy and union with the universe. This force wasn't a physical thing, or a spiritual thing, or any other specific thing. It was everything.

It is how we breathe and open to the limitless light. It is in our union with the ancestors and the singing-into-existence of the future. In orgasm, with every quiver and quake of the body, with every tendril of energy that embraces the other, the cosmos is born. This moment of consummation is the holy reenactment of the creativity that birthed all-that-is. The Divine feels their own power and love, their own passion and lust, through us. This defies all categories. We are the endpoint on a vast web of energy, reaching outward from one original orgasmic moment of divine self-love. For me, sex is about spirit, and communion, connection, and communication: the primal prime mover. Ultimately, I am a lover to the Divine manifest through the universe. Their wholeness is reflected in my wholeness. Their passion and lust, my passion and lust. My body, the vehicle for their breath, caught in their throat, the whole universe awaiting its release.

Such were my complex queer thoughts as I stood observing the love and laughter of my friends, celebrating fertility for pastoral peoples. To this day, I struggle the most with relating to the festival of Beltane, but because Druidry is a do-it-yourself spirituality, I am free to experiment with creating new meanings and rituals. The multivalent and dynamic qualities of myth and ritual symbolism are openly encouraged in Druidry, and so I still meditate on what the union of Goddess and God mean to me, and how I can use the festival to celebrate the raw creative power of sex and ecstasy in a way that is less binary. It is Druidry's flat organization, its lack of authoritative religious hierarchy, that permits this individual work without barriers of requirements of belief or faith. While all religions demonstrate variability in the private feelings and thoughts of practitioners when faced with common religious practice, many—particularly denominations of Christianity, which dominate the US landscape—publicly demand adherence to doctrine, to the beliefs espoused by authoritative leaders. Druidry, in eliminating authoritative leaders (and having only administrative or organizational ones), opens the door to individual experience and personal gnosis as sufficient, proposing that rather than agreement among practitioners, we settle on respectful sharing. In this way, myths, rituals, and practices that do not resonate with one's own spiritual needs or experiences can be dropped, reinterpreted, or reinvented. Druidry offers a liturgy, a form for ritual to take—a way to put the body in service to the art of performing the sacred. But the possibilities for the shapes this art takes are limitless.

Art

Ross Nichols (also known as Nuinn), one of the key founders in British Druidry, once said that "Ritual is poetry in the world of acts" (Order of Bards, Ovates, and Druids n.d.). Druidic ritual is meant to be art as much as spirituality, engaging the body in performance that is both transformative and creative. In ritual, the body acts as an artistic medium, through which movement, song, and poetry are articulated. Ritual is therapeutic and allows us to process the difficult parts of human life, composting them into something beautiful and sustaining. The body is the tool through which we can creatively express these transformative acts.

In 2013, I was part of two group initiation rituals: one for a new member of the Order of Bards, Ovates, and Druids and my own Ovate (second-grade) initiation. In both, the use of the body's sensations was integral to leading initiates through a process of separation, liminality—or the state of being between socially recognized categories, and reincorporation into the group. The ritual for the new member began with a small group of us walking out into the field away from camp. Leaving the sociable central fire and circle of yurts behind, we traipsed across the wet grass into an adjoining fallowed field. We walked slowly and carefully, leading the blindfolded initiate through the cold, damp November air toward our destination. At the beginning of the initiate's ceremony, she was asked to kneel in a small ball on the wet earth and was then covered with a large deer hide. Encased in darkness in the symbolic womb, she was both geographically separated from the group at the camp and physically placed into a liminal state—

both human and other, born and unborn—between light and day, ordinary and extraordinary reality. The birthing into becoming a Druid was both symbolic and literal, as she re-entered the world through emerging from the leather womb just as Taliesin was born of Ceridwen's bag of skins. The physical sensation of pushing through the heavy hide and emerging once more into the bright world outside it yields a union of physical sensation and magical transformation—like literal birth, it is an act that transforms both body and psyche.

In my Ovate initiation, the separation was more physical and the liminality more extensive. The initiation began with each of us waiting, blindfolded, in the woods at night. Far from the central fire, we could barely hear other Druids near its warmth. The Pennsylvania September night had a chill in the air and each of us sat in silence, far from one another, in deep meditation. This was our second initiation of three in the Druid order; we had encountered the basics of meditative and ritual work in our training in the bardic grade, and we were now embarking on the more inward journey of the Ovate. Minutes slid by as I grew colder and my consciousness slipped more and more into a dream-like state. The fire and social world seemed incalculably far away; I felt as though I might be lost in time and place. By the time a ritualist came to fetch me and lead me—blind and stumbling—to my initiation, I was half in the apparent world and half in a wholly different reality. This was, of course, precisely the state of consciousness optimal for a meaningful, transformative initiation. It had been accomplished through not only the use of my body (and others') through physical distance in a symbolic sense, but also through using limitations on my sense of sight to shift my consciousness and heighten the juxtaposition of the cold aloneness of the meditative wait with the cozy and warm welcome of the collective fire, with the initiatory ritual actions mediating between the two.

The body, then, is not simply a vehicle to drive mental or spiritual change but is also an integral part of the ritual process, used as a ritual instrument to shift consciousness. This is common across religions, but is perhaps even more significant in Druidry, because Druids have no permanent gathering place. Ritual is generally performed outdoors, usually in temporary locations. Altars are makeshift and transient, and frequently in remote areas or someone's back yard, constructed with items drawn from the entire group. Because of this, ritual art and symbolism are often expressed through the body—in movement, singing, and narrative speeches—as well as through clothing, staffs, drums, and other instruments carried and manipulated by the body. Ritual is both religious practice and performance art. From planning ritual and gathering the altar decorations to chanting, dancing, and storytelling, Druidic ritual is about honing the artistic crafts of performance as much as it is about connecting to the cycle of the seasons, to the spirit world, and to one another. The bardic arts are a key facet to Druidic training and practice. Just as Druidry proposes that every Druid is a priest, it also proposes that every Druid is an artist. This is most prominent in the adoption and adaptation of the Welsh tradition of eisteddfod, which was historically a competitive festival of music and poetry.

We were gathered around the campfire that was warming the Northern California chill. We passed a flask of whisky around the circle, each taking a gulp if the mood struck us. Though I was practiced in public speaking for teaching and presenting in meetings, performing in eisteddfod or functioning as a ritualist was a different skill. I took a shot of whisky and let its fire burn down my throat. I stopped reciting the poem in my head and focused my gaze on the fire, letting the crackling movement of light guide me into a light trance state. I wanted to *feel* the poem in my whole being when I performed it, not simply recite it from memory. I wanted the poem to emerge from the meeting place of the spirit world's inspiration and my mind the way it did when I had dreamed it:

> *Sky above and earth below*
> *It is through you all blessings flow*
> *Stars guide my path on moon's wavering light*
> *Through the cool embrace of night*
> *And with the sun red-gold of morn*
> *Crystals of dew on leaves are born*
> *Soft mossy banks beneath wise trees*
> *Are friends and gently call to me*
> *And river in its joyous dance*
> *Goes where it will by happenstance*
> *Masters all these spirits be*
> *If with my heart I choose to see*
> *Break free from veil 'tween thee and I*
> *And to your love my soul will fly*

Reciting was an exercise in memory and performance—but more than this, it was practicing opening my body and mind to connection with the spirits that inspired the poetry and sharing this with others. For American Druids, eisteddfod is usually non-competitive, but is instead a time for sharing bardic arts with others and, through music, stories, and poetry, generating a transformative magic for those in the group. Eisteddfod is both about sharing one's inspired work and also about building performance art pieces held in the community—teaching chants, songs, and stories that can then be incorporated into rituals with others.

Likewise, Druid gatherings frequently offer workshops in various arts and crafts, which are often a union of embodied skill, practical use, and magic. As I write this, on one of my altars a candle is burning in a holder I made in a metal-working workshop offered by a fellow Druid grove member at our annual retreat. Several years ago, as I began to realize that I wanted to become more creative in my academic work and live a more united, seamless life, the Druid retreat provided me a perfect opportunity to focus on this goal. A half dozen of us gathered at a mountain cabin at over a mile high in elevation. Each of us had brought at least one workshop to share with the group, providing materials and skill-building in an area of our Druidry that we felt comfortable with. I'd carefully assembled a wide range of materials and bound some small handmade journals for people to work on vision collages. A fellow grove member, skilled in metal-working and jewelry making, had brought thin metal circles, metal-working tools, and metal stamps for us to make candles and candle holders.

We sat at a picnic table on the deck in the warm late afternoon sun, trying our hand at working the metal. She explained the general process, then helped us as needed as we began to try our hand at it. I carefully fluted the edges of my candle holder, then began the stamping process. She had brought with her a number of stamps—a tree, a spiral—and also encouraged us to consider the candle holder process a magical one, in which we could stamp ogham into our work. Ogham is an alphabet composed of hashmarks on a single vertical line that dates back to as early as the fourth-century CE Ireland. Contemporary Druids use it as a mnemonic device and way of organizing magical associations (most commonly between trees and meanings) as well as a way to work magic using the symbols, which can be inscribed on the body, art, and other objects.

I thought carefully about how I had changed over the course of my time as a professor of anthropology, about my needs and desires, about the life I wanted to live. I considered which of the letters, the *feda*, would have the energy to help manifest these changes I wanted to make. One by one, I committed my body's energy to my goal, slowly and purposefully hammering out the letters with the small chisel. Again, the body was not merely the vehicle for getting the piece done. The body was also a vessel of energy that would be infused into the piece so that when candles were lit on it with intention, the energy infused into it would carry me forward— especially when it became difficult to sustain the work of transformation.

The body is more than a vehicle or a vessel for our spirit. In Druidry, it holds the power to transform one's consciousness and life. It is how we accumulate skill and wisdom, how we experience ecstasy, and how we connect to the natural world around us. We often close group ritual with feasting together, coming back fully into our bodies after focusing on the spirit. Together, we return from the challenging psychological, emotional, and magical acts of ritual to the vibrant world of ordinary consciousness. We share what humans have shared for hundreds of thousands of years— the pleasures of eating, talking, and laughing—feeding our bodies after we have fed our spirits.

CHAPTER 4

The First Spiral

Recognizing a Participatory World

Deep within the still center of my being, may I find peace.
—DRUID'S PEACE PRAYER FROM THE ORDER OF BARDS, OVATES, AND DRUIDS

In the study of religion, there has been a movement away from studying mysticism and consciousness toward the political, economic, and social, and from studying cross-religious commonalities to focusing on cross-religious differences (McDaniel 2018). Simultaneously, there has been a denial of personal experiences in academic work that limits studies of mysticism and embodied spirituality (McDaniel 2011). Avoiding such topics in academic work delegitimizes them in both our own culture and in others, and affirms a materialist worldview that is culturally constructed in the Western world. Even as academia generally affirms this materialist worldview (including in anthropology, a critique offered in Viveiros de Castro 2011), half of Americans report mystical experiences, which indicates that this is an important area of study in order to understand how people come to have and interpret religious experience (McDaniel 2018: 4). To this end, my own work moves away from the dualism too often present in contemporary academic study of religion. I focus squarely on religion (and magic) as I have experienced it—as mystical and as training in moving between states of consciousness. I do so through offering myself first as full participant, and afterward as researcher. This book's construction mirrors the way that Druidry is practiced by me and by many others—as a movement back and forth between intense relational spiritual experiences and analytical skepticism as a means to deepen my understanding of myself and the ways in which "self" is embedded in and defined by the process of being and becoming in which I live, move, and have my being.

Druidry is grounded in relational, magical, and participatory consciousness. It emerged from the responses Westerners had to the Industrial Revolution from the period of Romanticism to the contemporary climate crisis, combined with the influence of Western esotericism (Hutton 2009). Esotericism is defined by claiming directly acquired spiritual knowledge in metaphysics and practitioners seeking knowledge of hidden or invisible worlds (Versluis 2007: 1–2). Esoteric knowledge is generally kept secret, passed through either direct transmission in spiritual experience or through ritual initiation by other practitioners. Western esoteric traditions have six basic characteristics: a focus on correspondences between aspects of the universe; nature as alive and connected, forming the basis of natural magic; building perception of spiritual realms; transmutation (metamorphosis); analyzing for parallels between traditions and syncretic practice; and initiatory transmission (Faivre 1994). Most Western esoteric traditions are both magical and mystical—both focused on achieving practical, visible outcomes through supernatural mechanisms and focused on seeking experiences of union with a divine reality (Versluis 2007: 4). Druidry is more mystically than magically oriented, though like much of Western esotericism, it is a bit of both. This yields a different "feel" (as practitioners describe it) and focus than witchcraft traditions, which often center magic. Both mysticism and magic are approached through relationships in Druidry, and indeed, this entire work seeks to describe Druidry as a relational religion— as having a relational ontology, epistemology, and ethics. This relational orientation is not uncommon among mystical traditions, as seeking the deeper uniting processes beyond surface appearances and knowledge tends to generate a radically different ontology from dualist worldviews (Gill and Clammer 2019).

If we broaden how we define and describe magic, however, Druidry is very clearly mystico-magical—it is inherently participatory. Lucien Lévy-Bruhl (1949/1975) first described "participation" as being defined by independence from ordinary space and time, as encapsulating paradoxical experiences, and as producing a feeling of contacting a reality that differs from a normal waking state. This essentially describes what are altered states of consciousness, in which we experience in both dream and trance. To Levy-Bruhl, participation was essentially relational, without a sense of separation or individuation—essentially, the unitary experience, in which the boundaries of self and other dissolve and the self *is* other, and the other *is* self. This experience has defined my religious experience throughout my life, both prior to and after discovering contemporary Druidry and assuming it as an identity through my initiation into a Druid order. As described in the memoir chapters, my earliest memories of altered states of consciousness were when I was four years old. By the time I discovered Druidry as a young adult, the pervasive nature of such experiences in my life demanded I locate a framework through which to interpret them—Druidry was for me, and as I will explain later in this chapter, for many Druids, a way to belong to community and interpret one's spiritual experiences—not a rupture with the spiritual experience of one's past.

Druidry can also be understood through Susan Greenwood's concept of magical consciousness, the "mythopoetic, expanded aspect of awareness that can potentially be experienced by everyone; it is expressed in myriad varying situations and contexts, and it informs both the shaping of cosmological realities and individual behavior as well as social structures" (2009: 4). Magical consciousness integrates a spiritual other world with the everyday material world. Magic, then, is not only the symbolic ritual actions someone takes to affect the material world but more significantly a shift in consciousness from the analytical to the intuitive. Greenwood's magical consciousness is holistic, animist, and mythic, integrating the individual through time and allowing access to an ancient wisdom. As described in the chapters preceding this analytical chapter, space and time are experienced differently while in magical consciousness—one becomes aware of a collapse of the ordinary waking state linearity and distance, accessing new knowledge through experiences that range from subtle intuitive promptings to profound disruptions in ordinary reality.

However, as I will argue throughout the analytical chapters, it would not be appropriate to consider Druidry as magic and not religion. In fact, the differentiation between the two, while at times analytically convenient, is deeply problematic when put into practice. Marcel Mauss (1972) presented the classic differentiation: religion subordinates the human to forces beyond their control; magic uses forces to control events for human will. Greenwood (2009) argued this artificially differentiates between processes that do not have clear boundaries. For example, Christian intercessory prayer actualizes the will through asking for their God's blessing or favor, which is not different from a polytheist Druid like myself providing an offering to the Goddess Brigid in a request to overcome writer's block. More ritualized and impersonal actions happen in multiple religions too—the Catholic lighting a candle and leaving a charm at an altar is not substantially different from a Druid lighting a candle on the altar and placing an appropriate ogham stave on it as a form of magic. In reality, religion and magic both intersect with the messiness of human life, which is ever at the crossroads of both a desire for control and a necessity of letting go to a bigger, more complex process that we cannot escape or even understand.

Neo-Paganism, of which Druidry is one umbrella of traditions (as there are multiple Druidic traditions), formed within the context of post-Enlightenment marginalization of folk magic (Magliocco 2004; Hutton 1999). Just as academics and Christian clergy sought to differentiate religion from magic, magic was historically differentiated from science in the Western world during the Enlightenment, which left science with many of the traits common in complex, traditional systems of magic and which allowed academic treatments of magic to posit magic as inherently irrational rather than as a system that unites what we would now call empirical and intuitive ways of knowing and material and symbolic ways of acting (Henry 1997). "Alternate ways of knowing" were marginalized (Motz 1998), and combined with the influence of American Protestantism, this produced fear of the imagination (Le Guin 1985).

My own work posits a middle way—as a cognitive anthropologist who is also a Druid and nature mystic, I have wrestled for years to integrate two very different approaches to knowing. This book is another step along that trail, a way of understanding what my brain is doing in my Druidic practice and experience and simultaneously, a way of reframing and critiquing the materialism (and Western ethnocentrism) inherent in cognitive anthropology and cognitive science of religion. If we reframe such works away from the language of "how apparently rational people came to engage with irrational beliefs" (Greenwood 2009: 137) and toward *how people cultivate participatory consciousness and spiritual experience in a materialist and dualist overculture*, such work becomes universally applicable within systems in which science, magic, and religion operate as integrated wholes—and we are able to more clearly understand why these things our brains do may be adaptive ecologically.

Many of the experiences I describe in detail in this book could be glossed as shamanic under some universalist definitions of the term. These universalist definitions include: direct reciprocity and communication between humans and the spirit world (Siikala 1982) and altered states of consciousness that benefit the social group and is controlled by the person in the altered state (Peters and Prince-Williams 1980). Many of the universalist-oriented definitions and practices of shamanism stem from Mircea Eliade's description of shamanism as the oldest religion, which he characterized by "soul flight," a journey in which the individual feels they leave their body and enter a spirit world (1964). These early works inspired new religiosities that are expressed in non-authoritative, non-institutional ways, including "modern shamanism" (Selberg 2015). Michael Harner (1990) and Roger Walsh (1995) both described shamanism as a specific state of consciousness, and similar to how Druidry has been adapted to local contexts (White 2021), Harner advocated that neoshamanism could be localized. Later explorations of shamanism-as-consciousness categorized several "modes of consciousness" as shamanic, including spirit possession; communication with spirits without possession; sharing one's body with a spirit without loss of one's own personality (what various witchcraft and other Western esoteric traditions sometimes term spirit marriage or "carrying" a spirit); and soul flight (Sidky 2017: 29).

While soul journey, spirit communication, and even occasional spirit possession are common experiences in Druidry, and while some Druids call their experiences and practices shamanic (and though Druidry has been influenced by neoshamanism, including through Harner's work), I do not gloss the participatory or magical consciousness in the Druidic experience as shamanic. This is primarily because for most Druids, they do not perceive their social role in the same way as such universalist treatments of shamans depict. That is, their *inner experience* resembles some of the shamanic experience, but their *outer work in the world* is generally more mundane through political and social activism, education, and other ways that Druids integrate their Druidry with their vocation and at times, profession or occupation—something I explore at length in the concluding analytical chapter. Additionally, for Druids who function as spirit healers, diviners, or in other such capacities within their own communities, they may call themselves a variety of other terms—such as *filí* or *draoi*.

Additionally, while I am not of the mindset that there are no commonalities cross-culturally in the experiences and practices people call shamanic, I am deeply uncomfortable with conflating all of them. Cultural differences do matter in terms of understanding different cultures' worldviews, spiritual experiences, and the roles that spiritual healers and seers take (see arguments by Mayer 2008; Vitebsky 2010). While there are underlying universal neurological mechanisms at work, because shamanism, and more broadly what might be called *relationships with spirits,* are at the heart of specific ethnoecological and healing systems, and these are responsive to local natural environments as well as cultural and historical context, it is worthwhile to study diversity and context. Furthermore, if we wish to honor the requests of many indigenous peoples who have requested that we use their own terms for their spiritual practitioners and practices, we should be careful about glossing cross-cultural similarities in this way. Neoshamanism is tied to "a highly romanticized image of traditional indigenous societies for whom shamanism is the natural religion" (Lewis 2015: 129). Essentially, neoshamanism appeals to romantic primitivism. At times, such movements have been appropriative of indigenous cultures. Whether or not we personally agree that universalizing shamanism is tied to colonization of non-Western peoples or racist ideology (Kehoe 2000), we can appreciate that recognizing underlying universal neurological underpinnings of human experience does not mean that we cannot be equally attentive to diversity of those experiences and respectful of the concerns others have for context.

Finally, experientially, some of these practices—though all activated in altered states of consciousness—are not the same at all. Having personally experienced sharing my body with a spirit (though not full-blown possession), communication with spirits, and soul flight, while these are all experiences that arise out of trance states, they are profoundly different in how I experienced and interpreted them. As it is not important to my work to establish how universal or particular such experiences, practices, and roles are—but rather to discuss the specifics of Druidic experiences and how those experiences are embedded in individuals and communities, I will speak of Druids as Druids, avoiding conflating them with those who might have similar experiences or practices cross-culturally. I will refer to the experiences themselves as altered states of consciousness, where applicable, and as relational, participatory, or magical experiences.

Embodying Magic

As a cognitive anthropologist, my exploration of how Druidry works on individual and collective levels—as both individual training and religious community—is grounded in how magical and mystical experiences are embedded in our bodies and brains. Our brains are complex, developmentally plastic, in relationship with our body, and are hard-wired to be social; most of our brain processes happen outside our conscious awareness (Benvenuti and Davenport 2011). Cognitive Science of Religion (CSR) emphasizes brain-based mechanisms that are at the foundation of religious behavior. CSR posits that religion is natural for the human mind as a byproduct of our evolution (Boyer 2001, 2003) and that religious thought and behavior is therefore directly impacted by how our brains work (Whitehouse and Laidlaw 2007: 7). Religion is an aggregate computational domain— essentially, "religion arrived as a side-effect of other cognitive adaptations selected for prosaic survival reasons" (Smith 2014: 73).

Yet consciousness is not a thing we have, but rather a process we do. The brain creates our experience of being ourselves, largely through processes that are unconscious. We construct "a story of reality from the fragments of which we are aware at any moment, and we must construct a teller of the story, a self whose story we know" (Benvenuti 2014: 84). We co-create with those around us as infants and toddlers to develop how we relate to reality for the rest of our lives, within a cultural context (Benvenuti 2014). Largely formed from experimental psychological methods on Western peoples and with limited historical, theoretical, or methodological overlap with ethnography, CSR has significant limitations from an anthropological perspective, particularly with regard to understanding religion as a whole dimension of human life as opposed to piecemeal in individual computational modules or aspects of cognition (particularly addressed by Laidlaw 2016). In my own work, I offer analysis from a CSR perspective when useful, but also critique some of its underlying assumptions grounded in Western materialism, and offer bridges to understanding the individual-culture mutual emergence using approaches from cognitive anthropology, which emerged from the integration of cognitive psychology and ethnography, and particularly from early studies of language, kinship, and ethnoscience (D'Andrade 1995).

It should already be apparent—both in reading the chapters detailing my own Druidic experiences so far and in the centrality of magical or participatory consciousness to neo-Pagan (including Druid) religious practice—that understanding how altered states of consciousness (ASC) work is key to considering how Druidic experiences occur in individual

Druids and how this forms a foundation for the Druid's recognition of themselves in Druidry (as well as their subsequent refinement of such experiences), the subject of this first analytical chapter. The human mind can exist in various modes of consciousness, from an ordinary waking state (what you, the reader, are hopefully experiencing right now) to those that operate very differently from this waking state (as well as states in between) (Tart 1969). Altered states of consciousness (away from the ordinary waking state) shifts one's sense of identity and self-control (Evans 1989). It does this by providing us access to the unconscious, which is usually inaccessible (Winkelman 2014).

ASC is brought on by a variety of techniques that stress the body in various ways: through rhythmic sensory input (drumming, chanting, clapping, dancing, spinning, flashing, or flickering lights); stress (extreme exercise, trauma, sleep deprivation, fasting); certain forms of meditation (such as those using deep diaphragmatic breathing and visual imagery); and hallucinogens (Vaitl and Ott 2005). In such states, people experience a decreased awareness of surroundings (absorption); decreased self-control; heightened realness (vividness); distortion of time; lack of analytical or critical thought; and distortion of identity (such as possession or union) (Magliocco 2004: 160–1; Sidky 2017: 24–5). Maggie described how such moments are experienced within a Druidic context:

> I think it's both an inner and physical sensation that a god has shown up. I won't notice until I notice things in my body. My hands or my back will be moving and I could probably stop it if I wanted to, but I don't really want to. When we did that Samhain ritual with the grove—that first one—that was intense enough that I couldn't speak afterwards. I was perfectly fine and cognizant but I couldn't speak.

While "ASC are everywhere associated with revelatory (noetic) and awe-inspiring (numinous) spiritual, mystical, or religious experiences" (Sidky 2017: 23), culture shapes the techniques we use, the experiences we have, and the ways we interpret those experiences. This is why, despite universal underlying brain-based mechanisms for religious experience, understanding any specific religious experience requires examining its religious cultural context.

Ritual can bring about brain changes that produce spiritual experience (Newburg and D'Aquili 2001). One of the practices in Druidic ritual that commonly do so are rhythmic behaviors—dancing, drumming, chanting, and swaying, which affects the orientation association area—the part of the brain that differentiates self from the environment. This can generate religious ecstasy, including breaking down the self-other divide, resulting in the unitary experience—a feeling of oneness with all that is (James 1902). The unitary experience began happening for me from a very early age and was reinforced by my mystical Christian upbringing, which taught me contemplative forms of prayer from early childhood, becoming a foundation for my later explorations of Buddhist forms of sitting and breathing meditation and Druidic forms of visualization meditation. This experience was echoed among Druids I interviewed: "Through meditative states over time, I feel like belonging to one great energy source and I have experiences of the feeling of returning to that. So when you die, you return to that. It's very warm and very welcoming, and I feel very whole when I imagine it."

ASC activates the autonomous imagination, a largely subconscious stream of imagery (Stephen 1995). This enables communication between the conscious and unconscious mind without conscious control. ASC can also happen spontaneously, particularly through trauma-induced out-of-body or near-death experiences. These were not uncommon among Druids I interviewed as precursors to Druids seeking out a spiritual framework to make sense of such an experience—a trend mirrored in my own out-of-body experience I describe in Chapter 2:

> I do actually remember I was existing before I was born. I do have this pre-death experience—telepathic communication, a cessation of time, a feeling of love and bliss. I'm not afraid to die at all, It's kind of exciting and I'm rather looking forward to it . . . we're just going to continue in another form. (Fiona McMillan)

These so-called "anomalous experiences" help us understand the ways in which people initially come to seek outside their religion of origin (McDaniel 2018). The constructivist position is that mystical or ecstatic experience should be defined by the religion one is in, but it is not uncommon that this does not happen—and instead one has an experience that does not easily fit into one's preconceived ideas about the cosmos and self. This tends to spark a process of "seeking religious institutions into which to fit their experiences" (McDaniel 2018: 15).

ASC can also spark communicative and relational experiences with specific spirits. The process of discerning or knowing that an insight or experience is at a point of interaction between the self and the other is a sensory and embodied one in Druidry. Tanya Luhrmann discussed the process of discernment in evangelical Christianity as an individual development of their own patterns of recognition (2022: 51). Because of the complexity of the other-than-human world for Druids, they also layer the pattern recognition of different types of spirits alongside the "other" vs. "self" designation. Flashes of insight from the self is often thought to be the deeper, higher, or wilder soul providing insights to the immediate personality we have in the waking state. People may interpret this deeper soul as more expansive, wiser, or older than the waking state personality, which is often viewed as more limited. At the same time, we can also receive insights from our animal souls—from humans as animals, which carry different wisdom than our waking state. Then there are the insights or experiences thought to be initiated or supported by the "others"—and people often distinguish between types of spirits and between individual spirits through their own systems of pattern recognition that may rely on different sensory input. The presence of a spirit is often a very embodied one—heat and cold, hair standing on end, skin crawling, pressure on the body—or sensory through sight or hearing.

Western culture has largely marginalized ASC and more broadly, spiritual ecstasy, even though it is incredibly common globally (Bourguignon 1973). Yet one-third to one-half of people in such cultures that marginalize ASC have had at least one ASC experience (Wulff 2014). The perceived shifts in place, time, and the body experienced in ASC provide us with alternate ways of perceiving the self and the world. Rather than understanding these as symbolic visions that are in our minds, we should consider that they are lived realities on their own—a more inclusive way of understanding human experiences outside materialist frameworks (Viveiros de Castro 2011). Religious systems are realities that require development and maintenance; each operates on its own logic (Paden 1988). Many religious realities are not dualist or materialist. There is no "real" and "not-real." Instead, there are multiple "real" worlds—or in Druidic terms, multiple realms, accessible through different ways of knowing:

> We're just really tied to these bodies and this planet for this experience. I've always had a strong fantasy life, even before I was a Druid. I would wonder "What makes that not-real?" I go to my Druid [inner] Grove, and it feels real. There is a part of us that isn't stuck in our bodies, but sometimes we don't know how to get out and experience those other things. That's what I'm really working with right now: trying to get past the senses and navigation systems. I want to get out of the car every once in a while. (Kat Reeves)

While American overculture defines the real and not-real as a two-category system, reality is always mediated through the brain and body. The question is not "is it real" but rather the degree to which a group of people can participate in shared realness of an experience—it is an affirmative process, not a definitive one. Some things lend themselves more easily to a shared realness experience, such as a desk or a tree, but even then, perceptual differences can generate a different reality. Realness is more likely to be shared if the social group shares practices and interpretations of the resulting experiences. Druids share a toolkit of practices and few orthodoxic or orthopraxic boundaries, which opens up a library or archive of what is "real." Instead of trying to judge which realities are "really real" and which are not, there is instead a simultaneous generation of skepticism and openness that guides the Druid into greater and greater acceptance of the unknown and contextual instantiation of meaning rather than to a common doctrine, cosmology, or theology. This dovetails with the development of theories about consciousness itself.

In the mid-twentieth century, William James proposed that consciousness is not a single process, but rather an individual experience of a process (1950). There are many possibilities of consciousness, from which the individual creates and develops one—and that one changes over time. In recent years, theories about consciousness have increasingly posed an expansive and processual view, first positing that cognitive processes take place in and outside of the brain as a coupled system with the "other" (Clark and Chalmers's extended mind theory, 2010). Druids describe, at times, a reality in which what seems to be individuals—self and others—is in actually part of one process: "I think everything is one anyway. It's all energy; we're just pretending it's solid matter. At the end of the day, it's all one. And we're all part of it" (Joseph). Even more recently, Lambros Malafouris (2013) offered material engagement theory, positing mind as emergent property of brain, body, and culture through interaction. In this way of understanding consciousness, the focus is not on discerning truth but rather on holding multiple perspectives at once (including competing ones) that are useful in a variety of contexts. Holding multiple perspectives (even competing ones) at once due to their utility is how many Druids move back and forth between spiritual experiences and various forms of interpretation that yield different outcomes:

> When I think of the spirit world, of the Otherworlds, a lot of my understandings have to do with the breaking of physics. Time and place are just so wibbly wobbly, and two things can exist in the same place at the same time, which doesn't exist in the physical world. To access the Otherworlds, you have to do the counter-intuitive thing of not only going internal, to do centering and grounding, but that's also popping you out of your body to go into the external. Humans actually create the thoughts, the memories, the energies, the visualizations, and the understandings of the Otherworlds. I don't think they're god-created, I think they're human-created first, and then the gods are in relationship with us there. (Rev. Monika Kojote)

When we drop the materialist worldview central to the Western post-Enlightenment world and seek inclusivity of many other cultures' ways of understanding reality, we find theories that describe Druidic experience and Druidic experiences that illustrate such theories.

This orientation toward an integrated processual wholeness, of which the mind is only an ephemeral emergent phenomenon, has also been noted in some witchcraft communities (Best 2018). In such traditions, the individual and environment are one cohesive whole (ecocentric reality) and relational understandings replace categorical fracturing common in the Western overculture worldview. One Druid described the experience of spirit worlds as interconnected but different realities: "I do feel like I've seen spirits before. I do feel like they're around us, but they're like on a different plane, a different dimension. When you see them, they're like peeking through from this other dimension" (Siobhan). Rather than explain away such visions, which I have also had as a Druid, I offer that it is more inclusive (not only of Druids but of all peoples who do not conform to a materialist worldview) to understand realness as an emergent quality from individual sensory experience, affirmed by the stories others tell of similar experiences. That is, following Eduardo Vivieros de Castro (2011), visions of spirit worlds are not beliefs or cultural models (consensus views or interpretations of the world), but rather are objective experiences of other worlds. He argues that anthropologists have largely operated from materialist orientations, which affirms the primacy of a specific Western worldview, rather than treating as equal the experiences and interpretations of others. Once we operate from a position of equitable and inclusive treatment of other cultures, we can only conclude that first, no humans can access the fullness of reality as it truly is (due to our inherent limitations of body and brain) and therefore all human experiences are realities—some more common among certain cultural groups than others.

Yet Druids also acknowledge that these experiences of multiple realities are partially culturally constructed:

> It's the world next door, going into the sidhe, going into the Otherworld. It's hard to talk about. When you're there, you understand it. People can go and see different things. Just like we have different perceptions with our eyes, with our spirits we also have different perceptions. We bring our prejudices, what we think it's going to be. So we shape it into that. (Murtagh anDoile)

In this way, Druids often hold ideas about reality that mirror recent social theory: different worlds exist with no opposition between our representations and the world, no ultimate truth. We create different worlds through our differing representations (Henare and Wastell 2007). While such theory has been extensively criticized, it is useful for understanding how Druids hold multiple "worlds" or "realms" together at once, each with its own ways of knowing. The magical worldview creates the magical world. The waking state consciousness creates the waking world. Both are real, but they are differently real:

> There's a lot of wonderfulness in being embodied. I look for what I can and do enjoy. I'm going to try my large iced decaf americano with heavy cream in every coffee place I can possibly go to. Those are wonderful things. But also we talk about meditative and mystical practices . . . while being embodied you start to see behind the lathe and plaster façade of reality. And that is really entertaining: that you have a sense that reality is more than we thought it was. (Joseph)

There are different ways of knowing—some less conscious and some more (Samuel 1990). Knowing through ASC provides us with a mind-body form of knowing. Druids work on breaking the body-mind dualist split common in the Western overculture in order to self-consciously integrate ways of knowing—a work that is both practical and spiritual, a way of reconnecting all parts of the self as we reconnect realities.

Druids emphasize experience over belief (and even over practice). Beliefs are consciously constructed and lightly held, arising from experience. While Druids entertain beliefs they do not personally hold as equally valid (particularly due to recognizing the limitations of any one person's experience), they generally refuse to believe in tenets that are not affirmed through their own experience or reasonable extensions from it. While Druids' expressed experiential basis for belief is somewhat distinctive, Hufford (1995) has proposed that religious beliefs in general arise from experience, rather than driving them—something that dovetails well with the issue of anomalous experiences. Hufford offers that beliefs in spirits may reasonably be derived from experiences that are objectively real, but different from the ordinary material world. While such experiences are similar cross-culturally, they are interpreted differently based on culture and religious tradition (and between institutionalized forms of religion and folk religion). Culture provides a library or archive of sorts of others' experiences and beliefs. Through active engagement with the world using embodied techniques, we can spark experiences that develop belief (Morgan 2010). Initial anomalous experiences may set us on a spiritual journey, but after we have become a Druid, Druidic practices are actions that drive new experiences, leading to beliefs.

Taliesin and the Wild Soul

Druids often articulate the concept of the anomalous experience, the experiences that prompted their spiritual seeking, through the concept of the *wild soul*. This is the self who is wiser, older, and more in touch with nature's wisdom—the self who has lived before. The wild soul freely flows *nwyfre*, the life force, and responds in harmony with the world through intuitive knowing. The self as we experience it, in a waking state, is a limited and temporary instantiation of a much older and bigger being into which we develop ourselves—at times spontaneously and at times through effort. The process of unfolding into a Druid is a self-development process akin to Maslow's self-actualization, which develops character and well-being through a process that includes so-called "peak" experiences that are described as being like unitary experience: "We are again and again rewarded for good Becoming by transient states of absolute Being, which I have summarized as peak experiences" (Maslow 1970: 124). To achieve such states, people must overcome fear, self-indulgence, and other poor habits, as well as pursue learning.

Becoming a Druid is a self-selective conscious process, as Druidry is rarely available as a visible religious option. Most people discover Druidry as they seek out a new spiritual identity that can affirm and interpret anomalous experiences and beliefs and values that differ from the overcultural norm. The process of becoming a Druid is generally a recognition of these experiences, beliefs, and values in the Druidic community, a process that (like many neo-Pagans) Druids call "coming home." The Homecoming Narrative has been extensively described by Pagan studies scholars as coming home to a deeper self, to tradition, or to one's right place in nature (Adler 1979; Berger 1998; Berger and Ezzy 2007; Harvey 1999). One Druid describes this process using language common across Pagan traditions: "Being a Druid is a coming home. It's not about giving up what you were, and it's not about accepting what Phillip Carr-Gomm [a leader in a Druid order] says or someone else like him. It's 'Oh, I already think like that'" (Fiona McMillan). This homecoming is often linked by Druids to experiences and values they have had since childhood. The Magical/Spiritual Child Narrative is common among Druids as it is among other Pagans (Pike 2001). In my own Druidic journey, discovering the Order of Bards, Ovates, and Druids on the internet during my time in graduate school was a recognition that there were other people who were, like me, not indigenous but who held animist experiences and values. In my time following my initiation into the order, I reviewed memories all the way back to early childhood through a new lens, understanding my early and constant love affair with wild places as an intrinsic part of the wild soul I was—deeper, older, and more authentic than other aspects of myself.

While many Druids talk about becoming a Druid as a homecoming and not a conversion, Singler critiqued this differentiation, pointing out that conversion can be multiple models that describe a process of "transformation of self-identification." Focusing on Wiccan conversion, she explains that to be accepted as a witch, you must have a homecoming story. While many Druids have such a story, it is not an essential aspect of Druid identity for group acceptance. Instead, Druids speak of resonance with the centrality of nature—and especially trees—as the hallmark that someone is a Druid— even if they do not yet know it. The wild soul responds to the call of the earth:

> When I first got into OBOD and got into this group with my mentor, one of the things they talked about was what we had in common as Druids— We discovered that as children, we all had the top drawer of our dresser full of rocks, and shells, and sticks. And I'm thinking: "Is this how we recognize a Druid?" (Elizabeth Boerner)

Singler speaks to two conversion models: the Rupture and the Road. In the Rupture model, there is a moment of transformation of spirit. This is common in Christianity, when someone hears a calling to become baptized, prayed over, or confirmed in a church tradition. This is not common in Druidry; many Druids leave the religion of their upbringing long before they discover Druidry. In the Road model, conversion is a gradual process of becoming. While some of the features of the road model are apparent in Druidry, many Druids themselves would not use the language of conversion to describe their "return home." This is because many definitions of conversion are, unlike the one used by Beth Singler, far less broad and far more Christo-centric, including defining conversion as a sudden change (Pyysiäinen 2005); associated with feelings of guilt, anxiety (Atran 2002: 165–9); and as a result of significant personal difficulty or viewing the self as inadequate in some way (Pargament 2002).

The *wild soul* model is neither rupture with the past nor road toward the future, but rather a remembering and ever-becoming. One never arrives at a destination—the journey is the point, and it is a journey that will be repeated over and over again. As in my own initiation to Druidry, it is a discovering of a way to understand who one has been, who one is, and the underlying soul who one will always be. For many Druids, this is understood as part of a cycle of reincarnation and partial amnesia of one's past—and then a rediscovering of this past self in the current lifetime:

> In many ways, it's a sense that I've always been a Druid. I'm remembering my soul identity, not just my incarnated self. I'm living a life in this female body as this person, but the Druidry is where I'm from, it's who I am at the larger identity, my whole self, my true self, while I'm playing this role and having this experience. (Anon.)

In the Order of Bards, Ovates, and Druids, some of the first lessons focus on the myth of Taliesin—a powerful and wise Welsh bard. The Taliesin or wild soul model has no ultimate destination; recognition of identity is only one step in the journey. Initiation opens a gate to new influences, but the long and winding path has long existed, compelling the wild soul along—with or without the conscious current self's effort or even acquiescence—much as Taliesin is chased by Ceridwen into the fullness of his potential, but does so through becoming a sequence of nature-forms:

> The story of Taliesin talks about all these transformations he goes through, and to me it is symbolic of constantly becoming. I've grown so much. My life is so different. The way I look at the world is different. And it will be tomorrow, and the next day, and ten years from now. I am in process. I am becoming. (Kat Reeves)

The magical or spiritual child can be understood psychologically as "fantasy proneness" (Wilson and Barber), a tendency to have anomalous trance experiences (as we see, for example, in the Tellegen scales).

But if we consider the centrality of nature in the Druidic childhood, we find that Druids are re-membering the relationships between humans and nature as they are remembering their own wild soul. In this way, the Druidic journey is a transformation of both the individual consciousness and the collective human consciousness, undoing psychopathological interactions with the natural world. Some ecopsychologists have likened our contemporary crisis of the human-environment relationship as psychopathology in that it is destructive and dysfunctional, exploiting the other-than-human while also causing many humans to suffer (Metzner 1995). Others have drawn on Erik Erikson's developmental model (1994) to describe the Western overcultural human-environment relationship as a developmental psychological disorder, an "ontogenetic crippling" (Shepard 1982). The combination of acute awareness of this human-nature rift (and often, a deep empathy for other-than-human beings) with anomalous experiences yield fertile ground for agreement with common (though not orthodoxically required) Druidic models of reincarnation, kinship with all life, and sacredness of the earth. Conversion is generally socially, emotionally, and mentally costly. The self-story is generally fixed by early adulthood, integrated with culture in ways that guide norms for behavior and roles, prioritize goals and values, and provide the narratives and images the person uses to construct a sense of self (Benvenuti 2014). At that point, the person has invested a lot of time and energy into that self, so change is a serious cost that is avoided when possible. This is why "conversion" to Druidry does not feel like conversion to Druids: it does not contradict or disrupt the Druid's existing self-story, but instead provides a container and language for it. While being a Druid changes the person over time, it is grounded in preexisting experiences that are generally dismissed or demonized in the overculture, and that receive affirmation and belonging in Druid community.

Aside from a love of trees, why Druidry? Why not Buddhism, or witchcraft, or any number of other religions that Druids often explore and to which they also sometimes belong? Druids I interviewed echoed aspects of my own decision-making process prior to initiation: they were seeking a spirituality that affirmed embodied life as a good thing, that at least attempted to address issues of cultural appropriation, and that supported individual choice and diversity. The contemporary Western overculture, heavily influenced by various forms of Christianity, has largely rendered embodied life—both one's own body and the earth—as sinful, imperfect, uncomfortable, and undesirable. The dominant religious worldview of the United States, heavily influenced by Protestantism and capitalism, either treats the embodied life as something to survive—as a kind of test in order to get into a better, more perfect reality—or as something to exploit for short-term gain. Ecopsychologists have likened these relationships to the self and nature as pathological—as similar to addiction or compulsion (Metzner 1995; LaChappelle 1988; Glendinning 1995) or to dissociation, a kind of fragmentation of the self that results in perpetuation of negative interactions despite awareness of them (Metzner 1995). Druids, by contrast, expressly seek a spirituality that is affirming of embodiment: "When I started my search for something beyond this realm, I was turned off by ascension-oriented things. The idea of leaving the earth, the thing I find most sacred, doesn't appeal to me. I am an animal; I belong on this earth. I am not evil or bad; I am an animal with needs" (Dana O'Driscoll). While Druids recognize (and often studied in university) that many indigenous cultures and religions did not have this struggle with embodiment, many expressed conscious attempts to find a spiritual space that was open to white people and did not feel like cultural appropriation (while Druids are of many ethnicities, most identify as white).

This proves more difficult in practice than many anticipate. The three main Druid orders—AODA, OBOD, and ADF—have different approaches to constructing Druidry, but all of them borrow from the folklore of various European cultures and struggle with boundary-setting. Druids noted that if the group was defined too narrowly, it struggled to stay alive and functioning. But if it was defined too broadly, it became everything and anything—nothing distinctive at all. Hence, Druids tend to center on what Sabina Magliocco (2004) called the "Celtic Twilight Zone"—claims of Celticity without actual relationships to anything particularly Celtic. "Celtic" itself is so broad that it lumps together a number of different distinctive localized cultures, each with their own gods, sacred places, mythology, and practices. It is an ongoing matter of discussion and even debate how to define the boundaries of Druidry with regard to its cultural influences, and whether or not contemporary Druids are appropriative of subaltern European cultures. This is a matter that is very complicated in the United States, and often tied to ancestral trauma and loss. While ancestry does not generate ethnicity, in the United States, ethnicity was often intentionally obliterated by ancestors due to colonialism, slavery, and inequality. Among many U.S. citizens, both white and people of color, there is a sense of attempting to reclaim what was lost. White Druids often have no immediate ties to their ancestral past, but they also do not view white Protestantism or Catholicism as desirable either. For Druids of color, their ancestral traditions have often been stripped from them—and different contemporary ethnic groups respond in various ways (not always positively) to those who want to return. Druidry is a community that offers a sense of belonging in the journey toward uncovering relationships with the past, of honoring what was lost to the pressures of immigration and xenophobia, in a highly individualized way.

Even as Druidry develops relational awareness, it also affirms individualism. In any given religious community people will, despite outward appearances of doctrine and common ritual practice, have a variety of inner individual experiences of the religion (James 1902). In Druidry, this reality becomes outwardly displayed and expressly affirmed, and is one of the reasons Druids are drawn to Druidry as spiritual community. While American culture does not support a fully individualist-self isolated from the collectivist-self, the concept of the individual has a significant impact on shaping American behavior (Holland and Kipnis 1994; Strauss 2000 and 2002). This is reflected in American Druids' self-selection of a spiritual community that affirms individual difference and choice: "[OBOD] says if this feels right to do, do this. If it brings up emotional or psychological issues, don't do this. You can do this, or that. You get to choose the way you approach your practice" (Anon). In summary, Druidry appeals to people who have had peak spiritual experiences they could not fully wrestle into their existing religious options, who have long centralized a love of nature into their way of making meaning in their lives, and who want a sense of community without expectation of conformity to norms.

Cultivating the Druidic Experience

Druids often stumble upon Druidry in their spiritual seeking online or in books, recognizing elements of their own experience that resonate with descriptions of Druidry in these texts. Because Druid groups tend to be small and widely distributed, many people do not initially know of any groups except perhaps the larger orders that can be accessed online or through mailed materials. Druidic literature is often central to both self-recognition and socialization into Druidry, but there is no authoritative sacred text, leaving Druids to craft their own library of texts (Druidic and non-Druidic) that inform their spiritual journey (White 2021: 64–83). While Larisa White's analysis of a global survey of Druids revealed no significant statistical trends in specific books Druids owned or relied on for guidance, my own content analysis of eighty texts on Druidry indicated more commonalities in what Druids encounter (regardless of their selection of texts) than it would otherwise seem. The details regarding how Druidic community is developed, maintained, and transmitted through written works are extensively discussed in Chapter 8 (Druidic Community), but is important to note here in terms of how individual Druids, who so often stumble onto Druidry via books or websites, come to cultivate their Druidic experience.

If there is anything that resembles a core sacred text in the way that many of the world religions have a corpus that guides them, in Druidry this is not anything written by humans, but rather the "Book of Nature." The natural world is itself considered a sacred text every Druid should study, engage, and use for guidance. Because of the centralization of the natural world in Druidry, Druids will engage a wide range of texts in order to better understand it. One Druid explained to me that while there were a number of authors on herbalism, bushcraft, and indigenous knowledge about the earth who influenced her journey, "In the end you don't have to read anything to be a Druid. You have to spend time in nature" (Dana O'Driscoll). Druid orders and books offer practices that engage nature and cultivate Druidic relational consciousness—an awareness of relationships with all existences.

As in other Pagan traditions, Druidic spiritual practices "train the imagination to perceive visual and sensory images in ways that sharpen focus, increase the vividness of imaginary perceptions, and can lead to extraordinary experiences" (Magliocco 2018: 336). The extensive focus of building these skills within the context of engaging the natural world leads to a distinctively Druidic experience in which the anomalous becomes more common, weaving together the seen and unseen, practical and imaginative, sacred and mundane. Such practices result in a bodily learning process Luhrmann called "spiritual kindling"—experiences that become more easy to engage over time within a religious group (2022). Spiritual kindling engages a "faith frame"—a way of interpreting the world as if there are disincarnate others—in such a way that we experience a feeling of spiritual presence of these others, which reinforces the faith frame. While she extensively describes prayer as a mechanism of spiritual kindling (given her primary field context among evangelical Christians), such also describes other mechanisms that religions may use, such as mindfulness or visualization meditation. Among Druids, meditation and trance are offered as spiritual practices in many orders and texts, and form the primary mechanisms for "spiritual kindling" of an alive, sentient, powerful other-than-human (both incarnate and disincarnate) world that Druids encounter again and again over time. White's survey noted that trance work, for example, increases over the course of Druidic experience—the more years one is a Druid, the more likely it is that one engages in trance work (2021). Druids essentially train themselves, without any necessity for an authoritative leader or even a face-to-face social group, into an ever-more relational experience of life by engaging in practices that reinforce and expand the anomalous experiences at the start of their journeys.

While experiences can arise from consensus understandings of a social group, which frame our experiences and narratives, they can also arise from the body in its environment (Taves and Asprem 2016). Druid texts provide a common language and to some extent, common practices and concepts. However, because they are not authoritative and there are many of them, they afford considerable diversity of experience. It is likely that commonalities across Druids' spiritual experiences are primarily due to core practices that engage the body in the natural world and in the imaginal realms accessed through meditation and trance. The commonalities of experience that emerge from these practices are discussed at length in the second analytical chapter in this book, and the remainder of this chapter is devoted to discussing commonalities of spiritual practice and how they can be understood within a context of spiritual kindling. White's global survey of Druids found five universal themes in Druid ritual and devotional practice: meditation and/or visualization; prayer or other relationship-building activities with spirits of nature; ASC and magical practices; using a nature-based spiritual framework to structure rituals; and connection to and stewardship of nature (2021: 186). My own Druidic experience, text analysis, and analysis of interviews with other Druids affirmed these themes. Ultimately, Druidic relational consciousness is developed through mindfulness (practices that generate greater self- and observational awareness), which leads to a sense of interbeing; shifting consciousness (practices that build focus, self-control, and absorption), which leads to *awen*; and integration (practices that lead to flow, creativity, contemplation, and reflection), which leads to an experience of synchronicity and deep meaning.

Engagement in nature and attending to the body and its senses are practices encouraged by Druid orders and books. These practices build mindfulness. Humans have two forms of attention: endogenous, which perpetuates preconceived ideas about reality (useful but problematic), and exogenous attention, in which we are drawn to change and newness (Sewall 1995). Attention is dynamic, and while it feels automatic, it is a learned skill. Speaking of visual attentional focus, Sewall offered that our subjective reality—the only reality we can really know—is determined by how we focus our attention (1995: 206). Druidry offers many forms of meditation to develop mindfulness: attending to our bodily senses, muscle tension, and breath; discursive meditation, which attends to our emotions and thoughts in response to a text or image; observational practices in nature that hone our ability to attend to sensory input and intuitive insight from the natural world; and visualization meditation, which hones our attention to our inner imaginal world. These forms of meditation produce different states of consciousness and self-awareness, opening access not only to self but to other, and more importantly, to the space in between.

Rather than attempting to transcend the body, Druidic practices hone our ability to attend to it, to have control over how we use it, and to use our bodily awareness to cultivate spiritual insight. Druidry affirms the goodness of bodies—of our own, of others', and of the earth—as a gift for engaging fully in life: "This is the life we're living. Let the next one take care of itself. This is the one that counts. You don't get to do that again. It's built into the religion—body positivity" (Rev. Kirk Thomas). This positive engagement with the body helped me through my own journey, cultivating mindfulness of my own physical body, thoughts, feelings, and actions in ways that helped me come to a place of peace and care for my body—a queer, chronically ill body that transgressed in multiple ways the expectations the overculture had for me. Body, earth, and life positivity are connected to empowerment and personal responsibility, both for ourselves and for the impacts we have on others:

> [Druidry] is about the understanding of self and noting how when self is not resonating in harmony with the world and the divine, the ability to recognize wait, we've got something out of sorts here and being able to identify what that is and make corrections that end up more positive for me. If I can't be right with me, I can't be connecting and right with the world and the divine. (Joseph)

Ultimately, self-awareness leads to awareness of "other"—and the permeable barriers between us/other—leading to an awareness of interconnection and interbeing, our mutual dependence.

Awareness of one's own body is paired with observation of nature, which builds perceptual skill, the foundation of knowledge (Milton 2002: 43). We have "anticipatory schemata" that are expectations we hold that guide our sensory perception, which make us able and primed to receive certain types of information from the world around us (Neisser 1976: 20). These can be guided by culture (primarily through mechanisms that cause us to act in certain ways in the world), but we also learn them directly from engaging with our environment (Neisser 1976; Gibson 1966, 1979). Knowledge, then, comes not only from culture, but also from our perceptual experience, based on both our personhood in our natural environment (the "ecological self") and on our relationships with other persons without further reflection (the "interpersonal self") (Neisser 1988). Perceptual engagement is different from study of engagement, which is why Druids are supposed to directly work in nature (through tree-planting, gardening, hiking, walking, and nature observation) rather than merely read about nature. This builds a connection to the natural world and a personal knowledge and collective memory of it that is more similar to traditional ecological knowledge than it is to the distance between perception and knowing that characterizes academic researchers and political organizers (Nazarea 2006: 320).

While the Protestant-centric overcultural messaging in the United States often positions the body and nature as "fallen" and undesirable at best, and evil at worst, Druidic practices are designed for unlearning the message that nature (and we) are to be feared, controlled, or transcended. Ritual time is localized, connecting Druids with the immediacy of the natural world rather than a uniform global Wheel of the Year, as well as prompting personal reflection that individualizes ritual to the Druid's contemporary life, allowing Druids to emerge from the pastoral calendar and into calendars that make sense for their lives. Nature engagement unites spiritual and practical dimensions of life, overcoming Western dualisms that disconnect the various parts of ourselves, both in our immediate forms and in our wider expansive reality. By breaking down the self/nature and spirit/material dichotomies, Druidry teaches us that humans are connected to all other existences and that humans and the earth can be good:

> When people ask me what is a Druid, I very much am like, we're the ones who are always the voice for the land, for our ancestors, and the nature spirits, and the shining ones—all of the different deities. There is a seeking connection with what is around us, which is like the first or second impetus of a Druid. We seem to be very interested and concerned about this physical world, because it's such a gift for us. (Rev. Monika Kojote)

Practices that build mindfulness, of self and other-than-self, gradually "kindle" repeated experiences of connection, even union, between the Druid and all else that is. This generates both a sense of one's smallness in the vastness of the universe and a sense of one's significant uniqueness.

At times—often, for me—this sense of connection is so strong that it subsumes all other experience. This is absorption, the quality that is at the heart of trance, a psychological state that provides moments of complete and rapt attention, blocking out the outside world (Tellegen and Atikinson 1974). Related to capacities to trance, dissociate, and imagine or strongly visualize, absorption is tied to spirit experience. In Druidry, these experiences are not found through transcending the body and earth but, rather, in interconnection and immanence:

> The otherworld is here. It's just a turning, not a journey. It's that space in between breaths, where you're not inhaling or exhaling, or in between thoughts about this and that. There's a space in there, we can wiggle ourselves in there and expand that, and go there. It's always present but not always acknowledged. You have to have a sense of wonder and drop anything you know. You have to be curious. (Anon)

While few people across religious traditions have frequent or "full-fledged" mystical experiences, almost everyone who is spiritual has some nonordinary experience (Luhrmann 2022: 110). Most children look for social consensus about spirit experience (Harris and Corriveau 2014), training themselves into spirit experiences over time. But *some* people do have anomalous experiences without training, particularly those who score high on absorption as a personality quality (on the Tellegen and similar scales, as I do). Even for those who have more average experiences—perhaps only one or two spirit experiences—time spent in practices that hone absorption result in people experiencing spirits as more real (Luhrmann 2022: 72).

Druidic visualization meditation or journeying practices train practitioners in honing both their focus (their ability to block out the outside world) and their ability to enter altered states of consciousness. Harner posited journeying as a universal human capacity largely lost to the contemporary Western world (1990). This practice and capacity have been revived among contemporary Druids, and it is largely this capacity that, when paired with mindfulness and engagement of the natural world, allows Druids to experience a relational world. Druidry does not offer one specific suite of spiritual technologies to achieve journeying, but rather encourages the individual practitioner to try a variety of them and use what works for them, which results in common experiences arising from disparate techniques:

> We all do the trance-journey, but how deep we get into it depends on the person. There are ways to achieve ecstasy. The most common neo-

Pagan ways—and some of them are general ways, not necessarily just Druid ways—is drumming, dancing. And there are some of us, not that many, who go much further. I call it body stress ecstatic practices. I get visions from doing this that informs my personal religion. The unverified personal gnosis is very important, but it's separate from group [ADF] religion. (Rev. Kirk Thomas)

Ritual is a vehicle for cultivating focus and control over consciousness, integrating altered states of consciousness, bodily engagement, and aesthetics. Ritual uses aesthetic, embodied, and sensory stimuli to assist practitioners with attentional focus (Lewis 2004: 159). The forms of many Druidic rituals help practitioners transition from the ordinary waking world, filled with distractions, to a distinctively set apart time and place—even in the absence of a dedicated ritual space. The opening of Druid rituals typically helps the Druid demarcate ritual time and place and engage spirit or earthy others—the ancestors, the nature spirits, and the shining ones (the deities). Opening ritual actions also help Druids transition away from the chatter of everyday life and toward attentional focus on tasks at hand. This may be done through mindful breathing, bodily movement, attending to the senses, and singing, calling, or drumming. Likewise, after the central rite, designed to accomplish a designated purpose—often connecting, healing, envisioning, or receiving insight—the closing liturgy affirms mutual relationships by thanking the spirits, as well as helping the practitioner reorient themselves to the everyday world, often closing with a feast to fully come back into ordinary waking consciousness.

Magliocco, studying neo-Pagan witchcraft rituals, argued ritual was the most significant form of expression in witchcraft and was a form of religious art (1996, 2004). Druids clearly view ritual as art. In the OBOD coursework, Nuinn (Ross Nichols, the founder of the Order) eloquently put it: "Ritual is poetry in acts." Yet unlike a "commodified witchcraft" focused on consumption (as described by Ezzy 2006), Druidry has little "stuff" in its rituals. It often appears almost minimalist, easily portable into a farmer's field, a forest, an urban park. Its most prominent expressive art form is storytelling, drawing from its history of viewing ancient Druids as keepers of oral tradition, including history, folk science, and mythology. Druid orders and texts encourage or demand extensive use of writing for communication, reflective journaling, and artistic expression of experience through poetry and storytelling. Most often practiced outdoors, the Wheel of the Year positions the Druid within a non-linear experience of time and anchors the cycles of nature to the cycles of human life. The Wheel of the Year also reminds the participant of the union of imagination, creativity, and the goodness of the body and incarnate life. The Wheel of the Year's themes recur year after year, emphasizing the cyclical quality of the natural world, yet also providing an unending opportunity for new experiences and meaning grounded in the progression of the individual Druid's life (Lewis

2004: 163). Through facilitating shifts in consciousness within a relational context, Druids tap into *awen*, which provides wisdom that crosses the ordinary chasm between the conscious and subconscious.

This state of receiving *awen* is similar to the psychological concept of flow—intense experiences that affect our perception of the passing of time (as defined in Csikszentmihalyi 1990). Flow generates a sense of being filled with happy and productive energy, easily holding rapt attention for the task at hand, and forgetting a passage of time (McDaniel 2011). Like altered states of consciousness, flow changes brain wave patterns and makes it easier to link the unconscious and conscious levels of brain functioning (Wise 2002), which increases cognitive efficiency and creativity (Smith 2014). Religious rituals produce flow states that are interpreted as peak religious experiences (Smith 2014). Flow has also been linked to artistic creativity, uniting unconscious and conscious mind with the body. For Druids, artistic creativity is, like spirituality and life itself, about the journey and not the destination. Druids seek to improve bardic skills, but generally the focus is on inspiration, embodied practice, and joy. Through these practices Druids reinforce their unlearning of the body-mind-spirit dissociation and the ways in which embodied joy is thwarted. Artistic creativity is an avenue for cultivating both religious experience and integration of body, mind, and spirit:

> We know that in major world religions, [there is often an] emphasis of textualism, intellectualism, the stuff in the head. And for me, coming into Druidism was an acceptance of the body. We already are in heaven. We shouldn't fret about it, just be immersed, in love with being on this planet. There is a reason we're in bodies, there's a reason we're on this planet. If bodies weren't important, we wouldn't be experiencing reality in a body. (Fiona McMillan)

The practice of bardic and other artistic skills, part of many Druidic orders' studies, marry flow states (inspiration) with skill building (study, practice, and reflection). Druidry ultimately demands we integrate different states of consciousness and break down the dualisms of the Western world. We break down the body/spirit, self/other, spiritual/rational, and other dualist cultural models inherent in the Western materialist and Christo-centric worldviews in order to integrate all parts of ourselves, and to integrate self in its fullest meaning—as process and relationship rather than essence or personality.

Being a Druid is a journey through spiritual experience (including altered states of consciousness), inspiration and creativity, and contemplation and study—all simultaneously. Weaving these threads of the human experience together is the journey of becoming a whole human being, fully alive and in love with the earth. Experiences are wonderful, but they are also something to express and contemplate. Most of the Druid orders ask for processing one's spiritual experiences through writing—letters to tutors/mentors, papers turned in at the end of a grade or level, poetry offered in *eisteddfod* (a sharing of music, stories, and poems), and personal journaling. It is not entirely surprising that Druidry has both been shaped by academics and draws academic-oriented people to it. Spiritual experience is also paired with practical studies of ecology in order to unite multiple ways of knowing. Critical analysis and discernment regarding both experience and study of folklore, mythology, and ancient cultures result in a process in which the Druid self-consciously develops their own Druidry with articulations of not only experience but also choices in interpretation and use of sources:

> I recommend reading and study as a spiritual practice and I do it myself. Lifelong learning is a good thing. The trick is to not turn into a literalist or a fundamentalist about it. At the end of the day, what the ancient Druids did isn't nearly as important as what we do now. (John Beckett)

> I believe a Druid should never stop learning. To me they are the symbol of the wise ones. Druids try to be wise and balanced and by continually learning and not taking the arrogant approach of I know everything. It's a good stance to be open and willing to learn new things. (Rory Harper)

The confluence of inspiration and contemplation yields meaning-making, including a sense of synchronicity in life.

This book itself is an example of synchronicity at work. At about the time I received tenure, I began to envision—including through Druidic ritual and meditative practice—what my career would look like for my final twenty years before retirement. Through a process of inspired visioning and measured reflection, I came to conclude that I wanted to turn increasingly toward work in the anthropology of religion and autoethnography. Shortly thereafter, I was approached about the possibility of writing this book. For a Druid, this is how *awen* and material life work together— accessing inspiration helps us reframe our lives and vision a different future. Reflection helps us frame up how these visions fit with our current lives, what changes and choices have to be made, and what drives us. Action puts into play the necessary components for the universe to align with our visions. This process is not necessarily viewed as supernatural, but rather as a more integrated process of how the universe operates than our disconnected overcultural models afford. Ultimately, Druidry is about sacralizing the everyday, and reuniting parts of ourselves that Western society disjointed. The integration of spiritual practice and its attendant experiences and emotions with everyday life, as well as mindfulness of the joys of incarnate life, are key to moving from the dominant Western Christo-centric overcultural orientations that skip the present in order to look back at the past and forward to the future, and instead reorients Druids to the now.

Transformation of Self/Other

At the heart of Druidry, then, is a transformation of the self and the other such that one increasingly experiences both as a single united process. As Rev. Kirk Thomas put it, "All Druidry is a container. It's a way of holding it all together. It's a way that I can keep all the experiences in a way that I can understand them. Whereas before, they were just weird experiences." Being a Druid involves harnessing assumptions about agency that are inherent to the human brain in ways that cause us to seek further experiences of other-than-human agents rather than ignoring them. Anomalous experiences prompt a "feeling out of place" (Luhrmann 2022: 69). Whether we dismiss these moments or not leads to different journeys; many Americans dismiss those experiences, whereas Druids view them as openings to a more expansive reality. They come to inform the Druid's search for a community, even if virtual, that supports making meaning out of these experiences and offers practices to cultivate more of them. Luhrmann explained that if a social group views an experience as significant, the threshold for identifying those experiences decreases through socialization, and once a brain pathway is established, it is more likely for the frequency of the experience to increase over time (2022: 117–18). Druidic spiritual experiences are a union of both the neurological baseline of the individual Druid (susceptibility to absorption) and the Druid's choice to view those experiences as significant, to make meaning of them, and to cultivate more of them over time. Such experiences come to be fully embedded with everyday life, such that the Druid may have some spiritual experiences arising from altered states of consciousness and others from choosing to focus on and interpret observations in nature as more than material. This latter type of experience, while embodied and in waking state consciousness, still involves a perceptual shift (and not merely interpretive drift), training the Druid to see, hear, and feel differently (and more attentively) in the natural world (Luhrmann 2022: 134). Over time, these experiences build, affirming assumptions about other-than-human agency and deepening a relational worldview.

Luhrmann's theory of interpretive drift has been critiqued by a number of Pagan scholars (Reid 1996; Orion 1995; Ezzy 2004; Pike 2001; Pearson 2002), including by Singler (n.d.), as giving greater weight to phenomenological experience than socialization into an identity. In fact, it seems that for Druids, socialization in Druidry is part of a process that— through perceptual and interpretive drift—increases the frequency of phenomenological experiences Druids have of other-than-human agents. In the findings from my 2013 survey of Druids, non-solitary practice increased the prevalence of place-based practice by 55 percent and nature spirit belief by 30 percent. Gathering with other Druids reinforces nature-centric place-based practices and experiences of nature spirits, as well as belief in such spirits. Luhrmann's later work indicates that she includes perceptual change within her concept of interpretive drift, but it may be more helpful to differentiate between the two, particularly within the context of embodied nature-centric practice. Change in perception was noted by Sewall (1995) as being key to renewing a relationship with the earth, as it reshaped the deadening of our senses that contributed to the problem of our apathy in the face of the earth's suffering. Roszak offered a similar observation, arguing that "skillful perception" ("seeing differently") was a devotional practice that could help us overcome the disconnection between "in-here" and "out-there," between self and other (1993b: 203–4). Roszak called this ecological perception, a way of perceiving that breaks down the boundaries between self and other and leads to relational awareness. In both OBOD and AODA training materials, as well as in some of the Druid texts that are available, practices are offered that lead to ecological perception: learning to attend more mindfully; focusing on participation and relationships; letting go of expectations; recognizing that nature is within us and not outside of us; and honing visual imagery skill. Such perception can be a type of communion (Abram 1990).

Perceptual shifts afford not only repeated unitary experience but also an integration of experience with knowing. Mayer and Grunder (2010) offered two concepts particularly useful for understanding ecocentric religion that integrates ethnoecological knowledge with religious practice: *erlebnis* and *erfabrung*. *Erlebnis* is lived experience, our impressions on an individual level, whereas *erfabrung* is the social form of experience—interpreted experience and shared knowledge. Both are at play when we investigate personal experience and how they are socialized. Druids begin seeking out a community that will help them make sense of *erlebnis* that does not fit with the Western overcultural norms. People tend to only risk the stigma of an identity that does not work within the Western rationalist and monotheist overculture when they feel there is no other option, when their *erlebnis* is so discordant with the dominant *erfabrung* that they must seek a new identity and community. The core of the Druid *erlebnis* is a relational worldview, a permeable and flexible boundary between self and other, mind and body and spirit, material and spiritual. The core of this relational worldview does not change when a Druid self-consciously takes on a Druid identity, because it is grounded in the Druid's anomalous experiences that drove the search for a community that would affirm and expand it. Because Druidry is neither orthodoxic nor orthopraxic, it becomes a big tent that shares a strong orientation toward relational experience, practice, and interpretation. One can be atheist, monotheist, polytheist, and/or animist—but Druids take on a Druidic identity because the Druidic relational *erfabrung* supports, affirms, and builds on their own prior relational *erlebnis*. These two ways of experiencing parallel divergent religious modalities are brought together in Druidry. Doctrinal phenomena preserve traditions while imagistic phenomena motivate individuals (Tremlin 2005). Each exploits different types of memory: doctrinal phenomena rely on explicit training, while imagistic phenomena are tied to significant events (Day 2005). Druidry has no doctrine, but its orders' training materials and publicly accessible texts provide for religious structure and maintain common themes in practice and interpretation of experience.

Anthropologists have written extensively about spirit belief and experience, sometimes calling this animism, sometimes mysticism, sometimes shamanic cosmology. Sidky (2017) proposed that "shamanic" experience (basically, experience of spirits and spirit worlds) was a by-product of humans' brains to notice patterns of causality and agency, a useful evolutionary trait. Decrying postmodern anthropology and experiential ethnography as anti-science and non-academic, he argues that such approaches do not belong in the academy at all: "being a mystic and true believer becomes incompatible with the goals and objectives of academic anthropology, even when defined in the broadest terms" (204). He proposes that even entertaining that the ontological reality of other, non-Western scientific views could be at all true—albeit without the capacity of fitting into a Western scientific framework—is not appropriate to academic anthropology and that anthropologists should maintain atheism or agnosticism in their methodological approach. Those who have attempted to approach such experiences with vulnerability and honesty about what they literally *cannot* know (in terms of the boundaries of reality) as well as what they *definitively can know*, he reframes away from their own chosen description as experiential ethnography into paranormal anthropology. However, this shift in itself affirms a nature-supernature or real/not-real dualist worldview that is at the heart of Western cultures (both in terms of Abrahamic religions' focus on transcendence and on Western science's focus on materialism). This is a dualism that is not universal and is itself culturally and historically constructed and contextualized. In actuality, we cannot know that such assumptions are accurate, but rather only what we cannot know through a materialist scientific approach. We cannot say that what we cannot know through such an approach is less real, as reality is always subject to our limitations of sensorial experience and consciousness, regardless of how we boundary those senses and consciousness.

Rather than evading the question of spirit existence, we might instead embark on attempts to describe the experience of spirits, while simultaneously explaining that these experiences are attained through a state of consciousness incompatible with Western scientific materialist ways of knowing. At the same time, affirming the realness of spirits and the spirit world still begs the question of how we can define reality to begin with, which is always limited. Postmodernism points out this issue—that it is problematic to privilege only some ways of knowing and some realities, but not others—and that invariably, those privileged are the realities and ways of knowing of colonizing cultures, never the colonized. This is not anti-science so much as accurately contextualizing science as a particular culture's way of knowing, which like all ways of knowing in all cultures, is more useful for some tasks and not for others. Admitting that ethnographic data is constructed from interaction and dialogue, and not recorded as if we were beings capable of fully extricating ourselves from attentive and other forms of bias (Marcus and Fischer 1986) and that we might treat ourselves as data points and not as scientific instruments is not anti-science so much as pragmatic and realistic about the limitations of a human being (any human being) to behave as a scientific instrument. The act of participant observation is itself an act of collaboratively constructing a reality—reality itself is never fully observable because human beings are limited in multiple ways. If academic anthropology is only accessible if we deny any non-Western positivist worldview or experience, and reframe all experience within only that worldview—we essentially limit the practice of anthropology to a very limited and narrow group of ethnic and cultural peoples. This applies cultural relativism only to the other, and never to the self—as accepting one's own reality as real but not the possibility that other cultures' realities might also be real.

Fortunately, in both anthropology and Druidry, it is possible to move back and forth between theoretical approaches to the question of reality and the relationship of it human consciousness, entertaining everything from what we can know from positivist and materialist vantage points to what we can know from experiential ones—even while in altered states of consciousness. I would argue as both applied anthropologist and as mystic that asking what is *really real* is perhaps an interesting but not terribly utilitarian question. People create useful or dysfunctional patterns of thought, emotion, and behavior from their constructions of reality. To understand contemporary Druids, we must engage with the question of what is *really real* the way they do—playfully, but with a very solid grasp on the limitations of the human life. Consciousness is something to play with, something to temporarily engage in diverse ways, and to always— no matter how ordinary or extraordinary—to question. Because of this, as White notes: there is a "Druidic habit of seeking wisdom everywhere—even within the words and actions of those skeptical of or hostile to Druidry. It is one emanation of the cultural norm among Druids to respect, and remain open to learning from all systems of spiritual practice and religious belief" (2021: 50).

We can maintain two co-existing orientations to reality at once (Tambiah 1991). One orientation is participation (magical consciousness), in which we are not individuated, but rather connected. Participation is expressed through myth and ritual and experienced through emotion and intuition. The other orientation is causality (analytical consciousness), in which we are individuated and distance ourselves from events to analyze, critique, and reflect on experiences. In this orientation, we engage in self-conscious meaning-making, integration, and synthesis with other sources, and discernment. Druidry essentially unites both orientations in its positioning of the self-in-the-world and in its regular practices. This produces an interweaving, both individually and collectively, of experiences of what is generally termed unverified personal gnosis (UPG)—of mystical experiences that connect and relate, shifting our experience of self, other, time, and place—and of skepticism of those experiences. These two orientations are supported by observations by dual-process theorists that there are two modes of information processing, fast and associative (low-effort) and slow and rule-based (high-effort) (Barrett 2004). CEST (cognitive experiential self-theory) argues that the rational (rule-based) system is more recent evolutionarily and is analytical, deliberative, relatively non-emotional, and abstract and is expressed through language. The experiential system is automatic, rapid, effortless, holistic, nonverbal, emotional, and has a long evolutionary history (Barrett 2004: 72). Druidic training essentially builds skills in moving between these in order to have spiritual experiences (UPG) and then interpret and examine them.

This is similar to methodological ludism in religious studies: religious truth is not something to define, but rather religious truths provide us with roles to play. In this way, social context and spiritual experience are united. We *play* at being religious, building "the capacity to deal simultaneously and subjunctively with two or more ways of classifying reality" (Droogers 1996: 53). We behave *as if* these multiple worlds or realms are real because they feel real as we experience them—while recognizing that they may not be real in a material sense. In anthropological work on religion, this means the actor never forgets they are pretending. However, if you are phenomenologically studying magical or participatory consciousness or animism (or practicing Druidry), you will shift between states of consciousness, each of which provides access to different capacities for knowing and making meaning. We do not pretend to enter an altered state, we do it. But the way our brain works in that state is different from when we emerge and reflect on our spiritual experience. Druids move back and forth between the two, never fully denying or accepting one state of consciousness (or even all of them together) as reality itself:

> This meat computer is simply not prepared to comprehend the vastness of what Richard Boch calls the Is. I'm not going to get it. I'm in a meat-sack. It's not prepared for true understanding for the vastness of reality. (Joseph)

> I always say I believe in reincarnation every other day. I've interacted with an afterlife, but until I get there, I won't know for sure. And as humans we're so presumptuous that we always have the answer. There's an old Irish proverb that we admit that we don't know anything. (Murtagh anDoile)

> I especially like OBOD as opposed to some of the other organizations because the only required orthodoxy is being an environmentalist. We're drawn together by our love of earth. I can't swallow an orthodoxy. I've been wrong so many times, and I'll be wrong again.(Dawn)

Druids are not the only religious practitioners who engage in skepticism; doubt and uncertainty can play a role in religious life (Engelke 2007; Henkel 2005). Ideas or beliefs develop over the course of our experience as we examine our own experiences and resolve points of dissonance (Robertson 1996). Rather than belief (a destination), the goal becomes being active in a search for meaning and wisdom that is never fully resolved (Kirsch 2004). Because of the strong orientation to the natural physical world, Druids can be agnostic or atheistic, even if they often do not behave that way. In acknowledging human brain-body limitations, they neither judge others' experiences as false nor view their own experiences as true, and with the orientation toward immanence and the present, they transcend the arguments that often occur between Western atheists and monotheists (see, for example, Mair 2013). Realness of all experience is both plausible and partial.

In Druidry, religious tradition and folklore is for inspiration and critical reflection, not for wholesale reclamation. Druids generate deep experience and lightly hold interpretation of those experiences. Spiritual experience does not translate directly to words or even to concepts, and belief is not a description of religious experience (Needham 1972). The concept of belief does not exist in many languages, and belief means many different things even in the Western world. Druids talk more about working ideas they have to explain their experiences or make them more useful (but that might well be wrong) and ideas others have that might be right, but do not currently connect to their own experiences or are not useful to them. Many Druids talk about *behaving as if*, primarily out of emotional, social, or other utility— positioning themselves as agnostic but behaving as if they do hold religious beliefs. Even Druids who are not agnostic emphasize practice over belief:

> I have specific beliefs, but they are beliefs I hold loosely with the expectation that I'm wrong about at least some of them. I like to say "hold loosely but practice deeply"—remain open to new evidence and new experiences, but explore your working beliefs deeply, as though you were certain of them. See where they take you. If that works well, keep going. If it doesn't, try something else. (John Beckett)

As I will explore in later chapters, this means that when contrasted with the pervasive Christo-centric definitions of religion in the United States, Druids do not necessarily think of Druidry as religion. If we reframe the concept of belief (both religious and mundane) as different "cognitive attitudes," using different evidence and different reasons for holding them, rather than describing facts (Van Leeuwen 2014), we find Druids tend to differ from other Westerners, both atheist and theist, in their beliefs. While their working hypotheses vary, because Druids study a wide range of approaches to knowing and maintain these are equally valuable, depending on context, they tend to view experience as a valid form of evidence for all of them. In the Druidic framework, the reasons for all forms of knowing and experience are to come into right relationship with others, both human and not human, and to develop the self in those relationships. Druids approach beliefs-as-factual-representation-of-reality of all kinds with skepticism, viewing the human body and brain as inherently limited in a very complex and vast universe.

Because belief about the nature of reality guides perception (Benvenuti 2014: 37), Druids train themselves to have a wider openness to perceived experience and to self-consciously construct belief (or avoid such construction). The Druid self-story, as Benvenuti calls the construction of self, is developed to be flexible, to accommodate new experiences and interpretations, rather than to be rigid and to ignore or dismiss information that does not affirm the existing self-story (Benvenuti 2014: 115). Druids develop self-realization as "a process of self-examination in which one comes to understand oneself as part of a greater whole" (Wu 2019: 442). The union of these two orientations: the causal and the participatory; the analytical and the intuitive—are found throughout animist religions and traditional ethnoecological systems that generally paired sophisticated observational and experimental scientific folk knowledge with religious and magical relational worldview, experience, and practice. These systems developed planning horizons that were more supportive of sustainability for the entire social group, that were easier to learn and remember, and more compelling to follow (Anderson 1996). They did not work perfectly, but they worked quite well as integrated systems for relating to the material world, including to the well-being of both the body and its natural environment. Druidry, as we will explore in later chapters, is a new religious movement that is building an ethnoecological framework for the contemporary world. I say framework and not system, because as I will demonstrate later in the book, achieving the localized specificity, social support, and outcomes of traditional ethnoecological knowledge systems has proven very difficult. However, in the development of a non-dualist integrated framework for knowing within the context of a relational worldview, Druids are forging a new pathway forward for decentralized, non-authoritative religion and for the ecocentrism arguably necessary for a more sustainable lifeway.

The Second Triad—
All as Conscious

Relational Spirituality

*Three sources of wisdom and companionship guide the Druid:
the nature spirits, the ancestors, and the shining ones.*

The Second Triad—
All as Conscious

CHAPTER 5

A Congregation of Nature Spirits

FIGURE 4 *Communion with horse.*

It is early morning as I gather the grooming box, bridle, and saddle from the tack room. The horses are lined up at their hayracks, crunching contentedly. The Southern Californian summer sun is already beginning to warm my skin. I look over at my retired senior horse first, a gray Arabian with red freckles all over him. He is quite elderly now, the first of my teachers in the ways of living with Horse. He doesn't understand the passing of time. Inside, he still feels young and if I let him out into too big a pasture, he will run and buck and play until he can barely walk due to his arthritis. I sobbed several years ago when the vet told me that this best friend of mine, this spiritual teacher of mine, would never carry me again. I found the heart and soul of my religion on his back. Every day I am with him, I thank Epona, the Gaulish goddess of horses, that he is in my life. That Horse is in my life. And every day, I stop to breathe with him for a moment, to run my hand over his forelock and give it a tug and to kiss the soft, white muzzle. It's my form of gratitude.

I shed tears ever so many times I'm at the ranch because I'll never gallop on Eoin again. But this is how we know we have loved deeply: we grieve. Eoin has taught me so much about human cognition, perception, and affect by demanding that I learn his other-than-human ways. He's taught me so much about my wild soul: about full presence, intuition, mindfulness, body awareness, and unfettered joy. Eoin came to me before I knew about Druidry, and many nights when I felt alone and lost in the crush of the human world—too different to belong in Christian churches and too religious to abandon them, I would climb on him bareback and lay against his neck under the stars. Somehow, I felt understood and at peace again. Among horses or trees, in a thunderstorm or the mountains, I felt most thoroughly alive, most *myself*, and connected to divinity. Early in my twenties, I kept trying to find a pathway between the Christianity that was the religion of my family and friends and the ecstasy I felt in nature, but I could only seem to feel that sense of awe and great love outside of the confining walls of church.

Gradually over the years, the mountains became my church. A stand of trees, a chattering blue jay, an adolescent coyote—became my congregation. A light mist and plump, warm blackberries became my Eucharist. I walk over to collect my current horse in training. He's the opposite of the tiny, feisty Arabian who was my riding companion for over fifteen years, putting up with my learning curve with his stereotypically acute intelligence paired with sometimes overwhelming anxiety. This other teacher is an enormous, lumbering Percheron draft—the horse of knights and farming. Twice the weight of my little Arab, with hooves the size of salad plates, he has demanded I hone other parts of myself. I am learning strength of will, patience, courage, and clear communication. Less nimble and perceptive, as well as more dominant and brave, he is a new chapter in the dozens of horses I have ridden in a spiritual quest to become a better horse-person, to merge my body and mind with theirs. He is the fulfillment of my dream to train a horse from the first human touch, arriving years ago as a rescue from the slaughterhouse as an awkward sickly baby with a too-big head and gangly legs. Even then, when I was still steeped in Christian values, I could not shake the pervasive feeling that all lives were equally worthy of dignity, respect, care, and love. If I could not save all the beings that humans discard in the quest of consumption and convenience, I would at least occasionally save one. We amble up the hill toward the arena together, this now one-ton friend and I, as the sun brightens the sand. It is time for church.

Looking back, even in childhood my spirituality spilled out of the human-centered world of religion and into nature, recognizing and cultivating a deep kinship with animals and plants: relationships of student and teacher, of family and friends. When I was in elementary school, my father lived outside of Yosemite National Park while working for the National Park Service. He was Lutheran, and when I visited we went to church on Sundays, leaving by six o'clock in the morning to drive the winding narrow roads from the mountain cabin into town. I sat bleary-eyed and nicely dressed, holding his coffee mug out of habit, not fully awake until we reached the expansive fields where the Central Valley met the foothills.

I cannot remember exactly when it began, but I came to have two church services, two congregations: the human one with my father, and one in nature on my own. I sat patiently through the pastor's service, following along in the photocopied liturgy booklet they handed us, punctuating the silence with singing hymns. I loved religious ritual: the solemn and predictable cadence of the calls and responses, the beauty of the sanctuary with its stained glass, the introspective moment before the Eucharist. When we returned home, my father invariably settled in for a nap. I took the liturgy booklet from that day's service and head out into the woods in the backyard, carefully setting up a little altar on a tree stump with offerings of water and crackers or bread. I performed the entire service again, this time as priest, offering the holy communion to the animals and faeries. From the opening hymn to the benediction, I never felt alone. The squirrels and trees were no less rejoicing, even if they did not say much during our coffee break after service.

Trees and animals became my friends early in my life, so that when I became a Druid, it was easy for me to view them as persons—as they had always seemed to be as much so as humans to me. When I was eight years old, I moved from an urban poverty I barely remember to a picturesque rural town of chicken ranches and orange groves. I walked to school for the first time, swinging my arms freely in the early autumn heat, my fingers swelling plump. I loved the feeling of independence rural living gave me; I was finally safe from the prying eyes of landlords and the loud voices of neighbors. I walked the long mile to school and back and then climbed up, up, up into the waiting arms of a Redwood tree in my front yard. I climbed the branches laid out like a spiral staircase until I met, some thirty feet in the air, the three branches that wove together a seat just for me. Hauling up my snack and homework in a basket I rigged into a pulley system, there I sat in my little aerie like a bird, perched happily away from the noisy human world, feeling the breeze and protected just enough from the sun by the dense needled canopy. Back against the sturdy bark, I studied and read, tucked happily into my inner world of thoughts, away from the earlier pressures of the school day that demanded assessment of each social interaction and response.

The mild Southern California climate permitted a four seasons getaway into this perfect hiding spot, out of the reach of my sister seven years younger than me. I spent most of my afternoons for six years ensconced in the embrace of my friend, this massive Redwood. When my best human friend's parents divorced and she—the only friend I was fully comfortable with—moved several states away, my tree friend hugged me close, hiding my grief as easily as it hid chattering squirrels running from our dogs. And when my mother announced her impending divorce from my stepfather and the upcoming sale of our home, fourteen-year-old me, already focused on a future career in medicine and adjusting to the rapid shift from middle to high school, wrapped my arms around its rough trunk and sobbed. Its solidity had grounded me through the confusion of growing up in a human world. How could I let it go?

Druids often perceive the world through a contemporary animist lens: viewing all beings as persons who are necessary in the web of life and seeking relationships with them. For many of us, this way of seeing other-than-human beings began much earlier than our Druidry and was one of the factors that led us to becoming Druid. Druidic training and practice then reinforces this worldview, providing activities that allow us opportunities to encounter the personhood of other-than-humans again and again, confirming the roles of these other beings as teachers, kin, friends, and fellow congregants. Druidry was the first religion I encountered accessible to me as a white person that affirmed the personhood of other-than-human beings and encouraged me to put such relationships at the forefront of my spirituality, focusing first on the immediacy of relating to who surrounded me rather than on relationship with a powerful god. Even for someone like me, who had had a lifetime of close relationships with animals, plants, and rocks, it was revolutionary to re-center my spirituality on these relationships.

In the Druid's Prayer, common to both OBOD and the Ancient Order of Druids in America (AODA), the re-centering of the immediate relationships with those in the manifest world around us becomes clear:

Grant, O Great Spirit, thy protection
And in protection, strength
And in strength, understanding
And in understanding, knowledge
And in knowledge, the love of justice
And in the knowledge of justice, the love of it
And in the love of it, the love of all existences
And in the love of all existences, the love of Spirit and all goodness.

In Druidry, the center of spiritual work is how we relate to other living beings. The love of the divine or more amorphous, esoteric beings arises from how we relate to the smaller beings who are like us, enmeshed in the earth's ecology and its relationships. When we love the rocks, plants, animals, and other beings of the earth, we develop a capacity for loving the divine. This reorders the heart of spiritual work, standing in contrast to a Christo-centric framework common in the United States that puts a special relationship between humans and a god at the center of spiritual work, proposing that right and loving relationships with other beings arise from divine salvation or grace. In Druidry, the relationships with the other persons in our lives—including the rock persons we walk on, the tree persons who shelter us, and the animal and plant persons we eat—are the central, defining relationships that build and demonstrate our spiritual development. These are relationships that we act in every day of our lives, and at the heart of having good relationships with other beings, we must know them and honor just or right relations with them. Learning from them and honoring their personhood through mutual benefit and reciprocity—just as we would in healthy relationships with other humans—is the foundation on which spiritual growth toward loving the divine and all goodness is built.

Listening

I sat in silence, breathing deeply, practicing stillness. My back rested against the rough bark of a tree as I sat on the soft carpet of pine needles. The spring blue sky was mostly clear with only faint wisps of clouds, and the gentle warmth lulled me into drowsy half-alertness. My sketchbook rested on a mossy rock next to me, a pencil tucked underneath it, as I loved the crisp flat pages too much to leave it messily stuck in as a bookmark as some are wont to do. My backpack held a water bottle and snack to tide me over until I met my father for lunch. I was twelve years old, and I checked in midday to eat my sandwich and let him know I was OK. But for now, I had four hours to myself in the woods, and I was determined to cultivate the patience necessary to erase my humanness enough that the woodland creatures would come out from hiding.

A loud pop threatened to startle me, but I stayed still, heightening my senses—straining to hear and see what was making the crisp, cracking noises that punctuated the relative silence. Another crackle, and another. Across from me, fairly close, a doe stepped out from underbrush. Gracefully, she paused, checking for danger. Checking for me. I focused on breathing ever so quietly, entranced by her elegant slow steps, her dainty hooves, her large, searching eyes. And then, another step, and a tiny fawn—young enough to still have spots—stepped out behind her. The fawn's legs were impossibly long and awkward and its small tail wagged. As they browsed, I sat motionless, transfixed, recording as best I could a memory of their movements and form to sketch later. For just a moment, I was not a human in nature, but rather nature observing itself—one with the solid earth beneath me, the warm fire of the sun above me, and the magnificent deer who had deigned to feast in my presence.

I have been fascinated with large prey animals ever since the first time, at sixteen months old, I was plopped onto the back of a pony. My face split into an enormous grin, and that joy and fascination when I am around horses and other large prey animals has remained undimmed all these years. Deer seemed to be the ultimate challenge to get along with: beautiful and wary, sensitive and fleeting. For years, while my father worked and I was free to roam the valley floor of Yosemite, I would take some of that time to wander off-trail and sit very quietly, waiting for deer and other creatures to find me.

Deer became one of my spiritual teachers who, like horses, taught me patience, silence, and awareness. More wild and sensitive than horses, my time with them was ephemeral and so the relationship progressed more slowly as I learned how to translate what I had understood in relationships to horses—particularly abused or relatively untrained horses—to wild deer. When I became a Druid and learned about the Celtic gods, I was instantly drawn to Cernunnos, the horned god of the forest. The idea of a wild god, a god of the deep woods I so loved, was at once appealing and comforting. I related to these gods, so different from the Christian one, first through their connections to the natural world. Epona *was* Horse in quintessential spirit form. Cernunnos *was* the spirit of the forest and stag.

My first altars I constructed during my bardic studies in OBOD were focused on nature spirits. They held rocks, leaves, and feathers. Deer antlers and twisting manzanita branches spiraled outward from the central candle. Through the construction of my first shrine room, my meditative practice with the inner grove visualization, and sacralizing my activities with other-than-human beings—not only working with horses and hiking but also trimming my trees and cooking—I developed my sense of the centrality of the nature spirits in my spirituality and cultivated deep listening to their wisdom.

I sought the lessons Deer taught because like me, Deer was hypervigilant, easily started, and highly observant. Yet Deer was also powerful, graceful, and social. Studying horse behavior and working with horses, and then translating this when I could to wild deer was (and continues to be) a decades-long progression in pushing my human brain to see the world through the perspective of very different minds. Like Cernunnos, who is often depicted as half man, half stag, with great antlers emerging from his human hair, I pursued the ancient wisdom that is only available in the liminal space between my humanness and my animalness—between the separation of species and the inextricable truth of their entwinement.

I was twenty-eight years old when I was briefly accepted by wild deer. I was walking through Port Townsend Historical State Park in Washington state when I happened across a small herd of deer browsing. They startled and froze, looking at me with their dark eyes. For the first time, I was not still. Instead, I sunk instantly into working with them as if they were feral or abused horses. I advanced a step, and as they flinched, I then turned and walked three steps back. I turned, and they remained frozen, observing me. I walked obliquely toward them a few measured steps—neither creeping nor bounding forward. Then I walked off a bit to the side of them, looking away. When I turned back, one doe flicked her ears. I knew then that I had a breakthrough.

In this way, I patiently advanced and retreated until they no longer viewed me as a threat, and instead were curious. As I retreated, they advanced. As I advanced, they stayed still. We danced until, after a short while, I was browsing alongside them, spaced as far from them as they were from each other. I allowed myself to slide into an altered state of consciousness, imagining myself as half-human, half-deer—half in my world, and half in theirs. I tried to see the world as they did: the heightened senses, the instantaneous reaction to perceived danger. In that moment, browsing with deer, was a profound peace. From Deer, I learned more deeply what it meant to be human—the humanness I had deep in my blood and bone and gut, the humanness the modern world of busyness and noise trained out of me.

These were the foundational pathways toward wisdom Druidry cultivated in me: a blending of attentiveness to the immediacy of teeming life around me with tools to derive deeper meaning and knowing from it. Each time I tread the trail into the spirit world embodied in the other-than-humans around me, my perspective shifted and I reached new understandings of myself and my relationships with other beings. Sometimes enjoyable and ecstatic, other times disconcerting and disorienting, I emerged from each experience changed. Sometimes I gained wisdom from a kind of union, a becoming, a merging of self and the other. Other times, as I sought communication with other-than-human beings and humbly opened to listening, I received knowings—often in the form of visuals that popped into my mind. Trees, particularly, seemed to provide this type of insight. Single images held wisdom they freely gave me, making them my teachers as much as they were good friends. Years after my self-initiation into the bardic grade of OBOD, I was finally able to experience a group initiation at the first California Druid Retreat. In that initiation, our final assignment was to find a tree that seemed to have a message for us and sit with it to hear its wise offering.

In the smaller Redwood groves of the Central California coast, I felt drawn to one particular Redwood. Redwoods are very large, but because they grow quickly, this means some Redwoods are not particularly old. I sat at the tree's base, looking up into its lofty heights, opening myself to its "voice." Swirling through my mind was the uncertainty of the moment: it was 2009, in the midst of a recession that had seemingly killed academic hiring just as I had emerged with my doctorate. I had come to this gathering scraping together the funds to do so, having lost my home, truck, and savings in the recession. I was not sure what a tree could offer me in the way of advice on such an imminently human need, but at the moment, the most pressing question in my heart was not simply about the future of my career, but more deeply—how to actualize my pressing desire to be of service in the betterment of humanity.

In a flash, I saw in my mind roots pushing deeply into the ground and branches reaching wide to the night sky. My mind, seeing this image, translated to "Deep roots allow wide embrace." Yet the tree's message did not end there. One of the more interesting practices in Druidry is that it highly encourages, if not demands, ecological study. Unverified personal gnosis is all well and good, but only if it is interpreted through a body of knowledge that one also accumulates through more conventional means: reading extensively and studying the natural world through an ecological lens. It is through this other way of honoring and knowing other-than-human beings that I knew that the message of the Redwood was somewhat different than the image I had received. Because Redwoods, in fact, do not have deep roots. Redwoods have very extensive shallow roots. The way that they support themselves on such shallow root systems is that they rely on one another. They weave their roots together, entwining them, supporting the whole as a collective. It was not my own deep roots that would allow me to do my service in the world. It was forming a support network, a community, that would carry me through this uncertain time and eventually—through the trials of coming fully into my soul's work, into the service to the world that I was meant to do. I was inextricably entangled with so many lives—human and other-than-human—and I needed to consciously cultivate relationships in ways that nourished me so that I could go on to feed others.

Entanglement

In my early twenties, I briefly lived in a hundred-year-old cottage on a thirty-acre field. The house was inexpensive and permitted me to have my two horses with me, but it was rather prone to mice infestation. The mice who scampered through our kitchen were adorably small and round, with little coal-black eyes and impossibly tiny feet. I did not have to trap them, because my cat viewed them as rather fascinating toys. Too many days, I would hear her begin to run amok through the house, and I knew she had caught a mouse. She trotted proudly with it, head in her mouth, tail and back legs flailing. She would gently hold it, periodically letting it free so that she could enjoy the chase once again, then carrying it room to room until the next session of her game. Invariably, the mice died, but she never outright killed them. I imagined they died of fear or exhaustion.

I did not want mice in my house, but regardless of how carefully we kept our food, they came all the same. The surrounding ranches and orchards had been decimated, and it seemed a metropolis of mice had descended on our field—all of whom wanted to take up residence in our home. At the same time, I could not help but feel badly for the mice. They were simply trying to survive, and I could not take any pleasure in my cat's cruel pastime. The cat was rather trainable and already would come when her name was called. I began to train her to catch the mice, but then give them to me. I would hear her catch a mouse, and would take a paper grocery bag, opening it up close to the ground, its mouth pointed away from me. Calling my cat, she would come running, live mouse dangling from her jaws. I am not sure how she knew what I wanted, but she did. She would proudly let the mouse go in the bag, which I would quickly close and take outside, letting the mouse free again in the field. I knew that the mice may still be in shock and may not live, but at least I gave them a chance. I felt this was a compromise: I maintained the boundaries of mice and humans, and showed them again where their home was when they trespassed. But I did not abandon them to a cruel fate.

I know that my rescue of the mice would be viewed strangely by others. Unlike a Jain, I do not try to avoid all harm to all creatures. I call the exterminator when it is necessary to combat an invasion of roaches or termites. I eat meat. I pull the weeds out of my garden. But I do feel a sense of responsibility to these fellow beings I am interconnected with through the web of life that is the earth's glorious creative spark made manifest. I think of them as beings and not objects. Even when they are a nuisance or dangerous, more foe than friend, they are more like humans than things. And so I try to ensure my meat is from animals who are humanely raised. When I can, I "meet my meat"—I buy them when they are still living, "on the hoof," as the farmers say. I thank them in person. I cry over them. I give them the reverence I feel they deserve for sacrificing their life to feed mine. I warn the insects before the exterminator comes. I give them fair warning of their coming end and encourage them to move ahead of time. It does not take much from me, and it honors their agency as beings.

My obligations with nature spirits are both spiritual and practical, more familial than material. We are entangled together in both the manifest relationships of ecology and the veiled relationships of a divine mystery. I seek an ideal state of reciprocity with these beings, which means I have obligations to them as much as they provide gifts to me. It is a struggle to enact this reciprocity in our broader culture and economy. For many of us, this produces a long-term challenge in how to enact and embody our values in a social structure antithetical to them. As a religion, Druidry does not dictate how to enact shared values related to sustainability and mutual care with other-than-human beings as much as it offers practices to give us a motivation to enact those values. Through developing a sense of other-than-human beings' personhood, agency, and inherent worth, and our entanglement with them, feelings of empathy and responsibility emerge. The ways that these are enacted in the lives of Druids vary, but for many, gardening is an activity in which the values of mutual care, sustainability, and sacralization of place occur.

Even in the suburbs of Southern California, Druid gardens can become spectacular places in which pragmatic sustainability meets sacred space. Recently, I attended a group ritual for Alban Hefin, the Summer Solstice, at one friend and fellow grove member's garden. After two years of being absent due to the Covid-19 pandemic, I was struck by how much she had accomplished in cultivating it. When she arrived at her small California Bungalow on the edge of Los Angeles, the backyard was a relatively ample expanse of lawn. Two years of consistent work with the land later, the grass had been replaced by a more environmentally beneficial low ground cover and mulch. Trees, native shrubs, and vegetables pushed up through the soil, now rich with nutrients from compost. A cozy meditation spot had been added under the welcoming branches of a Coast Live Oak. She had slowly worked on her relationship with the land, healing its wounds and coaxing a healthier habitat out of its suburban ordinariness.

The garden is sacred space and also at the heart of spiritual relationship with other-than-human beings, especially in places that are more urban or suburban. It provides Druids a place to develop experiential knowledge both about and directly from nature spirits, to enact mutual care, and to cultivate understanding of the wild soul—the deeper, more intuitive, and connected human self. Having grown up in more rural settings, when I moved to Los Angeles, I felt deeply disconnected to both the nature spirits there and to the way I usually related to myself. Gone were my abilities to go outside and look up into the stars to feel expansive; gone were the quiet mornings spent listening to birdsong. I struggled to relate to the noisy expanse of concrete all around me and felt distant from the me who I knew best—the intuitive, quiet person who sought solace and wisdom from the woods.

When we moved to Pomona, some thirty miles east of Los Angeles, I found Sarvodaya Farms, a local bioregenerative farm that had managed to restore soil health and biodiversity, as well as produce an amazing array and quantity of organic food on a mere half acre. I signed up for a volunteer program, and through the guidance of the farmer-educator and executive director Rishi Kumar, learned new ways to conceptualize my relationship to the nature spirits in an urban environment through intensive mutually caring relationships. For the first time, I could see in practice rather than theory, what it looked like to bring together a community of people who valued reciprocal relationships with other-than-human beings in an urban environment. Thousands of pounds of rotting fruit from nearby farmer's markets were processed into salvaged bits that became canned compotes, ciders, and vinegars. The rest was hauled by hand, bit by bit, into compost mounds, mixed with the shavings and horse manure from local stables and the wood chips from tree trimmers. Rich soil was produced and shoveled by hand onto the long rows, building the earth where development had once stripped it bare.

In the garden, I found my wild soul again. I listened intuitively in new ways and took pleasure in the hum of bees busy in the fruit orchard and in picking ripe bright orange cherry tomatoes off the vine. I learned the muscle memory of staking and trimming tomatoes, of turning hundreds of pounds of compost, of checking the moisture of the earth until it was just right. Even though as an environmental anthropologist I had studied and read extensively on agricultural practices in many different cultures, on native plants and their uses, on the ecology of California—and even though I had already been a Druid with a relational spirituality for many years—working on the urban farm revolutionized how I saw urban spaces, human potential, and myself. I became more fully aware of how urban spaces could express the entanglement of human and other-than-human beings and could respect the personhood of the nature spirits that are always with us—even in seemingly dead, destroyed places.

While I eventually returned to a rural-suburban interface, my time spent learning how to be a Druid in the city transformed how I related to other Druids, to the land, and to my work as an environmental anthropologist. I began teaching my advanced environmental justice and anthropology of food courses in our campus community garden. Students learned about environmental and nutritional anthropology, but they also learned how to plant, tend, harvest, and cook. The practical work of teaching how to respectfully provide care to the earth in an urban environment, as well as how to derive pleasure from doing so, was a quintessential meeting point of my work as an environmental anthropologist and my spirituality as a Druid. It also pushed me further in viewing my own yard as the cornerstone of enacting my values of mutual care with other-than-human beings.

In early September 2020, after I had returned to living in a rural-suburban interface, on one of the hottest days of the year, a couple attempted a gender reveal at a nearby wildlands park and accidentally started a fire with a pyrotechnic they deployed. I saw it start from my living room window, a wall of glass that looks out over the northern plateau of the valley and the San Bernardino Mountains. My wife and I called the fire department but knew within a half hour that it would not be a simple fire to fight. In the hundred-degree weather and tinder-dry late summer conditions, the fire had already burned all the way to the base of the mountains by the time they arrived. For days, we anxiously slept in shifts. We had packed our documents, most precious heirlooms, and had the cat crates and dog leashes at the ready. Each night, we watched the fire's red trails expand like cobwebs over the dark foothills until it spanned tens of thousands of acres.

It had burned far from us and we thought we were safe. We did not unpack the boxes and bins that held our most priceless and important belongings, but we did unpack the cars. Our dining room looked like we had emptied a small storage unit into the space by the buffet. We had cut back all the Oleander bushes and trees in the back yard in preparation for greater fire safety around our home, and we had a pile of limbs in the center of a rock area near the pool, isolated from all the structures. We were simultaneously trying to have a new hot water heater installed, and our lives were a chaotic jumble of the mundane and the carefully measured assessment of what was extraordinary.

Then, quite suddenly one afternoon, the wind picked up and shifted. The fire roared back several miles back across the plateau at an astonishingly rapid pace. As I returned from the home improvement store with my new hot water heater, I faced a wall of flame a mere few blocks away, clearly visible from my driveway and advancing quickly toward my home. We began to throw all our boxes and bins back into the cars as quickly as we could. Within a half hour, the police were going door to door, telling people to evacuate immediately. It was time to go. We loaded cats and dogs into the cars and then I went back inside one last time. I looked out the window of my office, the room that also held my altars, at the fire line being set up on the street below ours, a mere block away. All that was between us and that fire line, if the fire jumped that road, was a steep embankment filled with brush and trees. I breathed deeply, calming my clamoring heart.

For just a moment, I sunk my awareness into the land, searching for the spirits—the spirits of the land, of the trees and plants, of the soil and rock that flanked the perimeter of my house, of the fire itself. And then I made a promise: "*Save our home—yours and mine—and I will protect and heal you the best that I can.*" We had only moved to our home less than two years prior. A deep connection had not been forged yet. But I had already envisioned the next twenty years until I retired: trimming and deep watering the trees, planting drought tolerant native desert plants, creating a small food and herb garden, composting and restoring the soil, offering healthy plants for bees and butterflies. I shared this vision with the land spirits and told them I had to leave for my safety, but if they could protect our mutual home, I would be able to keep serving in keeping them well. And then, as the wall of fire was at the edge of the cliff heading down to the fire line and the smoke and heat became unbearable, I drove away.

The firefighters held their line. The fire was stopped, and two days later we returned home to a layer of fine ash covering everything and chunks of charcoal the size of my hand in our pool. A year later, the mountains and plateau are still fire-scarred and mostly bare, slowly knitting themselves back together as the fire ecology of Southern California does. I kept my promise. The next spring, as a wall of weeds took over my rock perimeter and the normative way to abate the weeds would be to spray herbicide, I took on the cost—both financially and in time—of moving that rock, one shovelful at a time. Weekend after weekend, a little bit at a time with the help of a friend, I shoveled away the rock, pulled up the old rotting weed barrier, and pulled the weeds out of the soil with my hands. We are kin, entwined as one ecosystem. I will keep my promise: I will serve, body and spirit, the soil, the plants, and the pollinators. They protect me, and I will protect them. Our futures are inseparable.

CHAPTER 6

A Community of Ancestors

FIGURE 5 *The ancestral tree.*

Tonight, as I began to contemplate the ancestors, I knew right away that I had to begin with drumming. I had to call the ancestors to be present in order to speak of them, and they come to me through the drum. A couple of years ago, I excitedly brought home a large package shipped to me from Hungary. Inside was a handmade Sami-style drum made of deer hide. The drum was the size of my torso, egg-shaped, with beautiful natural spotting on the leather surface and a handle made of an antler. The beater was covered in soft rabbit fur and had been sanded until it was velvety smooth. I had been drawn to Sami-style drums for years, but the cost to procure one that was ethically and authentically made was considerable. Finally, this beautiful instrument had traveled halfway across the world to me. When

I need to feel connected to the old ancestors—the ancestors who live in my blood and bone, the unnamed ones who stretch back in time to before recorded history—I pick up this drum. So tonight, just as I did that very first night of its arrival, I lit the candles on my altars in the shrines. I picked up the drum, sitting cross-legged, resting it on one thigh. In this position, it was as tall as I was. I rested my cheek lightly on its wide, curved side and then began to play a steady rhythm.

Its deep, rich tones filled the room, echoing into and out of the shrine cabinets, filling the hall. Its reverberations pulsed through my body, bouncing off my chest. I invited the ancestors to be present. The images welled up in my mind—a herd of reindeer running across tundra, the stark contrast of ocean and rock and ice, the warmth of a communal campfire. My hand became independent of my consciousness, drumming ever faster as my awareness shifted. I could hear, distantly in the drum's cadence, voices that haunted me—unidentifiable words but unmistakable songs. The room felt full, as if it held the energy of a crowded party, though I was alone. I became warmer; my cheeks flushed. And then, I stopped. I breathed deeply into the sudden silence. I no longer heard them, but I felt them. Those people who, so many years ago, lived and died and were reborn until, so many generations later, I was born. Whether on this or the other side of the veil, they were my community. They never really forgot me, and I never fully forgot them.

The ancestors are more than our family. They are our history, we are their present, and collectively, we are the future. Whether we feel connected to our genetic ancestry or conceive of it more broadly as an imprint of memory and consciousness from the past, our bodies carry the wisdom of countless beings who came before us. Ancestors are defined in different ways—most commonly, the ancestors of blood—those to whom we are related through birth. But for some Druids, ancestors of adoption are more significant—persons and cultures who felt familiar, who welcomed us, who gave us a home. Sometimes, too, we connect to ancestors of spirit—to those for whom there are no recognizable contemporary ties, but for whom we feel particularly drawn.

Defining the ancestors can be difficult for American Druids because many of us have many cultures from which we came. Part of Druidic practice, encouraged by multiple orders and in books on Druidry, involves genealogical research—whether one does so through blood or adoptive relatives or both—to understand the people and processes that led to you, here and now. Many Druids believe that in some way or another—whether because we are literally our ancestors, reincarnated, or because the lives of our ancestors live on in a sort of spiritual and biological memory in our bodies—we are indelibly linked to the past in very personal and real ways. For Americans, who often have recent familial histories of immigration and pluralism, and who sometimes have indigenous or Black ancestors whose histories were suppressed, this process can be both logistically and emotionally challenging.

A couple of years ago, I hauled boxes of genealogical records my maternal grandfather had compiled when he was Mormon out of my mother's garage loft. We set up a pop-up canopy tent near her little creek under and hauled a couple of boxes back there to review them under the trees, bare feet in the warm grass. Ironically, though probably not unusually due to variations in historical circumstance and family member interest, I had more extensive records of my mother's side of the family, who had first arrived in the United States in the 1690s, than I did of my father's side of the family, who had more recently immigrated. On my father's side, I knew very little. My grandfather was entirely Czech but had been taught by his parents to avoid speaking the language and to strongly identify as American so that they could more easily assimilate. The only thing I had inherited from that culture was a handful of recipes that marked special occasions, dutifully prepared by my French-Irish grandmother who had been instructed on Czech cuisine by her mother-in-law. Each Christmas, my grandmother, father, and I proudly prepared kolache, a delicious sweet bread made with a sugar-walnut filling, using the old nut grinder she had operated, arms aching, since my father's childhood. Nothing whatsoever remained of my grandmother's own French-Irish Catholic heritage.

Similarly, nothing remarkable except a single bread recipe had survived of my nana's heritage. Both she and my maternal grandfather bore common English American names (Smith and Mills), and the lone survivor of her Norwegian ancestors' past was lefse, a potato flatbread which, like kolache, we made every Christmas (and then, like the Californians we had become, stuffed it with turkey, sweet corn, mashed potatoes, and savory bread stuffing like a Thanksgiving burrito). While my maternal grandfather had always told us we carried Native American ancestry, there was no evidence of it among the piles of records he had assembled in his time as a Mormon, seeking to baptize our past relatives so that they might be saved. His own lineage in the United States began with French Huguenots who arrived, stripped of title but not of wealth, and immediately began marrying their family off to Dutch people, since that was the colony that accepted them.

So many ancestors from different places and times presented a dizzying array of options for me to explore: French coming for different reasons in different centuries and from distinctly different cultural regions; highly educated Czechoslovakians who seemed to want to forget the old country; Scots-Irish who moved first due to Highland Clearances and then again due to the Irish Great Hunger; English and Dutch whose pasts were unclear; Norwegians who came first to Canada. I had had a range of reactions to these cultures over time. Even now, I struggle to feel that I can adequately grasp my ancestry. I become paralyzed by so many potential paths to explore. I would love to learn Irish or Scots Gaelic. I want to visit all these places, because I feel a sense of connection through land, through sensorily taking in the gestalt of a place. I have tried to track down some ancestors— is there any connection between my lifelong love of and fascination with deer, and my Norwegian ancestors? I go down rabbit holes, like trying to find a Norwegian ancestor in their national records. I spend an afternoon straining to read the digitized scrawling script of a pastor's church records from 200 years ago. I feel like my relationship with my ancestors is shallow in every way, but I feel as though all my attempts to deepen are limited by time and resources and incomplete records.

This is why, perhaps, I took to intuitively connecting through drumming. I picked up a bodhran a decade ago and learned to play (badly) via videos online. It is not spectacular technique, but having mastered a few basics, like a jig rhythm, gives me a sensory connection to my ancestral past. More recently, when the Sami-style drum arrived and I heard the ancestors in it, then did some research and found similar sounds in yoik, I felt a sense of the past reaching into my present—even if fleeting. I imagine my experience is not uncommon among American Druids: ironically, the more tangible aspects of my ancestors' pasts—their census and immigration records, wills, short news clips—feel shallow. The imagined deeper past I access through unverified personal gnosis, through direct experience—feels more meaningful, more *real* in a way than the very real people I can access but who chose assimilation.

This focus on deep-time ancestors and the American tendency to lump disparate languages and cultures into a vague but meaningful Celticity is understandably frustrating to some contemporary teachers from Ireland, Wales, Scotland, and other places who have more access to specific cultural and folkloric traditions. However, even knowing that this is an issue and understanding its importance (as an anthropologist), I have found it intensely frustrating to try to live in my Druidry. There is only so much time and money—to travel to ancestral homelands, to learn languages, to master folklore and mythology. The process for me, hailing from so many different places and peoples, feels scattered, piecemeal, and inadequate. For some, the answer is to do a little bit of something with every ancestor's heritage. For others, the answer is to pick just one, but explore it extensively.

These challenges can be even greater for indigenous and Black American Druids, whose ancestors' records may have been suppressed. Indian boarding schools and closed adoptions purposefully broke the cultural continuity of Native American peoples. Some people find, through admittedly problematic but sometimes personally meaningful DNA tests, that they carry more than half their DNA from indigenous populations—but due to closed adoption records, have an inability to ever reconnect with their tribal heritage. People with ancestors who were slaves were often not documented adequately, as they were treated as property rather than persons. Exploring one's ancestry can be painful, unearthing recent connections between oppressor and oppressed that haunt all of us to this day. The ancestors are indeed a community, but like any human community, they are filled with their own troubles.

Trouble

It is easy to say honor your ancestors. It is easy to say seek the ancestors'
guidance. I sat in the blue camp chair, holding a copy of the will of my
first ancestor to arrive in the United States, a French Huguenot who fled
persecution with his wife to New Paltz in the then Dutch colony. Upon
her death, she freed their slaves. I struggled with this. If she freed them,
she had some idea that they *should* be free. Yet she waited to do what was
humane until it did not inconvenience her. What do we do with troublesome
ancestors?

This fundamental problem faces most American Druids, who are
predominantly white and therefore must wrestle with the actions their
ancestors took—actions that have had real and lasting harm for others. My
ancestors held slaves, killed indigenous people, and settled on land that did
not belong to them. I do not say this as if I do not know if they did these
unethical things and am writing a standardized history of whiteness in the
United States. I say they did these things because I have the documentation
that demonstrates those facts. Druidry asks us to consider our ancestors—
to find ways to honor them and to heed their wisdom. This can be difficult
when one's ancestors caused so much suffering to others.

So far in my Druid journey, I have had to look primarily to modern
psychology and borrow from certain other spiritual traditions to find a
pathway I felt appropriately acknowledged the suffering my ancestors had
both endured and caused. I found that I could look at my ancestors with
compassion, but also with accountability, by addressing their suffering.
Hurt people hurt people. Many of my ancestors, like so many people in
the United States, had come here to escape persecution and privation.
Their bodies brought with them the trauma of war, famine, abject poverty,
religious persecution, ethnocide, and genocide. Unfortunately, in turn, they
subjected others to these same fates. I began to ask myself: *How do we heal*
the wounds of our ancestors—the wounds they caused and the wounds they
carried? If we are our ancestors, or carry our ancestral experiences with
us, honoring them (and ourselves) had to start with healing these festering
multigenerational wounds. This takes the form of healing ourselves (both
practically and ritually), correcting the suffering our ancestors caused (in
whatever ways we are able), and in ritually healing our ancestors who are
still hurting after death.

Each morning, my spiritual practice ends with blessing my ancestors
and my living family members. "Blessings upon the ancestors of my father.
Blessings upon them wherever they may be. Blessings upon their journeys . . ."
Each person in my family, from my deceased grandparents through the
youngest generation, is blessed by name or family household. I bless those
who are troublesome; they need it the most. Blessing all these people who
have led to my existence does not mean they only experience enjoyable, happy

things. Some of them need to experience a reckoning, an accountability, a change. I am blessing them with what their soul needs most. This pause makes me remember to reframe my own life in the here and now as well. I look back with disgust at the ancestors who harmed other people. What might those coming after me find unacceptable about my life right now? Remembering the ancestors each day seeks to heal them through spiritual means, but it also ensures I examine my current actions through the eyes of those who will one day be my descendants.

The practices I cultivated for deeper spiritual work on my troublesome ancestors were borrowed from the Anderson Feri tradition of witchcraft (the *kala* rite) and Orion Foxwood's Faery Seership tradition (the River of Blood practice). In the kala rite, I work with negative energy or patterns in my own life, transforming these into nourishing qualities. The River Blood practice works directly with ancestors who are trapped so deeply in the suffering and unethical actions of their past that they are unable to fully move on to the afterlife, join their fellow family, and begin the work of healing. Like the father-husband in the film *What Dreams May Come*, the practitioner enters the world of the dead knowing how to locate and then rescue one's ancestors from the hellish state of being trapped in their past patterns of suffering. The dead must do their own work to change the suffering they carry, but we can provide an outstretched hand and initial support along their way. In this way, our love for our family transcends death and we work together—ancestors and descendants—to heal our collective pain.

While my Druidry did not train me in these practices, as a religion without mutual exclusivity, Druidry allows and even encourages the simultaneous practice of other traditions. Alongside my Druidic coursework, I spent two years under spiritual direction with T. Thorn Coyle, who shared with me the revolutionary qualities of the kala rite. I also spent three years in the Faery Seership program, before my academic schedule got in the way of my attendance at the biannual workshops. Many Druids are influenced by non-Druidic religious traditions. Some practice two or more religious simultaneously and equally; others study another tradition and bring only a few elements of it to their Druidic practice. While less common, some Christians and Jews adopt Druidic practices without converting from Christianity or Judaism. Because there is no demand to conform to a specific set of beliefs or practices in Druidry, individual Druids vary considerably in how they view their religious affiliation and indeed, if they consider their Druidry a religion at all (some consider it a spiritual toolkit, philosophy, or way of life). While most Druids believe in reincarnation, there is no common pathway for how to handle the difficulties of one's ancestral past. Each of us embarks on a very individual journey to discovering and getting to know our ancestors and developing ways to heal and honor them.

Ideally, we handle our complex lives, at best filled with a fair amount of suffering and difficult decisions to make, with self-reflection and attentiveness to our own soul's development. When we do this, we spare future generations a troublesome ancestor to heal. Instead, we break the cycle of past traumas we carry with us, and in doing our own work to heal and grow fully into our soul's potential within our lifetime, we give an incredible gift to the future of humanity. Such a life and death inspires others to do the same. When we find this inspiration in a tradition, or among a wider group of people served by the person who has passed on, we call them the Mighty Dead.

The Mighty Dead include not only well-known teachers, such as the founder of a tradition, but also (for some) those who may have only been particularly significant to a smaller community of Druids, such as one's local grove. These teachers maintain their connections with their community, becoming a source of wisdom, comfort, and guidance from the Otherworld—and remaining as fondly remembered friends in their communities. For many years, I was a solitary Druid, and so I could not fully relate to the Mighty Dead as a lived experience. While I understood it conceptually, in practice, the founder of my own Order was not someone I had ever known—and indeed, I received no sense of his presence, just some utility from his writings.

I was already an Ovate when a fellow grove member was diagnosed with cancer and slowly but inevitably made her way toward the Summerlands. I knew her reasonably well, but we were not particularly close. We had different theological orientations in our Druidry and different ritual needs. However, I had hosted some of the events she led over the years, and she was a kind, peaceful, generous person. It saddened me that she was being called to the veil so early in her life, when she had only recently graduated from seminary and begun her ministry. She was significantly far along in her final grade of Druid study in OBOD when she reached the point that she struggled to focus and communicate. Her husband called me to inquire about leading a ritual to bring the Druid community together and honor the spiritual work she had done throughout her life. I do not usually function in the role of a priest, though I have occasionally led group rituals. While some OBOD Druids become chaplains and ministers through other organizations, the Order itself does not have a clergy-laity system and does not ordain priests. In this case, however, I felt a desire to be of service and had sense of what this ritual could provide, not only in terms of honoring her work and legacy but also in terms of bringing together—potentially for the last time—all the Druids who were closest to her, who she had effectively led for several years.

A sense of inspiration settled over my work, giving me the words and actions I needed despite a short timeframe to create the rite. I wrote the words for the rite easily because they were not mine. They were the words of the ancestors in the Otherworld, coming tumbling out onto the page as fast as I could type them, along with the images of the objects to gather and their associated meanings. Then, after the ritual had emerged, I sat with it, slowing myself to read each word, writing it in calligraphy by hand into a little book to leave with her and her husband.

I felt a bit of trepidation and uncertainty as I arrived at the hospital at the appointed time. It was Southern California, but still, I was obviously out of place—yet the formality of ritual was what this remarkable woman deserved, to honor her as she transitioned from living teacher to one who would journey to the Summerlands. I went to the hospital's main desk in my natural flax linen gown and tunic, holding my basket of unlikely religious objects in one hand—stones and antlers, cow bones and salmon skin leather—and a staff fluttering with pelican feathers in the other. They were expecting me and handed me the visitor badge without question. It was a relief to be in an inclusive place; the hospital had granted time for her to have the ritual, as well as allowing all her grove members to join together to perform it. As one person stood watch at the door, the rest of us filed in and honored the work she had so dutifully and valiantly performed. Her legacy lives on with us—her grace and good humor in the face of what does not seem fair. Each Samhain, she is named as we ask the spirits of our dead to join us. We raise a toast to her, for as we say, *what is remembered, lives.*

Transmutation

In Druidry, our relationships with our loved ones do not end with death, but instead can be maintained both through ritual (such as the annual rites of calling the dead and preparing food for them at Samhain) and through moments in which we feel we spontaneously receive wisdom, guidance, comfort, or requests for assistance from our dead kin. Death is not a wall so much as a curtain between the worlds of the seen and unseen, which sometimes becomes quite transparent. Death itself, then, is something to work at accepting rather than fearing—a moment the worlds meet, exchanging materiality for potential. The relationship continues but is transformed.

A few years ago, my last grandparent passed on to that other world. Each of my grandparents has had, what have been to me, remarkable deaths—all for different reasons. Each of them died slowly, knowing that death was coming, giving them time to prepare. While some of these deaths were challenging physically, all were testimony to the potential beauty of death's capacity to be used for healing and restoration. I lost my paternal grandfather first, a man I had struggled to know. He had worked during my childhood, as my parents were quite young when I was born. He passed away shortly after his retirement when I was only nineteen. Having had several debilitating strokes and diagnosed with stomach cancer, his time on hospice felt too long, as his body slowly became thinner. Yet inside, he was preparing—evident even then to me. At one point, he asked for work tools as he slid in and out of consciousness. My grandmother, ten years younger, missed him for the rest of her long life.

Grandma initially struggled to comprehend what happened to my grandfather after he died. Raised as a Catholic and converted to Lutheranism after she married, she could not sort out if Grandpa was in heaven or if he were in some sort of purgatory. While we assured her he was in a good place (he was an exceptionally kind and hardworking man), she often remained unconvinced. Several years after he passed, I was staying at my grandmother's house overnight. I was drifting off to sleep and then felt a sudden *not-alone* feeling wash over me. At the time, I still had little control over receiving impressions from the spirit world, which often frightened me. I sat up in bed, heart pounding, feeling as if my throat were closing. On the threshold of the open doorway, I could *feel* him. It was my grandfather. I loved him and wanted to be more open, but I could not shake the feeling of anxiety at the realness of his presence, knowing that he was long dead. His thoughts entered my mind, gently but firmly asking: "Tell her I'm OK. Tell her I love her. Tell her I miss her." My heart pounding, I nodded that I would. I promised I would take care of her and assure her for the rest of her life. And then he was gone.

Grandpa never returned to visit me again, and I often felt badly that the sudden sensation of his presence had produced anxiety and a lack of what I would later come to view as proper hospitality for the ancestors. But I kept my promise, and throughout the ensuing twenty years of her life, I reminded Grandma frequently that I was certain that Grandpa was in a good place, that he loved and watched over her, and that was waiting for her. Several years ago, at her bedside as she lay unresponsive in the final stages of dying, her pain finally mollified, I held her nearly translucent hand. And while she was beyond speech, I could see with my inner vision, her reunion with her beloved. As they had in their younger years, before I was born, her soul danced with his—effortlessly, joyfully. Their transformation was complete.

Druidry has no specific belief about the afterlife; while belief in reincarnation and some kind of ancestral home (the Summerlands) is common, there are some Druids (myself included) who believe that transmigration of souls—movement of souls between human and other-than-human forms—is possible. For me, it was impossible to think of my soul as *innately* human, particularly because I struggled so much at times to relate to the human world. In many ways, my drive to study culture arose from my tendency to view the human life analytically—to search for patterns that made sense of the social world around me, which so often seemed opaque compared to the clarity I felt in the natural world.

Because of this neurodivergent way of experiencing my own humanity, the ancestors were the last spirits to arrive in my spiritual experience. The nature spirits had been with me since childhood, and because I was raised as a Christian mystic—with the idea that God approached each person differently, and that the purpose was to find *my* God, as my mother put it—the divine was also present in my spiritual experience from early childhood. The ancestors were trickier. Humans often felt too noisy, too difficult. I startled easily, and the idea of dead humans popping up into my consciousness sounded frightening and invasive. From the beginning in my Druidry, I welcomed nature spirits and *shining ones*—divine and disincarnate other-than-human beings—into my life. But I firmly told dead humans, whether ancestors or ghosts, I did not want to entertain them any more than I wanted visits by door-to-door salespersons.

I was well into my Ovate (second-grade) studies in OBOD, in which there is a lot of spiritual work with the ancestors, before I invited them in. It was during a ritual I conducted to sever the ties to my ex-husband—essentially, a form of spiritual divorce preceding the legal one—that I finally, in part from my loneliness and pain, called on my ancestors to join me. I was kneeling on the living room carpet of my aunt's home while she was away on business; I was in a liminal space in every sense of the word. I was between the last mountain cabin I had shared with my ex-husband, and not yet to my first cottage I was to rent as I began my professional career and new life in Los Angeles. I had recently come out as bisexual to my family and friends, but felt uncertain about the future of my relationships. All I knew was that I was doing the right thing—the thing that had to be done: in order to give us each a chance to be happy, we had to be independent of one another. But it hurt, because I had not stopped caring for him—if anything, the decision to release the commitment was my last and best act of love, because we had tried to be happy for fifteen years and had failed at it.

As I walked the beach, day after day, in between preparing my classes for my first semester in my long-desired tenure-track position, I let my mind fly away from my left-brained, calculating, dissociated self. For a little while, I let my feet steadily swish through the sand, shifting my consciousness to open to the flashes of insight that came from a more mystical awareness. I came to see myself as bound to him in ways that were not going to be changed by a piece of paper given to me by the courts. I came to recognize that I had to move through a series of rituals to fully transition through this rite of passage—just as one does when starting a relationship. Eventually, there was a night that I came to be alone in my aunt's house, kneeling on the carpet, crying my way through a rite of passage. I envisioned myself free from the bonds of marriage, visualizing clipping through the heavy strands that wove between he and I. And yet something was missing.

I realized, quite suddenly, it was the ancestors who were missing. The bonds I was cutting were the bonds of the past—and I could not know how deep those bonds and that past went. The ancestors knew and could help me navigate how to let the past settle as I broke free into a new present. For the first time, I opened the door when the ancestors knocked. I invited them in. I had a sense that the room filled. I had the impression of shadowy figures across the history of my humanity circling around my exhausted and lonely body. A time-worn hand reached out, settling lightly on one shoulder. Some ancestors held hands; others lightly touched the person next to them. All were connected to me, their energy growing, filling the room, expanding until I was in a sphere of their love. It was then I could feel that I could begin the process of letting go. As Thorn had taught me to say, almost as a daily prayer, *I am complete unto myself, and I am sacred.* Complete unto myself, somehow human and not-quite-human, spirit and body. The ancestors lived in me, and in them there was a totality of human experience. When the divine could not console me because such beings did not live a human life, the ancestors offered the comfort only those who had loved and lost could give. Every ending was a beginning; every death, a birth. All of us, on this side and the other side of the veil, were caught up in the same process of metamorphosis, learning to let go of our attachment to the temporary details and to invest in the enduring power of *being* itself.

CHAPTER 7

A Covenant with the Shining Ones

FIGURE 6 *The Morrigan.*

Beginning at about four years old, I occasionally dreamed of wars and famine. The dreams frightened me, and I woke up suddenly in the middle of the night, leaving my bed to find my mother to chat until I felt better. Of course, this meant my poor mother had no rest. She began to teach me the Christian mysticism she practiced. "We can't fix these problems," she explained, "But we can ask God to help us fix them." She instructed me in a form of contemplative and intercessory prayer:

> You are feeling hurts in the world when you dream of these things. They're big hurts and you're very small. So for now, when you wake up with seeing those people hurting, tell Jesus about them. You will feel *your* God with you, and *your* Jesus with you, in whatever form they take. You'll feel comfort. And you can tell them all about what you've seen that

needs help, and they will help those people. Then, you can listen to the radio until you fall back asleep.

I began my own mystical practice. When I woke up in the middle of the night with a start, I asked Jesus to be there. I waited until I felt his kind, warm presence sitting on my bed. I curled up with my head in his lap, and his hand on my forehead, and I poured out the disturbing visions of mamas and children starving in the desert, of blood oozing from the men shooting one another on the battlefield. He took these visions and assured me that God knew about them, and that he was there for people in their suffering. And then, as I listened to soothing ballads on the radio, I felt his comfort ease my worries and I fell back asleep.

Those 3:00 am wake-up calls continued throughout my life, waxing and waning based on some pattern still unknown to me. Over time, the visions shifted so that they not only included the world's suffering but also a deepening and more expansive experience of selfhood and the Divine Mystery—the Great Something that integrated and connected everything but that felt so incredibly inhuman that I could not describe it except in fleeting and imperfect bits of poetry. Over time, the dream-visions also became populated with a greater diversity of other-than-human disincarnate divine beings, what Druids sometimes call the *shining ones*. These include gods, angels, fae, and other mythical beings (in anthropological terms, in which *myth* is used to describe sacred stories that carry deep truth).

Like many, if not most, American Druids, I was first introduced to these types of beings through a Christian lens. Perhaps unlike most American Druids, I was not introduced to them through doctrinal or even biblical depictions, but rather through experience. As a child trained into mysticism, I was taught from an early age that God and Jesus show up differently for everyone. We are diverse, so they are also diverse in the ways they manifest to us. Because of this, over the years, I built an internal classification system of beings based on experiences I had of them—the images that popped into my mind, the energy or feeling I had when they were present, the patterns in how they communicated. However, when I attempt to map this onto language, there is a challenge, because there are many different ways that people define such beings.

Some New Agers describe angels as human-like beings with wings who hang out with you and protect you. The Bible describes angels as fascinatingly odd and frightening, such as beings with many eyes and sets of wings, or interlocking wheels of fire. Cultures vary considerably in how they describe helping beings and harming beings, as well as those beings who, like humans, are both and neither—living out their own agendas and only partially touching our world. Interestingly, while Druidry does not demand belief in any divine beings at all, most Druids do come to believe in gods, and a smaller but still considerable number of Druids believe in fae. For most, this is based on experience. I knew based on my childhood experience that I believed in a Divine Mystery, what some Druids call the Great Spirit. However, it was not until I was seven years into my Druidic journey that I began to wonder about gods, about the individual more limited deities who populated the various pantheons of the world.

My first encounter with a god was not earth-shattering. I finally became curious, reading about gods in Druid books and training materials, so one April night I set out to encounter one. I lit the candles in my shrine room at each of the four directional altars to the elements, cast a sphere around the room, and sat in the center, waiting. Breathing slowly and deeply, I eased myself into trance and then asked if any god would like to make themselves known to me. Quite suddenly, the room felt much warmer and more alive. I knew I was not alone and welcomed the presence. The god sat facing me, cross-legged on the floor like I was. I had a clear image first: the god had a long red beard and hair, and warm, bright orange light emitted from around his head. He sat with his robes folded around him, neither young nor old— powerful and yet beneficent. "Here I am." His thoughts broke into my mind. "Thank you. I was curious. So the gods do exist." He nodded, then paused. "What can I do for you?" I inquired, offering the reciprocity and hospitality his presence required. "I want to be recognized in a ritual." The idea popped into my own thoughts. "I want to be honored at Beltane." "But who are you?" I asked. Into my mind three letters came: "Bel."

After I assured the god I would include him in the next ritual our grove did, thanked him, and he was gone, I jotted down the description I had for him. I still did not know who he was. I had an image and "Bel," but I had never heard of such a god. After I closed the ritual, I sat at my desk with a cup of warm tea laced with honey, grounding myself and consulting Google. The very first image that popped up was a carved disk that looked exactly like the image I had received. Bel was one of many variations of the god Belenus, a god whose presence spread across Gaul and into Britain and Ireland, who may have been particularly helpful in healing and who was associated with the sun and horses. The realness of the information, which I had never seen or heard of before, startled me. Belief is one thing; the gods showing up is another.

Druidry does not demand adherence to any particular set of beliefs so much as encourages experimentation with spiritual practice which may lead to experiences that percolate beliefs over time. For some Druids, unverified personal gnosis—personal experiences that are considered true in some deep (but not necessarily literal) way—leads to belief in gods or in the fae as real individual beings. For other Druids, they may come to think of the gods as manifestations of one underlying connecting divine process. Alternatively, they may think of the gods as mythical archetypes that speak to significant forces in the human life or in nature. There are many ways Druids think about the existence and nature of such beings, and many factors influencing those ideas, including personal experience, influences from other religious and magical traditions, and myth. What is perhaps distinctive is the lack of demand on Druids to agree on the existence or nature of these disincarnate other-than-human beings. Atheist Druids, Christian Druids, and Agnostic Druids are not uncommon, though in my own experience and research, the majority of Druids identified as polytheist or pantheist.

There is even less agreement about the fae than there is about the gods. The term is used by different American Druids to mean anything from specific beings in Irish, Scottish, and other Celtic mythology and folklore to a very wide category that broadly includes disincarnate other-than-human beings connected to, and often protective of, the natural world. When I began my journey in Druidry, I was surprised to find a rather widespread avoidance of them in literature for Druidic training. Many years later, my research data would show a lower level of experiential and other forms of belief about fae among American Druids, as well as a polarization over interacting with them. For some who believed in them, interactions were considered dangerous and undesirable; for others, a reciprocity and mutual respect had been carefully cultivated. In all cases, who and what are specifically referred to by the term vary.

I could not avoid beings that I consider to be fae. They pursued me from an early age. I had a sense of places in nature that felt like thin places, places where their world touched mine. At times, the feeling was so strong in my elementary and early adolescent years that I felt as if I could almost walk through an invisible doorway into some other parallel world. The divine and the fae blended together for me in visionary dreams, and I would enter worlds I could not identify to observe other-than-human cultures that felt familiar yet were unrecognizable to me when I woke. The distinctive quality was always an eerie feeling, a sense that time and space were sliding sideways into some otherworld that both was and was not connected to my own. It was years after my initiation into Druidry, filled with a building sense of impending obligation to these beings (one that I resisted), before I capitulated and began to center them more in my Druidic practice.

In comparison to the Abrahamic traditions (Judaism, Christianity, and Islam), which tend to heavily structure a collective agreement with a more narrowly defined divine, Druids tend toward highly individualized experiences and contractual agreements. I do not say "contract" lightly. In contemporary experience and in folklore, the fae and at times, the gods, have entered into contractual type arrangements with humans built on reciprocity. For some Druids, there is active avoidance of such engagements or these beings simply do not seem interested in forging a relationship with them. Both boundary-setting (including saying "no, thank you") and a lack of opportunity are not considered negative outcomes in Druidry, because the process of engagement is highly individualized. Likewise, an agreement may be temporary and minor (as mine was with Belenus) or lifelong and life changing.

Druidic orders offer texts that are more like laboratory manuals and libraries than they are like sacred canonized texts like the Bible. The rituals offered in them are meant to be experiments to try, change as desired, and adopt if found helpful. Neither orthodoxic nor orthopraxic, Druids are held together by common individual experiences rather than any authoritative voice on what to believe or how to practice. This generates a religion of priests who each express a unique facet of the Druidic tradition. The relationships Druids have with the gods and the fae reflect a diversity in spiritual experience and personal interest; each relationship (or none at all) is an equally valid expression of Druidry. Some Druids maintain strong beliefs, while others are atheist. Some center the gods in their spiritual practice, while others maintain relatively peripheral relationships with them. Belief in gods is not required or considered superior to those who do not believe in them. Instead, it is understood that the gods and humans are both types of beings with agency and preferences, who may or may not decide to initiate relationship.

Belief

I have been handling writer's block recently in the process of writing this book. This most commonly occurs as my anxiety ramps up, and it becomes a cycle: as I grow anxious, my creativity and productivity wane. As my productivity wanes, I feel more anxious. Tonight, I knelt before my shrine cabinet, gazed at the statue of Brigid—a goddess who, among many roles, provides poetic inspiration—and implored her for help. My relationship with Brigid is a close one, most often focusing on her capacities to help with healing and with creative inspiration. She rarely asks anything of me, but she knows that I try to help encourage and support others in their healing and that the creative pursuits—both in writing and in visual art—are areas in which I regularly express both my analytical and mystical experiences.

Staring into the statue's serene face, surrounded by a halo of light, lambs at her feet (a reference to her festival at Imbolc, which celebrates the first signs of spring in February), I felt the urge to light her votive as an offering and a request. It took striking the match three times to get it to light, but finally, the small flame flickered and I lit her candle—one that was given to me by a grove sister, procured from Kildare, Ireland, where there was a sacred flame that was supposedly kept perpetually lit in honor of Brigid stretching back to pre-Christian times. I looked at the small light, akin to the struggling light of creativity, so easily extinguished in me. I felt her prompt me to use her votive to light a candle dedicated to my own long-term goals. At a summer retreat in the local mountains several years ago, a grove sister with a special relationship to Brigid—particularly in her role as matron of blacksmithing and metal-working—hosted a candle- and holder-making workshop. The candle that represented my intentions for the next (and last) half of my career was one that I carefully wound of sheets of beeswax. It sits on a metal candle holder inscribed with *ogham*, an alphabet made of lines oriented around a central staff with associative meanings for each of the characters. The ogham I selected primarily focused on my desire for work-life balance and for deepening my spiritual and creative pursuits. I selected the leftover bit of a used match and carried Brigid's flame to spark my own. Only then, I sat down to write.

When they believe in gods or other disincarnate other-than-human beings, Druids most commonly do so based on having faith in their own spiritual experience. As there are no authoritative religious leaders or texts, belief comes to function more as working hypothesis than as litmus test. The Druidic journey is one of ritual experimentation and making meaning of our experience, and is always a process rather than an outcome. Because of this, Druids sometimes shift in their beliefs over the course of their spiritual development, learning from their own experiences and from one another. Rather than attempting to define the shining ones, it is best to learn to accept the unknown while pursuing wisdom and insight. We can only partially grasp beings so different from ourselves and so multifaceted in their nature, so humility and openness are key qualities to cultivate.

Even for polytheists, defining any god's boundaries and qualities is a difficult task. Some gods have common characteristics across cultures, begging the question of how culturally bounded or transcendent the gods are. The gods seem to manifest themselves in ways that share trends across individuals (both in the recorded folklore and mythology and in contemporary gnosis), yet they also show diversity in these manifestations. Many gods also shape-shift into animals who serve as omens, making it sometimes unclear how to separate the ordinary from the extraordinary. The universe is messy, and so are the gods. Without authoritative text or leadership, Druids are free to engage fully with the struggle to make meaning of a complex, diverse, and potentially ever-changing divine reality. In my own spiritual practice, which blends elements of both hard polytheism (there are many real gods) and monism (ultimately, all beings are part of one whole), I can identify three experiential origins of belief: beings for whom I have had no direct spiritual contact, but the relationship works in practical, manifest ways; beings for whom I have had direct spiritual contact that I initiated; and beings for whom I have had direct spiritual contact that the being initiated. As is the case for many Druids, it is far less important to me whether or not a god is real than it is that I treat the god with respect.

My relationship with Brigid is an example of a long-standing relationship built on practical manifestations of reciprocity rather than mystical direct contact. I have never directly encountered her in the way that I have, for example, Belenus. Yet my experience of Belenus was only a single incident, whereas I have worked with Brigid for more than a decade. Instead of direct spiritual contact, I related strongly to her qualities and roles. Because of this, I gave her space in my shrine, providing daily offerings and prayer cycles with the other gods with whom I have long-term relationships. Perhaps more importantly, I give her credit in supporting and inspiring my creative work and in helping to heal those I love. I acknowledge that while she does not manifest herself to me in visions the way that some deities do, she is deeply integral to my writing, visual art, and well-being.

Some of the other gods with whom I work were the result of mystical experiences—of direct spiritual contact that usually take the form of sensory input, particularly through sight and touch. I have visions of these gods, a bit like imagining an image I am about to paint, but instead of actively using my imagination, it feels as though the images pop up spontaneously. At the same time, I feel the room get hotter or colder. My hair stands on end. I feel a chill down my spine. The quality of these feelings and the visual input I receive help me categorize the disincarnate being who is present. Some of these experiences are—like Belenus—due to an invitation I extend to the spirit world. Others of these experiences are due to initiation by the spirit.

In 2013, I attended a series of gatherings for an ethnographic project on how Druids related to the earth in ritual and practical action. At the East Coast Gathering, a large gathering of Druids for Alban Elfed (the fall equinox), I attended workshops, *eisteddfod*, and grade initiations. The gathering was, rather hilariously, at a teen girls' camp in the Pocono Mountains of rural Pennsylvania. The set-up for teens was charmingly odd for a gathering of mostly middle-aged Druids. Even as a relatively small person, I barely fit in the showers. We slept in groups of eight in bunks with years of carvings testifying to teenage love: "Debra hearts David." "KS + TG forever." In the middle of one night, while the wind howled and the rain pounded the roof, I abruptly awoke to a soft light in the center of the room. A woman in blood-red robes was kneeling, one knee on the ground, the other leg bent, as if proposing. Her dark brown hair flowed in unkempt, voluminous waves over the rich red of her gown. She held a lantern from which the intrusive light shone while rifling through a black bag. As I blinked and came more fully awake, she turned to gaze at me—an inscrutable, penetrating look. My heart pounded and my throat closed. My rational mind knew that I must be dreaming, and if I was not, I should not wake the other guests in the cabin who were still fast asleep. Yet as a lucid dreamer, this did not feel like a dream. Usually, I can tell that I am dreaming, even when it feels very real in the dream. Usually, my otherworld sight is an inner knowing and vision I hold in my mind, not with my eyes. This moment felt as if I were completely awake, staring at this otherworldly (yet very solid) woman who had popped into the world of too-small bunk beds as if to extend an invitation to a place more appropriate to the coming half of the dark year.

As my heart raced faster, I propped myself up on one elbow and blinked again. With that, she was gone. No trace of her or the light remained, and I eased myself back onto my pillow, slowing my breathing and ruminating on what it meant. Who was she? What did she want? I had no answers but felt these would come in time. Eventually, I returned to sleep. The seeming realness of the encounter haunted me throughout the rest of the gathering and once I was home. No answers to my questions were forthcoming, no matter how much I reflected on the encounter or petitioned the spirits with whom I worked. Yet I could not let it go. I felt a feeling as if something or someone were initiating a process that would unfold slowly over time, revealing itself in bits and pieces, like following a winding trail with no sense of what was at the end of it.

Six weeks later I was surrounded by Druids in a yurt in Southern England for the Samhain Druid Camp. Some forty of us were gathered in a ragged-edged circle, waiting to be led on a journey to meet our psychopomp. I lay against the soft rugs on the yurt floor, lengthening my breaths, listening to the drumbeats. The horse that often carried me to the otherworld came to collect me, and we galloped through the woods, the drum hastening his hoofbeats. We began circling the yurt, spiraling outward, heading for the far hills. I knew I was flying to meet *her*—the woman spirit who had woken me up on that stormy night in the Poconos. Faster and faster I galloped until I shape-shifted into a raven, wheeling ever farther from the yurt and my inert human form. I landed at the base of a hill, looking up at a great tree on the edge of a forest. I knew that in the woods, she waited. My spirit moved back to a human form, walking toward her. She was instantly recognizable: the blood-red gown pooling against the autumn leaves under her feet, her lantern lighting my way. She was a priestess of the Morrigan, an Irish triple goddess of prophecy, death, and battle. The knowing flashed through me without any words from her. I walked steadily up to her and when I was within arm's reach, she took a knife and sliced open my skin, head to toe. My human spirit-skin slid off me as if it were an uncomfortable and heavy too-warm cloak, and I felt a sense of liberation. In this moment, I knew death as an ally.

Thus began my relationship with the Morrigan, which deepened over time, guided by prompting from the Otherworld—sometimes from this spirit-priestess, sometimes from the Morrigan themselves. Over time, they transformed my relationship to my bodily autonomy, to nationhood and the sovereignty of the land, and to the way I conceptualized and embraced courageously living and dying. Some of my experiences of the Morrigan tracks to their roles and qualities in myth, and some of my experiences seem uniquely contemporary, uniquely my own. Whether or not all of my experiences of the Morrigan are authentic to myth is less significant to me than the question of what the experiences mean and how they can transform my life. It is the consistent effort to express devotion, and its effects on my character and life, that is at the heart of relating to the shining ones. What I read or think about the gods and the fae is almost certain to be incomplete at best, as my human mind cannot fully comprehend them. Yet even within this acceptance of the unknown, I can grow deep and powerful relationships.

Devotion

In my shrine cabinet there is a horse vertebra, a symbol of my devotion to Epona, the Gaulish goddess whose namesake my Arabian mare bore. I know her only through my work with horses. She has never made direct contact with me, but every time I have called on her to help my horses, I have felt her power. My retired horse's bosal, a braided leather noseband from his last bridle, encircles her votive. My prayer to her is that I might claim some of her nobility and grace for my own. My commitment to her is that I care for the horses she has entrusted to me.

Only some Druids feel called to devotional polytheism, in which they commit to serve one or more gods or fae beings. For most of these Druids, the gods do not share the same character as the culturally familiar Christian God. They seek service, not worship; courage, not flattery. As one fellow Druid put it, "They want someone to stand alongside them for the fight for justice, not someone to bow before them." The old gods push humanity to its full potential, and they do not necessarily care if they break people in the process. Free will is a tricky and uncertain proposition. More than a few Druids had warned me: gods and spirits claim who they will, and time is on their side.

On the one hand, the gods are generally more limited in their power than the omniscient, omnipresent, omnipotent deity of the Abrahamic religions, and humans are generally believed to be more powerful than our overculture believes us to be. On the other hand, there is both a mythology and a collection of contemporary stories about the gods (and sometimes the fae) being quite persistent in calling some humans to their service, regardless of the interest or initial willingness of the human. In either case—whether the human being or the god initiates the relationship—devotion is most commonly understood in a framework of shared co-creative power, in which the human-spirit relationship drives change in human consciousness and in the world. It is the meeting point of human and other-than-human that serves as the springboard for human development, but the balance required between maintaining ego and surrendering to union can be challenging to attain.

It was shortly after I had stopping running from the fae being that I felt was pursuing me, tired of feeling as though I were in a perpetual race against change and my own higher potential, that I began to lose my sense of self. At first, I was too attached to the self, so much so that I ran from the changes I knew this spirit-relationship would bring. Then having opened to it, I struggled to put myself back into the equation. The enormity of this other-than-human being overwhelmed me, and I could not seem to find the balance between the two polar ends of the spectrum of relationship—none at all, or fully united in a way that erased me. Early into this process, I sat every day in meditation, trying to find the path forward. One evening, candlelight flickering against the wood grain of my cabin loft, I tried to translate the images that came to me: "Union. Tears. The sound at the edge of your hearing will come to fruition—will come into center. Remember? Radiance."

As I opened to the collective being's presence, its enormity engulfed my seemingly fragile humanity. I continued to journal in a sketchbook as I felt the primordial wave of the being swallow me: "I disintegrate—empty—a vessel for the message. I am only memory, only dream. There is nothing, nothing." I felt like an empty shell, a husk, a container for precious drops of water that only existed to ferry the drops back to the ocean, their source. In such moments, my human body and life seemed small and insignificant, my only worth in my reflection of the infinitely more beautiful and ancient being with whom I communicated. Yet this was not what the being desired from me, made clear through the images I received from them: "Feel the ridges of your fingertips, the soles of your feet. Your pulse. Invite us to join you. Feel your longing to come home. You are not lost. Remember? Remember and own your form."

The deep and difficult work of devotional practice is the union of the spiritual and the everyday, the human and the divine. Focusing too much on the spiritual is temporary escapism at best, and leads to dysfunction in the manifest, ordinary life at worst. This is, perhaps, why the mystics and seers from many religions seem to dance at the edge of insanity. Yet focusing too much on the practical, everyday ego does not permit the *something more* to transform one's life. At its worst, avoiding spiritual union felt to me as if my life were flat and devoid of connection. I missed the ecstasy of losing myself, even for a moment, in the connection with all-that-is.

It takes time, effort, and consistent practice to find the way forward in living in both realities at once: in devotion to the other-than-human, through the manifest qualities that devotion cultivates in everyday life. Devotional practice, then, includes at least two actions: spiritual practice (soliciting the attention of and listening to the gods) and practical action (actions taken on behalf of the god in the world). The former builds the relationship with the other-than-human and develops the skills necessary for communication, inspiration, and focus. The latter completes the devotional work as it manifests the wisdom, creative insight, and virtuous qualities of the shining ones into the human world. While all the other-than-human beings with whom I have consistent relationships spark both aspects of devotional practice, my relationship with Cernunnos is a good example of how the two fit together. I was drawn to the woods and wild creatures from the time I was a toddler. It was fitting that when I became a Druid and began to read about the gods of ancient Ireland, Wales, and Gaul that I would be drawn to Cernunnos, the horned god and so-called "lord of the wild things."

Before I personally and directly experienced him, I had long been drawn into the forest. My commitment to the earth and its creatures, nurtured from early childhood by my parents, had prompted my studies in environmental anthropology as an adult. As a child, I picked up trash on earth day and drew posters of endangered species for art class. As I moved through adolescence and young adulthood, my empathy for the earth only increased until it became nearly unbearable. In my early twenties, the rural agrarian towns around me accelerated in their development, stripping the land bare of its orchards and sending the small mice scurrying onto my property on the edge of town. The weight of losing the trees and the frantic fear of the little creatures who lost their homes overnight felt like an anchor on my heart. I could hardly crawl out of bed, so intense was my grief. A Christian at the time, I did not find Christianity offered me anything to assuage this pain. So human-centered, its promises of an afterlife without suffering did nothing for the small mice whose black-bead eyes looked at me from frightened little faces. When I became a Druid, some of my first offerings to the gods, long before I first experienced one, went to Cernunnos. I recognized that, even as an archetype, he was a god who was imminently useful to the wild souls like me, who found profound joy in the wild creatures' company and who felt their hurts acutely.

I had always collected ephemera from the forest and made little sketches and watercolors of its daily life. When I became a Druid, I gathered this woodsy flotsam and jetsam in my office to make altars to the four elements. My altar to earth rapidly became an homage to the woods—crisp autumn leaves, soft feathers, a pile of smooth acorns in a small pine needle basket. Eventually, the earth gifted me with antlers, and over time, the altar became one that honored Cernunnos and Elen of the Ways, an antlered goddess who helped me return safely from the mountain trails I hiked and the inner journeys to the Otherworld. Cernunnos helped me feel there was a deity who cared for the wild creatures I loved so much, at whose altar I could offer my grief as cars, climate change, and development steadily decimated their lives. Eventually, after the gods began to slowly reveal themselves to me, occasionally showing up at the edge of my ritual space as if they were interesting but strange guests to tea, Cernunnos came. His hooves sank into my carpet and his furry legs were rough with bits of twigs and live oak leaves that had become tangled as he had journeyed to my house. His chest was broad and tan, his hair long and curly and wild, and his eyes both ancient and perpetually youthful. He is beautiful.

Spending time with Cernunnos renewed my soul and soothed my grief. I could always lean into his embrace and let my tears pour down his bearded cheeks, and when I had finished weeping for the suffering of the earth's creatures, I was filled with renewed energy and hope in the work to care for them. I finally had found the path to productively processing the grief I felt. This latter half of devotional practice—channeling the spirit-human relationship into manifest human life—was the offering I could bring to his altar, forged from the gifts he gave me. The devotional practice had a circular rhythm: I offered dedicated space in my home, my time, and my focused attention; the shining ones offered insight, inspiration, healing, and renewal; I offered actions in my life that followed their insight and inspiration, drawing from their healing and renewing energy. Druidry is a spirituality that is intimately entwined with vocation—with a sense of employment in the world. Sometimes paid, sometimes volunteer, Druids often have a strong affinity for one or more paths of learning and service that unite the spiritual and the practical. Through pursuing knowledge, justice, and love in practical action, Druids manifest their spirituality into the world.

CHAPTER 8

The Second Spiral

An Ecocentric Community

Silently within the quiet of the grove, may I share peace.
— *DRUID'S PEACE PRAYER FROM THE ORDER OF BARDS, OVATES, AND DRUIDS*

While many Druids are solitary, that does not mean that Druids are alone. Since the rise of the internet, Druids have been in community globally through asynchronous virtual conversation; prior to that time, there were newsletters, books, and correspondence courses. I found Druidry through websites and books, as did most Druids I interviewed. In the first seven years of my Druid journey, prior to finding a grove in California I could join, my connection to a sense of Druid community was entirely through authors, websites, blogs, and the OBOD course—which I received at the time through the mail. While there is no authoritative text or even corpus of texts, many Druids gain a sense of what Druidry is and a feeling of connection with other Druids through some or another collection of texts they assemble themselves.

In order to understand how such texts might function to generate a sense of Druidic culture despite a lack of authoritative leadership or even face-to-face interaction among many Druids, I selected texts in the same ways that many Druids do when they are initially seeking out information and then analyzed the texts using content analysis, which is a way of evaluating themes across texts (see the Introduction for more information). Thirty-eight percent of the titles were books I would classify as introductions to Druidry, focused on broad basics for someone who may never have encountered Druidry before. Sixteen percent were still relatively broad but written for an already-Druid audience or in ways that clearly paired the book with specific foundational material. The remaining 46 percent of the titles focused on specialized topics, such as magic, deities, history and prehistory, or divination. Thirty-nine percent of the books were associated with a specific Druid order or written by a leader within a specific Druid order.

While, as Larisa White (2021) notes, Druids vary widely in the texts they consider foundational in their own spiritual practice, I found that there were strong themes across texts—meaning that it was likely that regardless of the diversity in which texts Druids bought for their personal libraries to inform their practice, they were receiving similar concepts, values, and guided practices. Half of the texts discussed cosmological and ontological topics, including the nature of time, the universe, and humans (38 percent described the concept of *elements* as an ontological framework for understanding the universe and humans, though they varied considerably in how they described them). Thirty-six percent of the texts specifically discussed the concept of *awen* and 31 percent introduced the concept of a grove as a group of Druids practicing together on a regular basis. While Druids often describe Druidry as this-world and this-life focused, more than a quarter of the texts discussed concepts of an afterlife, and almost three-quarters of the texts discussed one or more gods (more than discussed nature spirits or ancestors—both represented in about half of the texts). Sixty-eight percent of the texts discussed myth, most often from the Mabinogion and the Arthurian stories. Fifty-nine percent of the texts provided guidance on one or more forms of meditation, most commonly discursive, breathing/sitting, visualization, or trance-journeying. Forty-three percent of the texts offered suggestions for nature-centered practices, including walking in nature, herbalism, cultivating observational mindfulness, planting and tending trees, wildcrafting and foraging, and engaging in direct or political actions for sustainability. Half of the texts described types of sacred places, including liminal places, forests, and bodies of water. Almost two-thirds of texts offered guidance on Druidic magical practices, and more than half explored divination in depth—most referring to *ogham*, an Irish set of associations of sounds, symbols, and most commonly (though not exclusively) tree species. Nearly half of the texts described the Wheel of the Year and provided guidance on rituals for celebrating holidays.

Ultimately, Druid texts, despite not being authoritative, arguably socialize people into "rules of engagement" within the community, "special knowledge domains for these special worlds" (Luhrmann 2022: 34). In Druidry, because of the likelihood of being solitary for some or all of one's spiritual life, these materials also provide "shared elementary language" of Druidic ritual and discussion (Harding 2000: 19). Key concepts and the terms used to describe them, such as *awen* (divine inspiration), the circles of manifestation (a way of describing cosmology and reincarnation cycles), and elements (four forces that are thought to influence both nature and human life, and that are honored in some Druid rituals), are introduced through books, websites, and blogs—some more common than others. For a solitary Druid, these literary encounters, along with engagement in Druid social media groups or discussion forums, offer a shared language—and with it, shared conceptualization of the spiritual experience.

Druidic ritual practice, even when conducted as a solitary person, generates a sense of not being alone. It does so through a sense of communitas— intense bonding among co-participants—despite being practiced at different times and places. Ritual changes our experiences of time and place, opening a liminal time and place to produce spiritual experiences, which then bond participants in the ritual (Van Gennep 1909; Turner 1995). In Druid ritual, this is marked through casting the circle or sphere (in OBOD and AODA rituals, for example) or by providing in-boundary and out-boundary offerings (in ADF rituals). In AODA and OBOD, the transition to liminal time and place is particularly evident, as both provide opening and closing liturgies that flank a central rite or working. Druidic spiritual experience may be co-experienced by some only through the expressive works Druids offer to the community in the form of poetry, prose, books, online discussions, and training materials. At the same time, these expressions inspire and bond Druids in a sense of global community: "I love to watch Damh the Bard when he does his house concerts, because I see all the comments from around the world and I feel like we're all here, and the comments resonate with me, and I feel like I'm part of this big community who sing along in our homes and we're all connected" (Kat Reeves).

Druidic community is more than the humans involved. It is an ecocentric community, encompassing diverse living incarnate beings and a rich and varied spirit world. Ancestors—intellectual, embodied (blood/adoptive), and spiritual—form Druidic community through spirals of time. The ancestors can be specific kin, those we find in genealogy: "I think they live through me in a way. I'm sure they're watching me" (Fiona McMillan). Alternatively, the ancestors may be unnamed, from a deeper time: "If we go back far enough, we have a million ancestors. Those are the corporate ancestors" (Rev. Kirk Thomas). Though it takes myriad forms, reconnecting to the past is critical to Druidic practice and is part of overcoming the dysfunctional Western relationship between culture and nature, which some have described as amnesia or memory loss (Devereux et al. 1989; Metzner 1995). Druidic practices that center the ancestors serve multiple purposes: to remind us that there is wisdom held in us and the human past we have forgotten, to revive older ways (or new ways inspired by old ways) of relating to the earth and to one another, and to acquire a sense of support, guidance, and encouragement from a long lineage of kin stretching across time. The ancestors are the closest to understanding us as living human beings, even if they carry the same frailties they had in life:

The ancestors as a whole, in my understanding, along with the recently dead, seem to be a class of spiritual beings who have the greatest understanding of humanity—of our excellence, of our limits—because they were human. And they are helpful to go to because problems that have existed interpersonally have existed throughout times, cultures, and families. One of the caveats that I always remember when working with the ancestors no matter how long they have been dead, is just because they are dead, does not mean they are wise. (Rev. Monika Kojote)

American Druids have varying approaches to the ancestors as community, in part related to the challenges inherent in the history of whiteness in the United States. Some, like me, feel drawn to a role of trying to heal wounds their ancestors have caused: "I have trouble with my ancestors. . . . Part of what I'm having to do in this life is I'm doing ancestral remediation" (Dana O'Driscoll). Others do not feel called to do such work:

I don't worry so much like a lot of people do about the sins of the ancestors. It's very easy to stand in a more enlightened time to make judgements, but I don't think it's our role. Future generations may judge us for actions we take now. Once people die and go through the threshold, they deal with their own issues. It's for them to do their work. (Kat Reeves)

American Druids wrestle with simultaneously trying to revive practices our own ancestors lost, and recognizing that the most detailed information we can access about ancestor-focused spirituality is often from cultures our own ancestors marginalized and decimated—and from cultures we do not fully understand:

We get so much of our language from, especially around ancestor worship and ancestor work, from marginalized communities. And we get a lot of those ideas from communities who handle ancestors differently from how white America handles ancestors. So it is kind of trying to impose a different paradigm than the way we actually do things. (Maggie)

Druidry is multiethnic, but 90 percent of American Druids in the survey I conducted identified as white. Within the context of European colonialism, genocidal and ethnocidal policies against indigenous peoples in the United States, and chattel slavery and its legacy, working with recent ancestors (even ancestors of several hundred years ago) necessitates developing a sense of how one relates to the American historical and contemporary construction of race and racism. Druids do not uniformly respond to these issues, but most Druids with whom I have interacted have considered them.

Druid community is also more than humanity. The other-than-human is part of society. Places and objects hold community and energy (White 2021). Contemporary Druidry began as mystery traditions, similar to Freemasonry, but over several hundred years, morphed into a nature-centered spiritual movement: a unique form of contemporary Paganism. We know little about the earliest Druids at the time of contact by the Roman Empire, but we have a wealth of sources about how they have been imagined in the process of developing contemporary Druidry (Hutton 2009). For some a religion, for others a spiritual toolkit, contemporary Druidry is a conceptual place of belonging for those who, like me, found their deepest sense of self-development in communion with nature. Like many neo-Pagan traditions, Druidry is a body of interconnected new religious movements that seeks to reconnect us with the natural world, but it carries a distinctive focus in its practices compared to various witchcraft traditions:

> I don't know that they've [Druids] all phrased it this way, but for me, it feels—it's more relational than a lot of witchcraft. Witchcraft is very focused on what you do. And as a Druid, magic is a thing but it feels more like Druid magic is about building relationships rather than achieving a goal. (Maggie)

While foundational anthropological works about magic (such as Malinowski 1954) propose magic is inherently tied to what cannot be controlled in more pragmatic ways, the heart of Druidic magic is precisely about what is most within our control—the control over one's own consciousness. This is likely due in part to the strong influence of Jungian thought on the formation of Druidry, particularly in OBOD. The focus of Druidry is the development of the self and its relationship to the earth: "Druidry is having a deep connection with earth and communicating with earth first, and nature first, when it comes to figuring out issues, problems, and solutions in your life" (Siobhan).

Druidic ontology is ecocentric rather than androcentric, arguably a key orientation toward a spirituality more suitable for facing climate change and ecological degradation (see Kopnina 2012 for an extensive discussion on ecocentrism). Similarly to traditional ecological knowledge systems, Druidry emphasizes the connectedness and relatedness of all things (Pierotti and Wildcat 2000). The human is developed within the context of the other-than-human and is bound to it—there is no individual self or human species outside of its relationships to others. How can we understand the other-than-human as part of self and community? A variety of social theorists have offered a progression of new ways of understanding the subject-object relationship that offers descriptions for the ways that Druids describe a blurring of self and other in spiritual practice and experience.

Gregory Bateson (1972), in his concept of the ecology of mind, offered that the individual is constituted in part by the individual's environment. Tim Ingold (2000) pushed this further to propose there is no mind-environment separation: that consciousness is inherent in the body and the environment as one "indivisible totality" (19). There are no subjects or objects, but rather separation is an emergent and dynamic property of life (Ingold 2011). Subject agency arises from interactions, and in a specifically religious context of relational personhood, sacred objects are themselves sacred subjects

(Lynch 2010). This relational personhood is evident in Druids' experiences of objects and places as agents: "It's a relational thing. It's not that the place is sacred in itself, it's more like we recognize it and it's in relationship to us" (Kat Reeves). Sarah Best noted that natural landscapes form connections that affect Pagan "spirituality and sense of being" (2018: 32). Druids could describe both natural and human-made places that elicited a response in them. The place is itself a type of agent, in relationship with the person visiting it:

> It just seems to me that some places have a little bit more something. There's something about the place that makes it significant somehow. It can be someplace natural, that's always been there and always like that. Then there is a place that is sacred from use from ancient times. And nowadays you can create a sacred place through use. To me, a waterfall can be a spirit. A mountain can be. A cliff or a clearing, if there's something about it you can feel. There are places across the Indo-European world, but the ones that really struck me are in Britain. Stonehenge and Avebury. New Grange. Because they were sacred for so long, they still hold that magic or whatever. I don't have quite the word for it. My own stone circle. The one in Tucson, we did ritual there every week, that got really juicy. (Rev. Kirk Thomas)

Place also impacts Druids in patterned cross-regional ways that transcend individual emotional response. In my survey research, rurality made it significantly more likely that Druids communicated with nature spirits and constructed sacred places outdoors, as well as having experience of and belief in nature spirits. Being located in a rural area had approximately the same statistical effect on belief and practice related to nature spirits as practicing in a group. This suggests animist beliefs and place-based spiritual practice is grounded in forging experiential relationships with other-than-human beings embodied in practice, which can arise either from encountering such beings directly in the natural world or from being taught and reinforced through collective ritual practice, but that solitary urban Druidry generates a significantly different experience. Returning to Tanya Luhrmann's (2022) work on priming, these seemingly disparate mechanisms guiding Druids to an experience of ecocentric community are united in the psychological processes by which each of them spark—whether through interactions with human community or with nature. In these interactions, human-other boundaries are blurred and personhood expands (Rountree 2012: 314). This expansion yields biospheric altruism, in which our moral concern includes other species and ecosystems as a whole (Zaleha 2017: 290). One Druid explained:

> The land is alive. The earth is our mother. There are land spirits and nature spirits everywhere you go. I try to maintain a respectful reciprocal

relationship with the land spirits where I live, and I try to maintain this when I'm traveling. Even just giving a bit of water offerings when I travel. That's doing my part to embody a virtue of hospitality. But also, nature is powerful. I move almost seamlessly between spirits of nature writ large and spirits of nature writ small. They're all part of the same spectrum. As I often say, I don't love nature because I'm pagan. I'm pagan because I love nature. I am a spirit and so is the tree, and the river and all the other creatures in here and we're all a part of the universe. We're all connected on some level. (John Beckett)

Expansion of personhood is not only relational but also co-creative for Druids. We are part of something larger as a process with others. We are bound to one another through ecological and spiritual processes. We are differently gifted agents working together as part of this process. We are nature and nature is us, and our survival and spiritual potential are mutually entwined.

The Nature of Nature

Druidry can generally be described as animist, not so much in the sense of belief in spirit beings (Tylor 1970/1871) but rather in its understanding of the world as filled with sentient agents—beings that have consciousness, agendas, emotions, and the power to affect others. It is a religion centered on relating to the natural world in the here and now. Druids exemplify Graham Harvey's "new animism": nature is one spirit with varied and differing bodily forms (2005). What is sometimes called "Great Spirit" in the Druid's Prayer is more process than being, an unfolding of a universal process of creation and destruction into many interconnected and interrelated forms of being—human and not, incarnate and not. Most Druids practice as an animist and/or polytheist (whether viewing the gods as real individual beings or as symbols of significant suites of traits or forces) while simultaneously holding agnostic positions, primarily grounded in separating capacity for the experience and meaning-making inherent in unverified personal gnosis with capacity for accurately understanding ultimate reality. Divinity is beyond human understanding, but within human experience: "I'm an animist, and as an animist I recognize it's all a great mystery and I'm really happy not knowing everything" (Dana O'Driscoll).

Experience of nature spirits is trifold: as nature-as-whole, nature-in-part (forms), and as individual beings. I experience my horses as "Nature," "Horse," and "this particular horse." This is also true of humans and the self. I am self-as-process within Process Itself: I am a confluence of human consciousness as a whole and my particular ancestors living in and through me, both physically and spiritually, all in a specific incarnation here-

and-now as Kim the anthropologist and Druid. Similarly, another Druid explained:

> Animals, and trees, and stones—things I relate to here in the physical world and in the Otherworlds—yes, this individual piglet in front of me is its own being, with its own spirit and thing to communicate and interact with. And when its life has ended, it rejoins what is Pig—that oversoul. The same way that humans, when we die, join up with the sharing of memories and stories. Anything I interact with in this physical realm is both, at the same time. Depending on how it's evolved, it has the capacity to bring in different information. All coyotes are coyotes, but I've only interacted with two coyotes that were Coyote. It's an instinctual thing—there is a different feel in the body, a different sense when I'm looked at. I recognize individual autonomy as well as the connection to the oversoul. (Rev. Monika Kojote)

For many Druids, the spiritual experience of near death, prior life, or out-of-body events causes a skepticism about one's capacity to understand the totality of reality (even of the self) during incarnation. There is, then, an emphasis on the transient nature of immediate experience and the permanency of processes—but as processes, they are not fully comprehensible or immutable. Keeping this acknowledgment of human brain limitations in the foreground yields a spirituality primarily focused on connectedness and relatedness of all existences, rather than on cosmological certitude.

Druidry could also be described as Gaian spirituality (Clifton 2006) and as dark green religion (Taylor 2010); Druids do not think we are merely obligated to be environmentalists but rather view nature itself as sacred. On a spectrum in which human-centrism (anthropocentrism) is on one end, and represented by religions such as many Christianities, and biocentrism is on the other end (Johnston 2013), Druidry is firmly biocentric. There is a long-standing link between deep ecology and the history of divinization and idealization of the earth in Paganisms (Pike 2019: 133–7). Deep ecology integrates spiritual perspectives with environmentalist actions, viewing nature as sacred and the protection of it as a spiritual commitment. Nature involves moral and practical mutual obligations among beings: "[My view is] the idea of Gaia, that the earth is a living being, that we are all connected. When I die, I'm not going to be gone, because the rest of the body will still be there! Yeah, I'm not sure I like sharing it with cockroaches, but oh well!" (Dawn).

In a sense, Druidic practice taps into what Theodore Roszak (1993a, b, 1995) proposed as the "ecological unconscious" (or the "living record of cosmic evolution") or what Aldo Leopold called the "ecological conscience" or "ecological consciousness" (Metzner 1995). It is a Jungian sense of a collective unconscious writ large—tapping into not only the totality of human history and experience but also into the totality of the experience of nature itself. Like Taliesin shape-shifting, chased by the divine, we have in us all of nature, and we, in turn, are inseparable from it. This orientation is particularly at play in both OBOD, because it has been formulated with significant influence from Jungian psychology, and in AODA, which requires Leopold as part of the reading for the second degree. Such influences centralize the interconnections between land and humans, and posits that ethics of care for each must include the other. Ecological conscience proposes individual responsibility for the land's care, fueled by biophilia (Edward O. Wilson's idea about love for life, discussed first in Wilson 1984 and later in Kellert and Wilson 1995). From influential myths (not only Taliesin, but also Finn McCuill and the salmon of wisdom) to Druidic practices that encourage acquiring direct insight and inspiration from communications with trees, plants, animals, and places, Druidry emphasizes a cosmic connectedness that not only sacralizes the earth but also forms a wisdom that we can readily access as in and all around us.

While Druids generally feel emotionally close to and responsible toward spirits, there is no expectation that all Druids will forge the same relationships with the same spirits. Instead, spirits may call or claim different individual humans. This diversity in relationships is a product of relational ontology in a universe that is filled with distinct, different other-than-human persons who are relatively flatly organized in a dense network rather than in a hierarchical chain of command. This cosmology works well with the bottom-up, hypothesis-driven individualist approach in which the Druid maintains direct spiritual experience and skeptical reflection on those experiences as mutually beneficial for moving effectively in multiple realms or worlds. Rather than emphasize agreement to specific beliefs or commonality of practice, Druids share a common orientation toward relational ontology itself and a value of diversity in experience and thought. Druidry is not so much a particular belief system as a process of producing spiritual experiences and reflections on them. This approach affords the flexibility necessary to be responsive to changes in relationships with human and other-than-human others.

This responsivity to relationships is paired in Druidic animism with universal cognitive foundations permitting the relational experience itself, described by cognitive scientists as the Theory of Mind, an "intuitive tendency among all modern humans to attribute thoughts, intentionality, and beliefs (i.e., minds) to others so as to predict their behavior" (Sidky 2017: 95). Our species evolved this cognitive computational specialization to predict and explain other humans' behavior, but arguably, its side effect is that we experience spirits—and arguably, have religion as a whole (Barrett 2004). Additionally, it allows metarepresentation—"thoughts about thoughts" (Barrett 2011), which enables us to split our interpretive reflections from our sensorial experiences, entertaining multiple points of view—including what we posit internally as views that are not our own. These capacities are paired with an "Agency-Detection System" (Guthrie 1993; Sidky 2017;

Whitehouse and Laidlaw 2007) that is grounded in a combination of pattern recognition/seeking and Theory of Mind, which means we perceive relationships between events and we seek an agent behind them. In short, our cognition and perception are hard-wired to seek patterns and relationships with sentient others, which means that we are capable of readily perceiving sentient others outside of our own species.

Most cognitive scientists view animism as an evolutionary mistake, a byproduct of our sociality (Guthrie 2007). Yet, psychologists working on the intersections of human and animal cognition have argued that animals, too, have the mirror neurons that allow for empathy and rich emotional lives. They may have their own Theory of Mind—and the human requirements for animism and rich animal-human relationships may not require a fully developed Theory of Mind—we are closer to one another in the animal world than we think (Benvenuti 2014). Furthermore, animism and spirit belief has been extensively implicated in ethnoecological works as foundational in producing sustainable behavior, something sorely and obviously lacking in Western materialist cultures. Ethnoecologists (e.g., Milton 2002, resting on Gibson 1966 and 1979) have argued that it is inaccurate to say that humans personify nature, because it implies we construct them as persons, rather than discovering their person-like qualities through interacting with them. That is, rather than understanding Theory of Mind as an innate cognitive drive to see persons in an impersonal world, we could understand it as an innate cognitive capacity to perceive persons in a personal world (Milton 2002: 44–5). Druids are not fabricating experiences with other-than-human persons in nature, but rather building relationships with them in ways that are similar to how we build relationships with human persons.

In this relational understanding of nature, the self and the environment are mutually emergent conceptualizations that are part of one process of engagement. This is adaptive collectively in the form of sustainable engagement with the natural world on which we depend, and adaptive individually in the form of fulfilling psychological needs we have for attachments to animals, which help us connect to our own animal bodies and experiences (Benvenuti 2014). Such relationships reduce our abstraction and connect us to perception. The ways in which animals are like and not like us help us expand in our experience and knowledge. While these universal cognitive processes are held in common with indigenous persons, it is inaccurate to think of Druidic animism as highly similar to indigenous animist religions. Philippe Descola (2013) offered four categories that can describe ontological relationships between humans and other-than-humans. If we compare Druidry to other common Western ontologies, we find that it is animist in Descola's schema, positing shared intentionality and agency with differing bodies. Other-than-human beings have similar capacity for feeling, thought, agency and power as humans, despite different outward forms. However, shared personhood is integrated within diverse and unique other-than-human perspectives (perception, cognition), culture, and ways of communicating. In this way, other-than-humans are persons in Druidic animism, but are not humans-in-other-clothing, therefore differing from Amerindian perspectivism (Viveiros de Castro 1998). Druidic animism is relativist; the navigation of the relationships with other-than-humans rests on similar skills we find for navigating cross-cultural relationships in pluralist societies. Druids do this through empathy, imagination, and folkloric tradition. Much like cultural relativism in anthropology, Druids generally do not believe any being is superior or inferior, but rather that their diversity is united through and necessary for natural and spiritual processes. This is useful in personal development as it requires expansion of capacities to think through the lens of very different "others"—different perception, cognition, and culture. Experiences and beliefs of transmigration and shape-shifting capture the fluidity and unity of "life" and "nature," as well as how current incarnations as bodies shape experience of being.

More significant than ontological differences, the primacy of individualism in Druidry is distinctively different from most indigenous animisms, which emphasize collectivism. The American model of "mind" is highly individualistic rather than relational, including perceptions, thoughts, feelings, desires, intentions, and self-control or will (Bennardo and De Munck 2014: 104–5), but at the same time, it is the situational context that renders selfhood egocentric or sociocentric (121). This individualism limits the translation of a relational ontology to a common relational ethics, as I will extensively explore in Chapter 12. Indigenous animist systems integrate place-based knowledge, codes for behavior, and social sanctions for breaking ethical codes in ways that Druidry does not: first, due to its globalized and diffuse nature; secondly, because of its individualism; and thirdly, because of its lack of authoritative community. Individual Druids face greater social sanction outside of Druidry than within it. This means that while Druids hold in common nature-centrism and a desire to be sustainable and ethical in their relationships, there is no coherent whole in Druidry to guide, evaluate, or correct behavior. At the same time, Druids do hold a belief that knowledge is central to forging right relationship—which is why study (in a multiplicity of ways of knowing) is so central to Druid orders. We cannot come into right relationship with beings we do not know—this would be projection of our own desires onto them rather than coming into an emergent co-creative and co-agent space with them through a process of interaction and experience. Yet while Druidry deconstructs the dualisms of the Western overculture, it does not entirely escape its philosophical and cultural legacy. Druidic concepts and feelings about places and "nature," therefore, are not always internally consistent and instead may shift based on context—as well as simultaneously hold paradoxical experiential truths. One of the primary places we see this is in the way Druids view the sacred as it relates to place and to nature as a whole.

Wilderness in the Wild Soul

The Western separation of wilderness from the human world goes back to ancient Roman times and pervades the dominant American model of nature, which separates nature from the human world as a limited resource and idealizes smaller-scale societies as inherently sustainable (Bennardo and De Munck 2014: 124). In this division, which is foundational to both romantic and materialist orientations toward nature, there is a commodification of subjectivist nature (Coeckelbergh 2017). The Western world's conceptualization of nature as separate from humans is a minority worldview in the world, including nature's "disenchantment" that happened with modern Western science's rise and which made nature material objects and therefore outside the boundaries of moral and religious obligation (Harding 1994; Sullivan 2017). While modern Paganisms such as Druidry seek to re-enchant the natural world, they often simultaneously reinforce Western notions of wilderness as nature-set-apart. Yet we know through the ethnographic record that there is no wilderness (in the case of pristine nature); nearly everywhere has been extensively managed by humans for tens of thousands of years (Callicott and Nelson 1998; Blackburn 1993). This has led to reconsidering what is "cultural" and "natural" in anthropology, and instead viewing many aspects of both the physical world around us and the social world between us as "biocultural" (Posey 1999; Maffi 2001).

Arturo Escobar's (1999) work that defined "nature regimes" explained that the meaning of nature has shifted throughout history, and that we can now acknowledge how nature is both a constructed concept within a human context and yet also ecologically independent of human construction. Escobar describes "organic nature" as a foil to nature within a capitalist context, a construction of nature and society as ontologically interwoven and interdependent—and explains that ritual links the two. Druids are essentially working to unlearn a capitalist nature regime and return to an organic nature regime. However, the conceptual separation of humanity from nature is difficult to unlearn. The bridge in Druidry toward this return to an organic union of human and other-than-human is in the relationship between "wild nature," as some Druids describe it, and the "wild soul."

As was discussed earlier in this chapter, sacred landscapes are part of Druid community, and can be constructed or perceived. Sacred places provide an "immediacy" of the other-than-human, where it is easier to feel them, experience them, and engage with them (Blain and Wallis 2004: 241). Places are agents, persons of their own accord that facilitate spirit communication and communion. In this way, wilderness is not only a location but an attitude, a way of knowing, a state of being that Westerners largely forgot, but that is the legacy and birthright of all humanity (Roszak 1995). Druids "going into wilderness" or going to "more natural places" is not so much about the human-nature dichotomy as it is a spiritual practice to attempt to sew back together the rupture that we inherited:

> Up here in Northern California, it's not just forest. It's the quality of the whole atmosphere. Specifically, the beaches here have cliff faces and rocks and the ocean spreads forever and the sky is there. So you've got all the components of the universe: you've got earth and sea and sky. When we were down in Los Angeles, it was a little harder. But there are hidden pockets of parks in the Hollywood Hills and we used to go up and do rituals in them. (Murtagh anDoile)

It is not so much that there is a "pure without humans" Druid concept of sacred wild landscape as much as a "finding the wild human in the wild landscape" concept. It is a return to a deeper, more ancient self residing in the contemporary human body—a kind of shared memory between place, body, and soul. It's also the silencing of chaotic or busy "noise" of human urban Western life in order to more deeply listen to nature.

This Druidic practice of hiking, walking, or doing ritual in spaces away from the intensity of Western human life is similar to the "wilderness practice" described by some ecopsychologists (Greenway 1995; Harper 1995). Such practices have been demonstrated to produce perceptual and cognitive shifts, including toward the body, nature, other persons (human and not), time, and culture/civilization—allowing the practitioner to more easily shift away from dualism and to become mindful of cultural patterns at work in their lives (Greenway 1995). This is not all "love and light" as some Druids put it, because nature itself is also death, chaos, destruction, and upheaval—also noted by ecopsychologists as key to accessing our own messy, sometimes painful, wild natures (Harper 1995: 187–8). This messy, chaotic, dark aspect is the shadow in Jungian terms, and confronting it in both self and nature is an inherent part of the OBOD material. It is most visible at Samhain and Alban Arthan, which focus rituals and meditations on death, decay, and the dark and reorient the Western overcultural avoidance or control of these to one of fully embracing grief, sorrow, fear, and the necessity of death for life to go on. The bridge between wild nature and the wild soul is the pathway to integration and wholeness, as well as to sacralization of everyday life and of every place—a way of using wilderness to overcome dualisms that threaten sustainability.

Druids often note that certain "wild places"—as the mountains and ocean does for me—can serve as powerful agents in helping us re-center ourselves in our wild souls and as part of the integrated process of the universe, can inspire us aesthetically and spiritually, and can restore us psychologically. Yet the home and garden is also sacred; sacredness is everywhere:

> I'm quite drawn to the ocean. It's powerful energy places. Like when you go to the Redwoods—those giant Redwood forests are very powerful

to everyone and very restorative. I'm in suburbia in my back yard. The energy is [also] here because I've cultivated the land and taken care of it, doing restorative landscaping, mostly with native plants except the vegetable garden. I have a connection here, and this is home. (Elizabeth Boerner)

Druids do not necessarily take for granted that certain types of wild places, particularly forests in Druidry, are spiritually significant due to their inherent qualities. Due to reflexive practice common in Druidry, they also reflect on the influences that may make so many of them feel the woods are particularly special, acknowledging the influence of Western cultures:

I was talking to myself while driving yesterday, and I was asking myself why so many people like the Pacific Northwest and feel that it's somehow magical and mysterious. I used to feel that way as a child. Go back to their childhood when their parents told them stories. Where do they come from? Some European wood. And so the collective worldview of North Americans and Northern Europeans are that the mysterious and the faerie and the otherfolk come from that kind of environment. And by golly, the Pacific Northwest fits that collective kind of view. (Rory Harper)

There is a recognition that culture and folklore shapes spiritual experience, but that the experience is no less real because of its necessary subjective construction. The woods and sea are sacred because they are locations of encountering powerful other-than-human beings, but they are also sacred because we perceive them to be so when we are present there—and yet, in a less awe-inspiring but still significant way, so too is nature in our city parks, back yards, vegetable gardens. Even if the wilder other-than-humans, the sidhe (or fae), and the gods, are less immediately palpable there, our homes are the places in which we dedicate most of our time in spiritual practice and environmental action. They are sites of dedication, even if we seek inspiration and a reminder of integration in wild nature.

The Gods in and of Nature

As I have explained in earlier chapters, the gods in Druidry are not much like those in the Abrahamic traditions—both in terms of how Druids often think of their nature (or characteristics) and in terms of how Druids relate to them. Not all Druids believe in or experience gods as real beings. For those who do, some believe they are human constructions, archetypes, or symbols more than independent agents. It is common for even hard polytheists, those who believe and/or experience the gods as independent real agents, to have close relationships and surety of experience with only a few of them. This is not problematic in Druidry because the boundaries around Druidic identity do not have to do with belief or with gods but rather in the sacredness of the earth and the importance of right relationships with all beings on earth. The gods, then, are subsumed as a type of being that some Druids feel called to be in relationship with, but just as individual Druids may variously feel connected to a particular river, a species of tree, or an herb, so too are relationships with gods highly variable individual to individual. There are gods with whom I have direct mystical experience and deep relationship, gods with whom I have a long-standing relationship of reciprocity without ever having had mystical experience of them, and many gods with whom I have no relationship at all. In all cases, the gods are generally less transcendent and more immanent in Druidry, which is a part of the process of returning to what Michael York (2010) described as corpospirituality, in which dualism is eliminated and the material world is both sacred and profane. After all, the conceptualization of gods or spirits as supernatural, as somehow transcendent of the natural world, is a modern one (Apffel-Marglin 2019).

Druidic theology is, as Chas S. Clifton wrote about contemporary Pagan theology in general, "more poetic than systematic" (2006: 57), permitting many variations. Yet as a whole, Druids tend to maintain that all—including the gods and disincarnate spirits—are part of the natural world: "I do think there is a spiritual realm. I don't like to think of it as supernatural. I think that the world is the world, right? And there are parts of it we perceive differently than other parts. It's not so much separate as different to me" (Maggie). Therefore, while many Druids identify as polytheist (57 percent in the survey described a special closeness with deities), this closeness can take many forms that are not grounded in worship or even in surety of the gods' existence. Relationships are more frequently collegial or familial than hierarchical. Druids "work with" or are "taught by" a deity, rather than "believing in" or "worshipping" the deity. The gods may be intimately related to ancestors, and likewise, humans may be capable of becoming gods, as one Druid queries: "Where are the boundaries of gods and not-gods? I don't know. We know that humans can become gods. Apotheosis is a thing. At one point does someone go from human to ancestor to god? How do they do that? I don't know" (John Beckett). In Druidry, theological orientations are also not necessarily mutually exclusive: 63 percent of hard polytheists are also animist; 93 percent of soft polytheists are also animist; 80 percent of pantheists (the 38 percent of Druids who believe the universe is divine) are also animist. And while many Druids have their own individual ideas about the nature of gods and other spirits, they generally openly acknowledge they really do not know and affirm that it's entirely possible for many reasons for different people to have different equally valid and real experiences of the matter—which may be framed as not knowing how such experiences are differently felt due to personality and sensory differences, cultural background, immediate context, and the agency of the other-than-humans themselves.

Druids often openly describe the concept Luhrmann (2022) called the *faith frame*; that is, behaving as if something were true (that a spirit or god exists) even if they are not sure, and taking ritual seriously—though often playfully. Because the gods are not necessarily viewed as fully independent from humanity, Druids sometimes feel that new gods may be discovered or developed:

> Humans with the energies that we have, create our god-forms, which is what allow them to evolve and shift and change, depending on which human they're working with. So there is an infinite number of spirit worlds and Otherworlds, but also through cultural and philosophical understandings and group-mind, there are structures of certain Otherworlds that get put into place over linear spacetime of hundreds if not thousands of years. (Rev. Monika Kojote)

While Luhrmann posits that the relationships forged with spirits is grounded in the imagination, which in turn emerges from the stories in which the god is embedded (2022: 30), that is not necessarily the case in Druidry—where experiences may arise that do not have any stories associated with them at all, in which the person does not yet know who the god is (Bel in my own spiritual experience, for example) or where the god or spirit seems to be new or unknown. The concept of the faith frame is relatively visible at the surface in Druidry in the conversations Druids have with one another without seeking consensus.

The gods, then, pervade nature—and conversely, nature pervades the gods. There is an interrelationship of divine and incarnate other-than-human beings. Personhood and agency are embedded in both incarnate and disincarnate beings, which may emerge in both worlds at once (gods as having incarnate forms or sending their messages through incarnate forms). Nature spirits and deities are fuzzy-boundaried, as are deep-time ancestors and deities. In the survey, 42 percent reported experience of or faith in gods who shape-shift into natural forms and 46 percent believe natural processes personify the gods. The distinct categorization of the natural and supernatural, human and other-than-human, we find in Christo-centric overculture breaks down in Druidic experience and cosmological thought, as one Druid described: "Druids in general have a lot of things in common. The reverence for nature. We really like trees—for us, that's an axis mundi, that connects all the worlds. A reverence for the earth. Nothing is outside for nature. The gods are part of nature. We're all in this together" (Rev. Kirk Thomas). In my own Druidic experiences, and in the reports of others, while both gods and sidhe or fae are part of nature, the two are not the same type of spirit being. Interestingly, quite a few Druids view the gods as aspects of human consciousness or as distinct and real spirit persons created by human consciousness, but do not view the Fair Folk (or sidhe, or fae) in this way. Instead, fairies are generally viewed as distinctive beings that existed before and outside of human imagination and consciousness. Some think this is why the gods play by rules understandable to humans, and the Fair Folk do not. Yet while the origins and relationships with humans may differ between the two categories of spirit beings, both are part of the natural world and nothing—even these powerful other-than-human beings—supersedes or transcends it.

Even so, once spirits are treated as social actors with agency, people may experience the relationship in ways they did not expect, and it can go sideways and become psychologically detrimental (even abusive) (Luhrmann 2022). There is a lively discussion among contemporary Druids what healthy relationships between humans and more powerful disincarnate spirits (such as gods or fae) look like—are they always entirely consensual? How can one discern projections from past trauma or psychological distress from experiences of powerful beings who are agents with their own purposes? Remember, in the context of myth—such as that of the making of Taliesin— the gods might pursue and transform a human who is initially unwilling or unwitting. The Fair Folk are even more potentially dangerous. It can be difficult to discern what arises from unhealthy interior projection from that which generates spiritual development, especially as gods and spirits (as well as astral places and processes) are often viewed as changing over time just as we do. However, unverified personal gnosis can be "checked" in various ways: against folklore and mythology or through discussion with others in order to tease apart the psychological, social, neurological, and spiritual dimensions of an experience. Druidic practice is both spiritual experience and critical reflection, sifting through experiences to make meaning as a self-conscious act rather than against a backdrop of doctrine. In Druidic ontology, humans are viewed as more powerful vis-à-vis the gods and spirits than they are in monotheist systems, usually (though not always) with freedom of choice to reject specific experiences, relationships, and requests. It is part of the Druidic work to work through the abuses, traumas, and other problematic patterns from one's life and to come into a position of healthy relationship. What healthy looks like varies considerably, from those who entirely do not work with categories of spirits (not uncommon) to those who feel called, claimed, ridden, or married to specific spirits or gods. However, a big part of training is choice and boundary-setting.

In its elimination of dualism, polytheist and agnostic leanings, and its affirmation of the power of individual humans in the deity-human relationship, Druidry serves as a countercultural movement to the pervasive assumptions of American Protestant traditions. Sabina Magliocco (2004) wrote extensively about witchcraft as a countercultural movement, and Druidry is positioned much the same way vis-à-vis an American overculture heavily influenced by both Christianities and capitalism. The spiritual ecstasy of direct mystical experience, particularly of and through nature, likely gives rise to new religious movements like Druidry because the overculture denies or dismisses such experiences, while they tend to demand meaning-making of those who have them (McDaniel 2018: 21). Druidry is less a revolution on the outside as on the inside, within consciousness. As one Druid put it: "Your whole purpose of being here is to transform yourself into the best version of self you can be. I definitely see that in OBOD Druidry—being at peace with who you are, and if you're not at peace with who you are, transforming yourself to where you want to be" (Joseph). Druidry first recognizes, usually from childhood memory, the sacredness and rightness of relationship with earth, with trees, with animals. It then comes to recognize community of Druids who share that primacy of the earth despite a materialist and anthropocentric overculture. Then, it provides practices that sacralize and re-enchant life, especially everyday life—the seasons of nature and of human life, the small details of living—of eating, of gardening, of care-taking, of working. This is revolutionary in an overculture of busyness and consumerism. It is a consistent work on reorienting oneself to relationship. Druids are also interested in social change—they discuss it; they work in it through interfaith councils, professional work, and volunteering; they build skills they think will be useful for it. But Druidry's impact on social change is less visible as protest and more as an infiltration—a patient work on replacing the pervasiveness of what is perceived to be unhealthy and unsustainable lifeways with humane ones—with lives that uphold right relationship, and therefore forge peace and love where there is strife, hatred, fear, and apathy.

Religion as Culture

So how, then, do we understand Druidry as religion? And how does Druidry as religion open a doorway to critically examining our definitions of religion? There is no academic consensus on how to define religion. Defining religion positions the study of religion in multiple ways: as ideas/thoughts/beliefs; emotions; experiences; practices; functions; or integrations with power. Variously, religion has been defined by its functionality for social solidarity and integration with the rest of culture (Durkheim, Geertz); as a mechanism for personal development (Jung, Maslow); or as counterintuitive and counterfactual thinking in the face of fear and uncertainty (Freud, Marx, Atran, and Feuerbach). For most definitions of religion, any scholar of religion can readily point to examples that defy the boundaries of the definition. Defining religion can come dangerously close to reifying what is actually emergent phenomena of patterns integrated with and inseparable from culture more broadly. As a consequence, some theorists have defined religion in existential terms, rendering all humans religious (Zahela 2017: 289–90).

To define religion is to theorize religion (Bielo 2015: 2; Taylor 2010: 1–3; Clarke and Byrne 1993: 26). Definitions of religion in Western academia, as a category of human life separated from the rest of social life, have been steeped in colonialism and Christo-centrism, a product of a specific cultural, historical, and ideological context (Asad 1993; Van der Veer 2014). Religion as a concept is not value-neutral, nor has it ever been, and it is not objective so much as instrumental. Each definition that has been made has generally been made grounded in Western discussion of what differentiates this facet of life from others, but this differentiation is itself a product of its philosophical history. This is complicated by the issue that the public conceptualization of religion is even more interwoven with Western materialism and Christianity as a philosophical legacy. This is true even of Druids' conceptualization of religion, even as they attempt to extract themselves from a Christo-centric, dualist, and materialist foundation of the overculture. The distinction of religion as organized and institution and spirituality as individual—so often discussed by Druids as they wrestle with the question of whether or not Druidry is religion—is itself problematic, as the distinction makes categories of what are actually interrelated processes of individual development and experience in a mutually emergent pattern of collective rituals, representations, and meanings.

Druids' assessment of Druidry is not infrequently informed by Christo-centric definitions: religion as having authoritative leadership and text paired with orthodoxy and doctrine. As a consequence, Druids sometimes show resistance to the concept of categorizing Druidry as religion, but acknowledge that Druids vary in their evaluation and that the question is a difficult one:

> For myself, I would not say it was a religion, because OBOD has no dogma and I like that about it. I don't see that as being a religion, but maybe it is. I would think of it more as a spirituality, and being able to commune with what's around me. You have free will, and no one's telling you want to do or trying to convert you. There is no recruiting. No one's asking for your money or time. (Elizabeth Boerner)

> I said I didn't think Druidry as a religion, because in my brain, religion has dogma, a certain source everybody goes from. I think of it as a spirituality and a way of life. [But] there's the Parliament of World Religions, and I would say yes, Druidry needs to be included. There's not a central book or a theology or a leader. So it's kind of a trick, so initially I'd say no, but then I'd differ if someone said to exclude [us]. (Anon)

Within these complex inner debates about Druidry as religion, the overcultural Christo-centric norms defining religion are apparent: the foil against religion that has doctrine, that seeks to have everyone join it, that is demanding of investment rather than supportive of personal interest. Others contrasted Druidry from religion by virtue of its emphasis of the sacredness of and integration with everyday life: "For me it's a way of life. It's not really a religion. It's a substitute for a religion. It gives me something to hold on to in bad times. But mostly it gives me something to celebrate in good times. I've been in it so long, it's just part of who I am. It's the way I view the world" (Dawn). Dawn's description speaks to the Western conceptualization of religion as separate from everyday life, but when we define religion in ways that speak to all cultures across time, rather than the narrow contemporary Western way of viewing it, we find that in most cultures, most of the time, religion was in fact inseparable from the rest of life.

Some Druids spoke to this issue—recognizing that our limited Western definitions of religion were themselves problematic. Siobhan offered, "The Druid's Prayer and certain things we do, on the surface, are religious, but I mainly look at that part as being ritual. Ritual has always been a thing before organized religion made it a part of its thing." Addressing the concept of religion from a historical perspective, Maggie argued: "the way it turns out in how these words [religion] were used in context before late antiquity are all social relationships. Your religion is a way to be social. The gods are part of society and they have a role in society." Maggie points toward the value of Druidry for critically examining the validity of definitions of religion, rather than attempting to categorize Druidry within the typical academic and vernacular Western conceptualizations of religion as a distinctive set-apart domain of human life. When we examine Western definitions of religion, we find that they frequently fall short of including both religions in antiquity and also contemporary non-Western religions, particularly indigenous animisms. This is because such religions were not distinctive domains of human life, but rather total cultural systems that integrated domains of human life. As Dorothy Lee argued, "Religion is an ever-present dimension of experience . . . to behave and think religiously is to behave and think. To describe a way of life in its totality is to describe a religious way of life" (1993: 12). The categorical dualisms so prevalent in the post-Enlightenment Western world were not, in fact, how humans in most times and places functioned. Indigenous animisms, for example, are both religions and folk science systems. Traditional ecological knowledge systems generally integrate religious and scientific approaches, which impact how people view themselves within the other-than-human world as well as their knowledge systems of the environment, including classification systems, uses, and resource management (Anderson 1996, 2010, 2014; Berkes 1999). In many indigenous animisms, there are no words for nature or for religion (see, for example, an extensive treatment of this among the Chipewyan in Smith 1998). There is no transcendent religion/mundane or human/nature divide. Druidry, like many other earth or nature-centered religions, are more aptly termed "spiritual ecologies"—a term proposed as more inclusive than religion and used to describe the interfaces of religions or spiritualities and ecologies and environments (Sponsel 2017: 132). Druidry is not orthodoxic or orthopraxic but rather a community for sharing approaches, perspectives, and skills for refining a body of ecospiritual knowledge—that is, how to understand and engage in a complex, highly relational, very alive universe.

What I argue is that Druidry is one of many examples of religions that demand us to (re)define religion itself away from assumptions that are deeply problematic when we examine the breadth of human spirituality, both individually and collectively, across time and space. Further, it asks that we eliminate the individual/collective dualist distinction between religion and spirituality, offering that both the individual and the collective are mutually emergent patterns. We are never alone, never truly independent, never truly isolated—in Druidry or in any other cultural context. A pathway forward to understanding religion in this way is to define religion as culture—not as an aspect of it but rather as culture itself—as inherently integrated with the rest of human life. In smaller-scale societies, everyone may share one religion-culture. In large, highly complex societies like the United States, religions are subcultures, intersectional with other subcultures and identities. Cognitive anthropology offers a pathway forward for understanding the emergent patterns we recognize as religious traditions (and as religious cultures) without reifying any attributes of particular religions in defining religion as a distinctive domain of human life.

At least as early as Charles Frake's (1980) work on spirit classification, cognitive anthropology has provided a way to describe the ways universal foundations for the human experience of religion are instantiated in specific cultural, ecological, and historical contexts to produce religious culture. Cognitive approaches seek to understand norms, which are both social and cognitive phenomena (Conte et al. 2014: 177–8). Norms demand compliance out of a collective sense of obligation that drives internal motivation. Norms articulate mental representations with observable conformity of behavior within social groups. Cognitive anthropology is primarily interested in the relationship between the individual and culture, within an understanding that these are mutually emergent. The individual is an emergent pattern arising from brain-based mechanisms, agency, and the sociocultural environment and context (D'Andrade and Strauss 1992; Holland and Quinn 1987; Kronenfeld 2008). Culture is "distributed cognition" with its own compelling features and lifespan not coterminous with any one individual (Kronenfeld 2008: 3, whose work explains how this definition of culture was developed from the 1938 Durkheimian theory about "social facts"). Culture does not reside in shared codes for behavior so much as it is a model that describes a distribution of emergent patterns across individual minds. Culture and cognition are process, not mere content—a description of a constantly changing and emerging mutual relationship between the individual and the social group. Thus, integration of psychological and anthropological approaches—uniting how people think (process) and what people think (content)—is necessary to fully understand how they function as an inseparable whole (Nisbett 2003; Shweder 1991), even as this integration has been fraught with debate and difficulty (see, for example, the discussions by Shweder [2012] and Unsworth [2012]).

Returning to religion, a cognitive anthropological approach seeks to describe religious culture through one or more patterns apparent in the behaviors and ideas of those who claim it as their own, breaking a barrier between the spiritual/individual and religious/social group by examining these as part of a whole process. Likewise, variation within a religion is approached as a normative and important part of religious community, neither as heretical (as when religion is defined by authoritative body) nor as statistically insignificant (as when religion is defined only by the majority of practitioners). Instead, the breadth of variation within a religion speaks to intersectional influences, differing social contexts, individual agency, and neurodiversity. Religion becomes a rich and fertile ground for understanding the most basic of questions about the human experience: how our brains and cultures influence each other and how our consciousness and motivation yields creative use and development of collectively held practices, ideas, and stories.

We can investigate the emergent patterns in culture through cultural modeling, a method and theory that describes the widely shared, often subconscious patterns of emotion, thought, motivation, and behavior present in social groups that help us to interpret our social world and choose actions (Holland and Quinn 1987; D'Andrade 1995; D'Andrade and Strauss 1992). We can think of cultural models as a kind of script that allows for a lot of improv, providing a sketch of a domain that can be adapted to many contexts for making meaning of our lives (Bang et al. 2007). A domain is a boundaried aspect of human life. Domains can be objects, concepts, processes or tasks, activities, events, emotions—just about anything we mentally process and respond to. Cultural models organize the information from the world around us, reducing our cognitive load. Cultural models can be more or less consciously held and can conflict or work in complementarity (Kronenfeld 2008; also see Barrett 2007 about reflective and non-reflective beliefs, which provides a similar conceptualization of variation in consciousness of our models). Multiple, even competing, patterns can exist in communities and in individuals, providing a variety of perspectives and approaches to diverse contexts and situations, but there are often statistically prevalent patterns that describe significant trends in a culture (Atran et al. 2005).

Multiple domains are associated with religion: supernatural, morals, group identity, action, emotion (Boyer and Walker 2000: 152). Cultural modeling as theory and method is useful for examining religion in general, and particularly ecocentric religions that engage participatory consciousness, because it has been successfully applied to understanding dynamics of thought and action in both environmental domains (Kirner 2017) and magical and religious domains (Sørensen 2007; Smith 2014). Rather than describing "a religion," cultural modeling permits the description of patterns of nested and interrelated *schemas*, or smaller aspects of larger models, that are at play in a religious tradition. Aaron Smith, for example, described an extended model of religious cognition that included emotions, symbols, rituals, experiences, meaning-making, commitment, rules and doctrine, and consequences (Smith 2014: 201). Cultural modeling integrates individual religious experience with social processes of identity formation and affirmation. While Smith's model is Christo-centric by assuming doctrine and authoritative experts, we can apply his conceptual framework within a cultural modeling approach, which does not require authoritative experts for cultural models to be developed and maintained. Cultural models can arise organically from the bottom-up through common experience and interpersonal communication. Examining Druidry as religious culture, using a cultural modeling approach, illuminates how commonalities and a sense of community can arise despite a lack of authoritative text or leadership, and even without face-to-face interactions.

Religion as culture does not require orthodoxy, orthopraxy, or authoritative leadership or text if it is understood through a cognitive anthropological lens. The sharing of techniques, strategies, ideas, and experiences to grow individual understanding and practice is sufficient (even when virtual) to generate commonly held patterns over time—that is to generate cultural models, and therefore culture itself. Cultural groups can be self-selective; Druidry and other ecocentric new religious movements draw people with specific pre-identified experiences and then provide practices and community that socialize, regenerate, and affirm those experiences. The contemporary United States has few mainstream venues for altered states of consciousness and intuitive ways of knowing, much less animist ontology. Druidry provides a "home" for such people, providing those with such anomalous experiences a "homecoming." Subsequently, the shared ritual forms and practices, Wheel of the Year, and communications between Druids (through gatherings, groves, workshops, blogs, books social media, and international orders) build religious culture—some aspects of which are consciously learned and visibly performed as Druidic tradition, and some aspects of which are the subconscious training of perception and cognition in participatory consciousness and relational worldview. That subconscious training in Druidry is in part, those developed in ecocentric community—in relationships with the natural world—shaping, over time, not only our core values and commitments (both within human society and to the earth), but also our attentive biases (so that we notice and interact with nature in certain ways).

Perhaps, then, Druidry is religion—if religion is defined sufficiently broadly to move away from Christo-centric ideals, and if we acknowledge that religion is, for many people of many religions, a way of perceiving, interpreting, and enacting—in short, a cultural system for living. Without any authoritative body determining standards by which we determine what Druidry is, and who Druids are, what then is Druidry? As White asked in her recent survey-based work: "Is modern Druidry defined by a set of formal, shared rituals and celebrations, or is it defined by the spiritual meta-practice of connecting with and celebrating the land upon which one actually lives—

guided by a shared philosophical framework?" (2021: 104). In keeping with a cultural modeling approach, I was more concerned with how Druids define Druidry for themselves than in imposing my own definition—however it might be informed by social theory. I posed this question to fellow Druids and found their responses illuminating. Spiritual ecology—a concern for the earth tied to viewing all of nature as inherently sacred—was the only common core at the heart of most Druids' description of what it means to be a Druid:

> Recognizing the really important role that humans play as caretakers and guardians of the living Earth. My own definition of Druidry includes practices of deep gratitude and reciprocation. (Dana O'Driscoll)

> It's communing with nature and being able to coexist and respect our world around us on many different levels. (Elizabeth Boerner)

> I think a common thing is wanting to be connected to the earth around us in some way, shape or form. (Joseph)

> It's when people have the nature spirituality part, but it's not from a strictly humanistic standpoint. There are spirits there. (John Beckett)

> It's a love for all things nature. All things true. All things healthy. All things united. All things in love. (Anon)

There were two other interrelated thematic patterns: first, Druidry is inherently diverse and respects those differences as a "feature, not a bug" (as a strength, not a weakness) and second, as a consequence, Druids do not tend to think of themselves as the prototypic Druid, regardless of their beliefs or practices. Because Druidry permits multiple religious identity and does not demand exclusivity, every Druid's Druidry is informed by cultural models they have carried with them from other traditions, experiences, and practices:

> I am a Pagan. I am a polytheist. I am an animist. I am a magician. I have a bit of leftover Revival preacher in me. And these are parts of my religious identity. And they don't fit real well with anyone's Druidry. It took time because I came to understand that I am a Druid, but Druidry as it is commonly understood doesn't entirely describe my practice. (John Beckett)

> I'm probably unlike many Druids because my entire Druid career besides the past five weeks, I have been a city Druid, and not the city Druid who hates being in the city and has to go to Central Park to find the spirits. (Rev. Monika Kojote)

> I don't assume every Druid is like me because I'm kind of eclectic and different. But most Druids are different in their own way. (Kat Reeves)

There is no aim in Druidry for conformity. Rather, the purpose is the ongoing conversation within a diverse community. The journey, not a destination, is the whole purpose of being a Druid, and the people who tend to become Druids do so out of a desire for this model of spiritual engagement.

Performing Druid identity is a dialectical process. The universal cognitive foundations for Druidry exist in all of us—the Theory of Mind and Agency Detection System provide all of us with a hard-wired motivation to perceive sentient persons throughout nature. For so many Druids, compelling anomalous experiences of other-than-human persons in nature and/or unusual ways of experiencing the self (generally in an altered state of consciousness), often experienced in childhood, motivate them to find a framework to help them make meaning of it. As the US overculture does not offer affirmative frameworks for such experiences, their search leads them eventually to Druidry—often through accessing websites or books as a first glimpse into Druidic culture, community, and conversation. Engaging these sources affirms and cultivates further spiritual experiences, effectively kindling and training the neurological pathways that give rise to participatory consciousness. The individual Druid's discovery of Druidry feels like a homecoming rather than a conversion because it offers affirmation of old experiences, not necessarily because it sparks new ones. The individual Druid feels as though their authentic and truest self is the "wild soul" because *it is*. Druidry is a way of relating to the very foundational universal experience of being human in an interdependent, relational natural world.

Then, because Druidry is contextualized within global, highly individualist Western cultures, it manifests as a countercultural movement rather than as a religion with a specific set of beliefs. Druidry trains practitioners to have spiritual experiences, hypothesize meanings, challenge assumptions, and critically reflect on beliefs. The global conversation among individual Druids, within a context of skepticism, agnosticism, and relativism produces Druidic cultural models, but these are held as a library of options and possibilities, not as doctrine:

> Coming out of conservative Christianity I was raised with the idea that there was a way of doing it wrong. Shifting religion away from this monolithic way, I'm able to recognize ways that you're not doing it wrong, you're doing it differently. The question is not am I doing Druidry correctly, and it's the question of am I leaving the legacy I want to leave. (Maggie)

> Druidry spoke to me more because it was something that you could develop who you are, and it wasn't rigid. It wasn't you have to read this and follow and if you don't follow it this particular way it's not going to work for you. It is really whatever you're into you can find it in Druidry, you can make it a part of Druidry. (Siobhan)

Druidry is best understood as a cultural, epistemological, and spiritual nature-centered movement that functions differently from Western Christo-centric models of religiosity. US Druids form a community of practice, grounded in shared human-brain-in-nature experiences that organically lead them toward shared beliefs, practices, and experiences—and that challenge them to enact a relational ecocentric worldview in the context of profoundly disconnected, materialist, and anthropocentric overculture. Rather than differentiate between categories common in Western ideology (religion vs. science vs. magic; religion vs. spirituality vs. philosophy) to understand and define religion, studying Druidry leads us to ask what orients people to the big questions and meanings in their lives. What gives their life meaning? What guides their most significant processes of being and becoming? The processes and patterns that do so, regardless of how they are categorized, often share common features and effects. We can address the phenomenological, cognitive, social, psychological, and other dimensions of these *orienting constellations of becoming and being*, recognizing that they are, regardless of what we call them, at the heart of being human.

The Third Triad—
All as Worthy

Living Druidry

*Three actions are held as the Druid mission:
to become wise, to work for justice, and to love.*

CHAPTER 9

The Foundation of Right Action

Knowledge

FIGURE 7 *Learning.*

A few years ago, I interned for a few wonderful months at an urban bioregenerative farm, the Sarvodaya Institute. One hot early autumn day, I pruned and trellised tomatoes for the third time. On one of my very first days on the farm, I learned how to remove the lower branches that touch the ground and to select one strong shoot and trim the others, so the plant could put its energy into producing more tomatoes. In one of those first days, I also learned how to use string to wrap the plant loosely and provide it with support as it grew toward the trellis. In that very first session, I was unsure of myself. Was this a branch or a shoot? How low was too low for a branch before I pruned it? Was I wrapping this plant correctly? After a few times, I found myself noticing on my own when the tomatoes needed more pruning and trellising, able to leap in with doing the task. It felt gratifying to be able to complete it on my own, and I also noticed that I was less clumsy in doing it: my body was beginning to have its own memory of the task.

For Druids, the acquisition of both our capacity to learn and reason, as well as knowledge itself, is central to our spiritual development. Indeed, the central turning point in the Druid's Prayer (see Chapter 5) utilized in OBOD ritual is the shift from being protected and therefore strong enough to open to learning, to the process of gaining understanding and knowledge. We must know things in order to make decisions about what is just and right. In a relational worldview, knowing other beings—their personalities, needs, and role in the wholeness of all-that-is—is key to advocating for justice for them, and this is the demonstration of loving other beings. If we do not know what or who we love, we imagine them as what we wish they were. This is not love, and it is not justice. Instead, it is self-serving, making other beings into objects of our needs and desires.

Druids, then, put wisdom and discernment at the heart of right action in the world. It is from wisdom that other virtuous qualities arise. A commitment to study and share knowledge with others is a basic function of all three of the largest Druid orders. OBOD has a study course that engages narrative, poetry, and practical exercises, as well as recommending extensive other literature as part of one's practice, ranging from spiritual to ecological works. AODA requires both practical exercises to hone skills and engagement with a range of literature, including studying book-length works in Druid revival, AODA ritual and curriculum, and ecology in its second-degree coursework. ADF offers multiple guild pathways that allow a member to gain knowledge and practice in various skillsets, including religious and magical skills areas (magicians, seers, liturgists); practical skills areas (brewers, artisans, warriors); scholarly skills; and naturalist skills. At Druid gatherings, workshops on plant identification may be held sandwiched between an ecstatic ritual and a practical workshop on making and using magical staves and wands. Learning knowledge through various ways of knowing, and integrating the process of understanding across ways of knowing, is central to Druidic religion. This process is not confined to Druidic community, but instead positions the Druid in a role of learning from and teaching to a broad and diverse group of others in the world.

I have met Druid public school teachers who use their bardic knowledge and skills to teach storytelling to their students and Druid nurses who use intuitive insights alongside clinical skills to meet patient needs. Druidry is not a religion that is sequestered to one place or time but is rather a way of reframing the way we move through the world, at the same time we restructure how we do so. Druidry reframes my own work as an environmental and medical anthropologist and college professor as the outer, actionable work that arises from my inner passion for understanding human-natural systems and teaching what I know to others. At the same time, anthropology has provided me with process and content knowledge—skills and information—that other Druids sometimes find interesting and useful on their own path. Teaching in the classroom is reframed as my vocation, integrated with my Druidic worldview that values knowledge. The way I learn and teach has been restructured by both anthropology and Druidry to be holistic, integrated, and to honor multiple ways of knowing—both in myself and in the knowledge other people and cultures produce.

Over time, my engagement in Druidry shifted how I taught environmental anthropology (combined, of course, with deepening my pedagogical understanding and skill). My environmental anthropology classes are now taught half of the time in the campus community garden, asking students to learn not through reading, writing, and listening to lecture—but instead through putting their hands in the soil and tasting ripe vegetables. I provide garden notes that are little sketches I make of key garden processes and native plants to help with identification. I encourage them to engage with the land not only through our readings and discussions but through practical effort and creative expression.

In 2018, I was teaching an Anthropology of Food course when a tree gifted my small class with a cornucopia of walnuts. My students had just finished reading about hunting and gathering, including food processing. They excitedly asked if they could try their hand at processing walnuts, with the idea of making walnut flour. I thought this was a wonderful idea, and because we had limited space where we could crack walnuts with stones, I added a few other food processing stations, including harvesting ripe amaranth seeds. One spring afternoon, sunny as is usual for Southern California, students clumped in small groups. One group gathered and cracked walnuts, trying to ease them out of their shell. Another shook and beat amaranth stalks over a tarp, then winnowed them using shallow baskets, exclaiming how tiny the seeds were. At the end of two hours, we traipsed back to the classroom with a small portion of walnuts and amaranth seeds in a couple of jars, windblown hair a bit wild, dirt under fingernails, a bit sore from bending over for too long.

The students engaged with their readings—and with relating to hunting and gathering cultures—differently than they would have without this experience. They understood the effort that it takes to make flour and realized the embodied skill they lacked. They marveled at more advanced processing techniques, such as leaching to make acorn meal edible. We all wondered together about the relationships that people have with the land that enable them to work with hundreds of plant species, the way that Mayan farmers do in their home gardens. The way we were able to engage using a combination of relational and practical approaches was entirely different from how we would have engaged had we only read academic articles about the topic and looked at photos, the way I taught at the beginning of my career. Druidry drove me to learn differently—in a more integrated, relational, and holistic fashion—making scholarly work one part of a larger, more diverse process of knowing. In turn, Druidry allowed me to imagine a different way to teach.

As an educator and cognitive anthropologist, the way I came to think about the concepts of *understanding* and *knowledge* in the Druid's Prayer was the intersection of process knowledge or meta-cognition (i.e., learning how to learn and skill development) and content knowledge (information). Together, it allows us to grasp both the big picture and the details of reality in ways that afford us wisdom, which leads us to actions that are just and loving. In the Druidic relational worldview, the foundation for ethics—for right action—is in valuing all beings, understanding the role of beings in the ecological whole, and knowing how to respond with action that maintains the integrity of the ecological whole. This is true for both incarnate beings like animals and plants, and for disincarnate beings like the fae and the gods. In the Druid's Prayer, our response to *all existences*—to places, humans, plants, animals, even seemingly inanimate objects—comes before our response to the divine. How we respond to the smallest, most vulnerable, or seemingly unalive existences demonstrates our commitment to living out relational spirituality through empathy, motivation to uphold the worth of all existences, and wisdom in how to do so through our actions.

Recently, this was brought home to me in my interactions with a spider. My wife and I had hauled in a small step stool that had been sitting on our porch, needing it to reorganize the top shelves of the kitchen cabinets. It was dusty, so we plunked it into the kitchen sink. As my wife turned on the spray of the kitchen faucet, a large black widow spider came hurriedly scampering out of the bottom of the stool. We squealed, both from surprise and because black widow spiders are venomous. My wife turned the spray toward her for a brief moment, but the spider scampered all over the sink, repeatedly trying to return to her spot under the stool. "Stop!" I cried. "We can't do this. We have to get her back outside." My wife stopped and the spider ran back up under the stool. We looked at each other. "You're right," my wife admitted, "I feel badly for her." "We just have to figure out a safe way to get her outside. We'll use a chair to get to the cabinets," I commiserated.

We carefully tipped the stool on its side to get a better look at her. And then we understood. Her large black abdomen with its hallmark red hourglass was sitting on an egg sac in the corner of the stool's base. She started, but did not move. It was as if she knew we now meant no harm. I crooned to her: "I understand now. I'm sorry. We'll make a deal: we'll put you back outside and you and your babies need to leave our house as soon as you can." Her feet stomped out a small response, or perhaps a retort. We carefully and quickly carried the stool back outside, depositing it away from our house in a bed of bark. I wished her well. It was not her fault that evolution gifted her venom. Regardless of my own fear of spiders, I could not kill a mama who so valiantly tried to care for her babies. And besides, even inconvenient or dangerous beings are valuable within the context of the whole.

Inspiration

In Druidry, knowing includes both understanding relationships within the whole, which gives us a sense that all existences are worthy of acknowledgment and care, and the natural outgrowth of this understanding, which is a curiosity to know (about) existences. As we recognize ourselves as complex, whole beings, we come to understand that we can know in different ways. Broadly speaking, Druidry trains us in both spiritual knowing and intellectual knowing, as well as the holistic integration of these different approaches to learning about self and other in a relational worldview. Spiritual knowing comes through both informal, spontaneous means (intuition, flashes of insight) and through Druidic practices that hone and activate such ways of knowing (divination, devotion to spirit beings who provide insight). It is difficult to describe how the individual differentiates between their own knowing—an outcome of critical thinking—and *inspired* knowing, a way of knowing something that feels as if it falls into one's mind from the deeper subconscious self or from another being entirely. For me, inspired knowing feels as if it has suddenly entered from outside myself, and as I am a highly visual thinker, it usually enters as an image, diagram, or symbol.

When I think about spiritual knowing, I inevitably remember one particular image that pops up sometimes in my meditations: a web of light. I am caught in a web of cerulean light that stretches into infinity. Each node on the web is connected to other nodes, and the image carries with it a strong sense that what is truly significant is the connection—the strands between nodes. The nodes are temporary, but the strands endure. For me, spiritual knowing is connected to the flow of information along those strands. When I let go of focused attention on my own node, constrained by my sense of self, and sink into the strands, knowing comes to me—seemingly without effort. Knowing in this way is tied to my animism and monism: everything has a consciousness and way of communicating (though it may be very foreign to me) and everything is connected as one divine mystery. Relationality, if at the foundation of worldview, extends into a responsive universe that can inspire insight and creative impulse.

Spiritual knowing, just like intellectual knowing, can be practical as well as transcendent. It does not always mean philosophically meaningful wisdom. It is found in knowing how to soothe a rescued feral animal, where to plant herbs in one's garden for them to thrive, or how to keep your bees calm when you are checking your hive. For me, many times, it has guided me when I have been lost while hiking off-trail. An appeal to the land spirits and Elen of the Ways—a goddess of roads and paths—often helps me *feel* the way to my destination. Of course, it could be that, after a lifetime of hiking in forests and mountains, my subconscious notices subtle features in the landscape that form an idea of how to reach my destination, that only feels as if it comes from outside my mind. However, in Druidry it hardly matters what I *think* is the mechanism by which I gain the intuitive knowing. More important is the process of practicing and refining my ability to merge biophysical sensorial hunches and a sense of intuitive knowing that together, yield positive outcomes.

Flashes of insight, a sense of disparate pieces coming together spontaneously, are also common in Druidry. We often call it *awen*, which is divine inspiration—inspiration that comes from the ancestors, nature spirits, or gods. Our capacity to cultivate and receive *awen*, particularly in creative pursuits such as writing, art, and performance, is a central part of many Druids' training, particularly at the very beginning of their journey. Training materials from OBOD, for example, include both triads (tripartite wisdom sayings) and poetry from other Druids, as well as directed exercises to practice writing poetry, telling stories, and creating visual art. I had always enjoyed the visual arts and writing poetry and short stories. As I practiced Druidry, I found that my interest in trying a wide range of arts and crafts expanded, and the barriers between imagery and writing broke down. The more I connected to the spirit world in my Druidic practice, the more I received inspiration through images and symbols. As Druidry encourages us to maintain journals of our experiences, I would often sketch the images that came to me, and later unpack them into poetry and prose.

In the spring of 2010, having been in OBOD training for five years, I was out in our local mountains on what I think of as spiritual hikes—in which I set off with the purpose of meditating in our national forest, journal and pen in my day pack. The earth had recently warmed, sending the meadows into a flurry of colorful activity—the delicate reds and purples bursting forth in the bare patches between the still-white vestiges of deep snow under the trees. I lay down on in the sun, surrounded by the scent of springtime grass and rich soil, eyes squinting from the dazzling blue of the sky. Sinking into my breath, relaxing my thoughts away from the tasks of life, I sunk into the earth, feeling a unity between her fiery core and my own. And then the images and the sensorial feelings came, one after another:

> *come back to me*
> *   precious child*
> *let your bare feet be*
> *   light*
> *in step upon warm earth*
> *and your tangled locks*
> *   windblown*
> *eyes bright*
> *   dance*
> *with abandon*

sing to me
  my beloved
and drink in my heady gaze
feel my ancient rhythm in
  your heartbeat
my breath stirring in
  your soul
roll on my meadow
  as a gangly colt
and snort your response
to the blossom-laden scent of spring
pausing only a moment
before spreading your wings
  for first flight

The spiritual knowing felt like a co-creative act that happened where I connected to the *something—someone—more* that is the earth, and in turn, her creatures. Druidry teaches us that the arts are both inspired and a craft— the outcome of where connectedness to *something more* meets dedication to honing skill. The process and artistic outcomes are unique to each Druid, but the way in which creativity and art play a central role in Druidic spirituality across practitioners is a distinctive feature of Druidry as a religion.

While inspiration can happen spontaneously, it is also cultivated through specific practices that hone one's capacity for stilling the chatter of one's thoughts, focusing on a particular intention, and opening to co-creative response. This is the case with divination, which is not so much telling the future as perceiving factors that play into possible futures. Many Druids learn one or more forms of divination, most commonly *ogham* (a historical Irish mnemonic device and alphabet of associated hash-marks on a centerline with entities in nature, most commonly trees, and their qualities), runes (a Germanic, and later Norse, alphabet that came to be associated with specific meanings), Tarot (a historical set of archetypal images associated with meanings), and oracles (e.g., the Druid Animal Oracle, which provides folkloric-based associations between animals and qualities or meanings). Practicing divination involves much more than learning the associations between the symbols or images and the meanings or qualities. More significantly, it is a way to access subconscious thoughts and cultivate new perspectives on a problem in order to make decisions from a more holistic and comprehensive understanding.

Druids tend to find one of the divination systems speaks to them most and hone their skills in that particular system. For those who become highly skilled at it (not me, I am afraid), watching them "read" the potential future for someone is a highly engaging and inspiring event. While many perform divination using cards pulled into a specific pre-determined pattern (which assists in crafting the answer to the querent's question), a small number of highly skilled diviners using runes or ogham will toss the entire set of symbols at once, reading not only the symbols but also the relationships between them. At one gathering, around the central campfire one night, a diviner sat on a large log, taking questions from others. He spread a leather hide on the ground in front of him, revealing a set of ogham staves— slender sticks about six inches long. He explained that he had spent years gathering each of the woods from various places in England, Ireland, Scotland, and Wales—sitting with each tree to connect to it, asking its permission to cut the wood required, and presenting offerings to its spirit. Then, as someone came forward with a question, he tossed the entire set of staves gently onto the hide, reading the connections between the symbols in an impressive display of integration—part life coach, part psychic, part storyteller.

For those who work intensively with specific spirits, new perspectives can be gained through cultivating the capacity to receive messages or insights from them on demand or spontaneously. Such insights can occur through brief interactions with the other-than-human, or they can happen frequently from a particular spirit with whom one has a close, enduring relationship. In a march for peace and nuclear disarmament during Holy Week of 2010, a spirit I often receive insights from and with whom I have a close relationship came with me on the walk. The spirit is other-than-human, quite old and elemental, and their perspective (as they are too primordial to have individuated) often comes as textures, sensory input, images, or symbols. Sometimes, I manage to receive a translation into words. Other times, the meaning remains a mystery.

We walked along the highway, an interfaith string of practitioners dedicated to peace: mostly older Catholic monks and nuns, some young atheists, a handful of Pagans, a middle-aged woman who walked in honor of her mother, a lifelong anti-war activist, whose ashes she carried. Footsore after several days of walking some ten miles per day on the roadside, bundled up against the desert wind, our feet trudged out a loving commitment to the earth and to the potential for humans to one day learn how to resolve differences without violence. We carried signs: against war, against nuclear weapons, against taking what had been sacred ground to the Western Shoshone and making it a wasteland, separating the living from the ancestors with government fence. In silence for hours, save the crunching of the gravel underfoot, the wind had exfoliated both my skin and my mind. "You work hard to suffer." The knowing entered me as a series of images my brain rapidly translated to English. The perspective of a spirit so old that disconnect and violence were unthinkable, but with a distant, observational quality to it, entered my mind. Humanity, such a young species, worked tirelessly and with great effort and creativity at generating ways to harm itself and the planet upon which it was utterly dependent. While I had been raised on non-violent resistance, the absurdity of my species' efforts had never occurred to me. That we took the pain that illness, injury, and death brought us and worked so industriously to increase it was so strange from this otherworldly perspective that my humanness made it laughable, a grim humor in the face of great grief.

Study

In my experience, spiritual knowing often provides perspective and motivation, but intellectual knowing provides detailed information necessary to take action. While the depth of absurdity of human suffering was a spiritual revelation, change-making takes many details: psychological and social theory on why humans struggle with violence; historical trajectories of when, where, and why humans become violent at various scales—from the individual to the society; and practices and conditions that have reduced violent conflict. Similarly, a tree occasionally will tell me it is thirsty and wants water, but it helps if I learn the needs of plants in my garden and attend to them before it comes to that point. In Druidry, *knowledge* is more than spiritual—it is scientific and practical information combined with skill. There are no boundaries around Druidry that differentiate the religious from the not-religious. Instead, Druids cultivate a relational worldview and an openness to inspired knowledge, while simultaneously practicing a variety of skills and learning information about a wide range of topics—history, archaeology, genealogy, mythology, folklore and magic, botany, biology, and ecology, to list a few.

It is for this reason, as well as the lack of an authoritative sacred text, that Druids often refer to themselves as the "people of the library." Most Druids I have met have rather extensive book collections or they read extensively from a local library. Their interests include books on Druidry, but also a wide range of other topics—and all of it is considered related to Druidry. Druidry is a large container for one's life, not a separate category of specific interests. Because Druidic training and community encourages the study of many topics and skills, it tends to attract people who also have wide-ranging interests and for whom engagement in study and practice are desired activities. For me, as someone who is an "idea factory" and for whom new interests pop up incessantly, the encouragement to engage in studying and practicing skills in many areas has led to very slow progress through the OBOD training, the primary Druidic training I have engaged in. My spiritual practice has been largely consistent, but my studies and spiritual training have meandered. If we think of spiritual training as a hike up a mountain, I am often wandering off-trail to explore some enticing waterfall, meadow, or stand of trees—often staying a while before making my way back again.

At the moment, I am in my eleventh year of the Ovate course (the second of three grades). I have restarted it three times and wandered off into many side pursuits sparked by the training. The coursework prompted me to do some work with ancestors, so I meandered off into a few months of genealogy at one point and pursued several years of training in a different spiritual tradition to fill in some gaps I felt I needed to work on in my capacity to understand how to work with troublesome ancestors. I spent six months at a bioregenerative farm learning how to co-create beautiful, productive soil with urban places. Each of these adventures off the Druidic path was fruitful and enhanced my Druidry, often connected with the Druidic training across time in ways I did not anticipate, but which were clearly beneficial forms of synchronicity.

It is easy to meander into little side-tracks in part because of the wealth of sources for Druids to draw from in their spiritual practice, and the ways in which spiritual practice bleeds into everyday life. Aside from training courses and books, there are podcasts, workshops and gatherings, and online groups and forums. Largely lacking authoritative religious leaders, Druidry supports and encourages an organic, bottom-up type of learning. The reduction of publication requirements and the increase of platforms on which to share one's practices and thoughts—blogs, self-published books, online discussion forums, online workshops—leads to a high degree of sharing between practitioners. Many of these sources blend the spiritual, scientific, and pragmatic. A book on herbalism for Druids may include both folkloric information on magical, spiritual, and practical uses of herbs as well as the Latin name for the plant and some scientific information, such as its growth cycle and range.

Not only are sources often holistic, drawing from both spiritual and intellectual knowing, at least one of the Druid orders—the AODA—also trains Druids into a practice of integrating the two approaches to knowledge. Discursive meditation encourages one to spend time thinking deeply about what has been read, and in the AODA training, required reading includes both spiritual and ecological reading. Discursive meditation unites spiritual experience and practice with processing its meaning in light of what others have contributed on the topic. In this way, one cultivates a union of reason and intuition, relying on both to inform choices about action and construction of meaning. The blending of spiritual and intellectual knowing is evident in Druid workshops and gatherings as well. Most frequently, such gatherings are contributed to collectively by Druids in their community, rather than relying on a religious leader. Even in gatherings that include a prominent author, this person usually hosts one or two brief sessions over the course of three or four days, leaving the rest of the programming to be generated by other Druids attending the gathering. Druids often draw from multiple forms of knowledge, which they blend together in single workshop sessions, which may have a practical focus as much as a spiritual or magical one.

At one gathering, Philip Carr-Gomm, the former Chosen Chief of OBOD (the organizational head) and a transpersonal psychologist, led a session on the challenges people had in connecting to the earth and one another in the crush of the modern world. More facilitator than teacher, he encouraged Druids to share their feelings, struggles, and practices that helped them create a positive and productive life. At another gathering, a small group of Druids retreated to an organic farm for a series of workshops, one of which focused on identifying practical skills necessary and existing in the group for handling an anticipated increasing number of natural disasters in the face of climate change. At a Druid camp in England, a professional botanist led a plant walk, informing people of both common and scientific names, distinguishing characteristics, and practical uses of the plants—along with folkloric knowledge of the plant's spiritual and magical qualities and uses. Meaning and practical action, intuitive guidance and detailed knowledge— these come together to form a virtue many Druids value and to which they aspire: wisdom. It is from wisdom that we are able to secure justice and win peace, and ultimately—it is from wisdom that we are able to love in a whole and healthy way. Justice is impossible if we do not understand what it is and how to achieve it, and justice is at the root of love.

CHAPTER 10

The Foundation for Peace

Justice

FIGURE 8 *Peace-making.*

It was December 2014, and I was raw from counseling students through their attempts to process their feelings, past experiences, and fledgling anthropological analyses of the protests and riots in Ferguson while teaching a class on diversity in the United States. I was the ritualist for Alban Arthan, the winter solstice—a time to enter the darkness of the womb and then celebrate the returning light, ending our mourning we carried with us from Samhain. In the central working of the rite, we sat in a grove member's mountain cabin, circled in front of the fireplace, shrouded in darkness. I guided the group to connect first to their breath, and deepening the breath, to feel as though they sank roots through their feet into the earth. I began to drum, relaxing into its rhythm, letting it carry me from thinking about ritual into becoming a vessel for it. I began to chant, lifting a prayer to the gods for our hurting world:

> *In a world gone dark, our lands are dying*
> *We call Cernunnos: help us rewild them!*
> *In a world gone dark, we Druids lift our voice to you*
> *In a world gone dark, where people suffer*
> *We call Brighid to us: help us to heal them!*
> *In a world gone dark, we Druids lift our voice to you*
> *In a world gone dark, so full of conflict*
> *We call great skilled Lugh: strengthen our service!*
> *In a world gone dark, we Druids lift our voice to you*
> *In a world gone dark, plagued with injustice*
> *We call the Morrigan: please give us courage!*
> *In a world gone dark, we Druids lift our voice to you*
> *In a world gone dark, we call the Mabon*
> *In a world gone dark, we seek renewal*
> *We call the Light Within*
> *We Druids lift our voice in love, in love*

I stopped chanting and silenced the drum. I was dimly aware others were with me, but I had slid into embracing the deep hurt I had felt for months—for my students, for my fellow citizens, for humanity. I drew in a deep breath, and let the words for the meditation pour out of me, barely aware of what it was I was saying—allowing awen to guide me.

I guided us all to reach into the seed of light in our core, to let that ripple through us, transmuting the reflections of suffering—our own and others'—into healing light. "What is our vision of hope for the world? How can we find the courage to give birth to a new world?" I relit the central flame, and the room came alive again with candlelight as we passed the flame person to person. We settled into cascading awens, filling the room with the sound, singing together and reaching into a wellspring of healing in our bodies, in our voices, in the earth.

> Hope is a choice—it is a magic we bring forth from our own powerful central flame, deep within us . . . a flame fed by the stars and the hot iron core of the earth. We are the enduring hope of thousands of years of wisdom. We are the peace that is brokered on the battlefield. We are the justice, the poetic voice of the ancestors, the bringers of light and love to the world.

The small flickering flames bounced light around the dark room, and I felt once again that we, too, could be small lights in the world.

Justice, broadly defined, is a central pillar of Druidry-in-action. One Welsh Druid explained to me that in the Druid's Prayer, in which *justice* is the central pivotal point between knowledge and love, the word might equally be understood as *rightness*. In a relational spirituality, rightness (or justice) describes a way of ethically and properly relating to other beings: human and other-than-human. Environmental sustainability is justice. Compassion for vulnerable humans is justice. When we are in right relationship with other beings, peace fills our lives and the lives of those around us. There is, then, an interweaving of justice, peace, and love. Each is not fully realized without the other.

Rightness in relationships can be achieved at various scales, from global to individual. Druids seek to behave virtuously in their individual relationships, with particular concern for attempting to select actions based on wisdom and careful consideration, and for being honest and careful with one's words. Words have power, particularly in a spirituality in which the mythology describes bards whose poetry could broker peace between warring factions and sustain history over time. On an individual level, justice involves knowing the other—their qualities and characteristics, needs and desires—and then acting from this knowledge with integrity. At the global scale, rightness is actualized through the ways in which our actions support right relationship with other beings—that is, how our economic and political choices affect humans, animals, plants, and places.

Working for justice is a co-creative act with other beings, both human and other-than-human. Actions to put things right are magical, spiritual, and practical. Druidic ritual provides a container, a structure, through which we can symbolically enact rightness—which can include setting boundaries or binding harmful events or actions, healing wounds in the earth or in humanity, and transmuting our wounds or negative qualities into positive or more balanced states of being. In the first OBOD Druid gathering on the West Coast in 2009, over one hundred Druids gathered in a large grassy field at a Buddhist retreat center in Central California. We each brought creative symbolic pieces to a collective ritual working for healing the earth.

In the face of climate change, Druids mourned the loss of habitats dear to them and committed themselves to the work of sustainability. In reflecting on the changes wrought over the course of my life to my dear mountain woods, and over a longer history, the ways in which California was shaped by concrete water canals and suppression of indigenous ecological management, the loss of plants and places and peoples—I wept. I grieved for and with the earth. But then, I also dared to hope. Here I was, surrounded by others who held the earth as sacred, who held relationship as more important than profit. I was surrounded by others who felt a deep empathy for all the earth's creatures, and who vowed to make what changes they could.

Ritual for justice, whether for humans or other-than-humans, is a way of symbolically enacting commitments. Ritual generates motivation and when done collectively, reminds us that we are supported and not alone in our values. Many Druids engage in rituals that are not only spiritual—connecting us with one another, with the earth, and with the spirit world—but are also magical. Magic is distinct from spirituality in that it imposes our will on the manifest world: on our own consciousness and, from a magical worldview, on the larger energetic patterns and probabilities that shape our lived reality. Magical ritual both symbolically enacts our intention, which aids in shifting our consciousness, and also—for those who believe magic is real—games the probabilities in the universe in our favor. As such, it differs from spiritual actions by imposing our own will, which like practical action means that we must have clarity in what we want to achieve, focus on our intention, and take responsibility for it.

After the recession in 2008, when my first visiting professorship ended in 2009, I was not sure where I was headed in my career. While the pause in my employment was frightening, it gave me the opportunity to focus on deep spiritual and magical work for an extended period at a level I never had time for before. What arose from this process was a focus on integrating all the disparate parts of myself and coming to recognize and then actualize my sense of purpose in the world. This was work that was intimately tied to my core values—particularly, to work for justice for human and other-than-human beings. As I tackled this work of knowing and integrating myself with the assistance of a spiritual coach, I worked through a series of magical and spiritual rituals—to come into connection with the spirits who could guide and assist me, to understand my soul's work in the world, and to face the parts of myself who were wounded, difficult, and an obstacle to self-actualization. Magic was a pathway to "putting right" what had gone awry, beginning with myself, and then rippling outward into the ways I would move in the world.

Of course, magic or religious ritual alone is only half the work in a relational, embodied spirituality. The other half of working toward justice is practical actions in the world: voting, writing elected representatives, learning as much as one can, selecting just and sustainable purchases and investments, volunteering, and so on. These acts are no less spiritual than giving offerings to the land spirits or doing magic for healing the earth. The symbolic and the direct are two halves of a whole process to transform ourselves and our world—to re-enchant and re-member—to weave together what has come undone.

Harvest

It was Alban Hefin, the Summer Solstice, in 2017. Usually, I would spend part of the day in ritual, but I was a bit tired after day upon day of scorching hot weather and a week of serious overwork. I had a 6:00 a.m. wake-up for hydrating adequately before I arrived at the bioregenerative farm at which I was volunteering and from which I was learning how to forge a relationship of mutuality with the urban land. Usually, when I overwork myself, as I had that week—and it comes at the cost of my meditative and ceremonial time—I feel much more of a sense of inner resistance and discord. But on the night of Alban Hefin that year, I kept thinking—there was no need for ceremony that day. Connection to my wild soul and to the Divine Mystery was in the garden.

It was all right that I was tired, and instead of doing my prayers and meditations, I went to sleep. Because in the morning, as I wound trellis string around tomato shoots, I was giving offerings to the land spirits and attending to that great Mystery of which I was a part. As I watered newly planted pepper plants, I was showering the green veil of the Divine with nourishment. As I sweat in the sun as the temperature soared, I felt the heat and fire of the stars, and my body responded with its own microcosm of a whole world of cells working together in unison. And I felt the connection to my ancestors, who farmed for thousands of years until my grandparents decided to leave the soil, and before my mother, my aunt, my sister, and I started to reclaim it as our inheritance. There was no better way to celebrate the solstice than this.

As much as the garden reminded me of my connection to life, it also reminded me of the consequences of living—death. Two gophers were trapped and died shortly after the solstice. They were terrifically destructive little beasts. One of them took out fifteen tomato plants before he succumbed to his love of peanut butter, smeared on a trap. I had uncomfortable, mixed feelings about this. Food is the result of a cycle of life and death. Plants can manufacture their food from sunlight, soil, and water. We are not so fortunate. Our lives are the result of the death of many, many beings. Even vegans' lives depend on the death of not only plants but also of pests. Without control of any kind, gophers, beetles, and caterpillars would consume our crops. Even an organic farm with a respect for life must consider how it will control its pests so it can yield food for humans. Still, it was uncomfortable to witness.

It was uncomfortable for reasons of both empathy and cognitive dissonance. As a person who is highly empathetic (and also animist, believing all living things—and even some non-living ones—have souls), I feel for the beings I eat. I can imagine their feelings, their suffering, their desire to keep living. All beings have an innate desire to keep living, and my desire to do so takes that capacity from others. With every gopher trap, inside I said a little prayer to the gopher. I said I was sorry. I told the gopher that it could live if it would leave the farm. And I hoped that if it did not leave, and were trapped, that its death would be swift and without suffering. A gopher's death, or a chicken's death, or a carrot's death—should make us pause and reflect. We should feel a sense of the sacredness of these beings' sacrifice for our own lives to continue. Perhaps if we felt this, we would be more insistent on farming in ways that are humane as well as sustainable. We can't live without death. But we can treat death with the respect, sanctity, and compassion it deserves.

Rightness, or justice, is not always what is comfortable. It is right that pests die only as much as is necessary for me to live. In an ecocentric, relational ethics, this cycle is not only right but also necessary to sustain a planet teeming with diverse life. Druidic ethics have core values that are grounded in the concept of right relationship and observations of how the natural world functions to sustain itself. Death is necessary; cruelty is not. Consumption is necessary; greed and waste are not. At the heart of ecocentric ethics is a world that operates on natural consequences: the Law of the Harvest is that what you sow, you will reap. This fundamental principle speaks to a process, not a judgment. Rather than specific codes for behavior, core values are enacted in diverse ways without any universal deity judging one's actions. However, the universe keeps the score automatically. In a relational universe, harm to others is also harm to self. As humans have become unsustainable, we are building our own pathway, brick by brick, toward our own species' potential extinction. On an individual scale, if we harm others in our relationships, we often find ourselves alone. The balance is always in patiently learning as much as we can—about ourselves and about others—and then discerning what actions lead to rightness.

There is no ultimate judgment, but the process of the harvest is unavoidable. If we want to have a good life, and a good death—a journey that is easy and transformative, that returns us to the fullness of ourselves in the company of our loved ones—we need to do the work of sowing virtue. We need to heal ourselves while we live, to become our full potential while we live—because no one will do it for us when we are dead. We will come to live again without learning the lessons we could have, and so we will repeat these again, often with the same suffering we had experienced before. If we want to reap a full and bountiful life's harvest, it is best if we work diligently on sowing what we wish to grow in ourselves and the world around us. It is then that we can find peace.

In our busy and consumer-oriented society in the United States, it is relatively rare we can witness the transformation of a person, even when they are given warning of their impending death and time to do the work. Too often, people dwell in anger or fear at their mortality and never dig deeper into the fullness of what they could be, of the ways in which death recycles us into a greater, more liberated, and perhaps truer version of ourselves. I have always been grateful that my nana, my maternal grandmother, showed me what an easy, transformative, and ultimately good death could be. Facing the imminent harvest of her body by nature's inexorable march forward of time, she accepted its transformative process easily and gently.

When my aunt called me and explained she had had an episode and the paramedics had come, I knew intuitively that her chronic health issues were ending. I drove to my aunt's house, where she had spent several years playing Farkle, a dice game, at the kitchen and basking in the warmth of the Southern California sun on the garden patio. She sat propped up in the bed, her face wan. I climbed onto the bed with her and held her hand. She smiled just a small, peaceful smile, like the Mona Lisa I had once stood in front of in awe at the Louvre with my aunt, who now bustled about in the other room. Her eyes closed, resting. Her body was with me and her soft, wrinkled hand was warm. But I could see, in my mind's eye, her spirit floating high above her—like a spirit of air, a kite, a bird—connected only by a thin cerulean blue thread, the color that always symbolized life in the messages I received. I knew she did not have long left. Her spirit tugged at the thread, yearning to break free, to return to birdsong and gentle breezes.

When I left the room, I called my mother and sister immediately and told them to come right away—to begin the journey from Oregon to her deathbed. Her children flew in from all over the Western United States to meet her last wish: to be surrounded by her family one last time before her journey to the ancestors. She had met years of increasing debilitation with a genteel acceptance. I am sure it was not always as easy as it appeared, but as she met each challenge with dignity, she cultivated a transformation that would enable her to let go of her existing self to become something more. Her last day was gloriously full, with three generations taking turns sitting and chatting with her as she watched us, radiant, from her newly arrived hospital bed in the living room. In the early morning, my aunt reported, she left her body, smiling and reaching toward some unseen beloved.

My nana had not lived a bad life, but she had had her share of losses, grief, fear, and suffering. Even so, on her last day she reaped what she had sown over many years of gradual, patient acceptance. Her harvest was a loving family and immeasurable peace. Each day, I bless her with my other family members, both still embodied and in the Summerlands. I ask that her journey may be blessed, but she had already done the work to ensure that it was. Her soul would continue to learn, to grow, to love and to be loved, but free from its thin tether to its former body, perhaps now she could now find greater happiness, peace, and freedom. I like to think of her as one of the songbirds she so enjoyed listening to, the late afternoon sun on her face, its warmth on her back.

For some who are very attached to their current personality, station in life, or body, it seems difficult to imagine transformation as desirable. But as we sow, so we reap. If we do not sow acceptance of the most constant characteristic of the Divine Mystery, so evident throughout the universe— change—we become bound to our life in ways that thwart our capacity to grow, to develop, and ultimately—to peacefully return to the great recycling program of which we are inevitably a part. Druidry offers a humanness that is temporary, permeable, and dynamic. Only partially bound by our bodies and brains, mythic reality is filled with shape-shifting and those who travel back and forth between the worlds. The ancestors are human, but so too we might have ancestors who were animals, plants, or even Otherworldly beings. We carry in us the lessons from these lives, as well as the traumas we are still working to heal. When we do the spiritual work necessary to deepen our wisdom—both arising from our own bodily memory and from the wisdom ancestor spirits offer—we cultivate not only a better life but also a better humanity. We help human consciousness develop a relationship with its potential, recognizing its current limitations do not represent the total of its past or future.

Peace

When we sow the seeds of justice, we reap the bounty of peace. This is true on individual and collective levels. When we are honest, when we seek to do our best, when we are open to learning and growing, we develop a deep and abiding peace in ourselves, a contentment with our lives. When we have this peace, we live without regrets, because we know we have done our best in all that we have done. While this is challenging work on an individual level, it often feels nearly impossible on a collective one. The United States was built on hundreds of years of injustice: injustice that brought diverse immigrants to this land, and injustice that shaped a nation from land already belonging to someone else. Not surprisingly, there is often a discord between Druids' ideals for society and government, for relationships to the land and to one another, and the reality that we live in. How we handle that discord varies, but across Druids is a central valuing of peace and attendant work for justice. Peace-making is relatively countercultural and revolutionary in the United States and feels like it has only become more so over the last decade, as the nation becomes more and more polarized (or at least appears to be in the media and on social media). OBOD Druids embed peace-making into the opening of every ritual, and this serves as a symbolic reminder of the central importance of peace, as well as a magical working for forging peace in the world.

A group of us led an inter-Pagan spring equinox ritual on the patio of a local Unitarian Universalist church—what for us is Alban Eilir and for many Pagans is Ostara: a time for symbolically planting what we wished to harvest later in the year. Opening the ritual was an invitation to shared peace: first, a cleansing of the trials and worries of the outside mundane world—bells were rung around each participant before they joined the circle. Then, after all had made their way into the circle, we were guided by one Druid through collective deep breathing, first with the earth below us, then with the sea around us, and finally with the sky above us. We fell into a relaxed rhythm, orienting ourselves individually and collectively to the quiet solace of the universe's great forces. My feet put down roots into the solidity of the earth. I felt the crashing waves of the sea wash away the last remnants of my worries. I tilted my face up to the sun like a flower opening to its life force, letting its warmth melt away the strife of the outside world.

Only then was I ready to fulfill my ritual role of giving peace to the world, because I could not give what I did not have. The order of ritual is meant to assist in the transformation of our individual consciousness so that we can shift into a collective working from that solid foundation. Having connected myself to a wildness that bound me to the earth and brought peace to the messy, wrinkled shroud of my humanity, I moved to face the North. Oak staff in hand, I raised my right hand toward the North as the others in the circle turned to face the mountains in the distance. "May there be peace in the North!" I called. Bringing a deep peace up from the earth into my solar plexus, I pushed the wave of peace northward, imagining peace settling across the intermountain states and Pacific Northwest, sweeping across British Columbia and into the snowy tundra of northern Canada and Alaska, until it seeped into the sea.

I walked across the circle to stand in the South, raising my hand to greet it. "May there be peace in the South!" As I called it out, I once again drew up the peace from the earth and sent it cascading out in front of me toward the South—toward Mexico, Central America, across the Amazon, and down throughout the wild mountains of South America until it too reached a land of sea and ice. When I felt that it had crashed over Antarctica, I walked to stand in the West. Greeting the West, I called "May there be peace in the West!" I felt peace leave the shores of Southern California, ripple outward toward China, Korea, and Japan, across the South Pacific and India in an ever-widening embrace. I turned to walk across the circle, and standing in the East, I finally called to the last corner of the world: "May there be peace in the East!" I sent peace across my struggling nation and onward to Europe, to the Middle East, to Africa. I imagined every willing heart receiving its small spark, a moment of calm and clarity. Turning to face the other Druids, we once again circled, as I firmly stated, "May there be peace throughout the whole world." Only in this peace: inner and outer, individual and shared, were we able to begin the central working for our individual plantings.

The Druid's Peace Prayer orients many Druids to what we could say are three ripples of peace, beginning with the individual and moving to the wider world:

Deep within the still center of my being, may I find peace.
Silently within the quiet of the Grove, may I share peace.
Gently within the greater circle of humankind, may I radiate peace.

(Order of Bards, Ovates, and Druids)

Peace begins in stillness and centering in each person. We cultivate peace first in ourselves, or we have no way to share it with others. Cultivating a deep abiding peace is the work of a lifetime, particularly as one faces the challenges and stresses of life. Because of this, Druidic spirituality includes forms of meditation, which allow the practitioner to practice calming and centering techniques. Many Druids practice sitting and movement meditation, becoming mindful of the breath and the body. Druidic training includes visualization meditation as well, developing one's imagination and capacity to create inner spaces that feel soothing and safe when the outer world is overwhelming or worrisome.

For me, the inner grove meditation—providing me an inner place filled with all that I love about the deep woods—did much to help me generate an ability to face pain and suffering with peace. It is imperfect because I am a work in progress. At the same time, the more than fifteen years I have visited this inner place has transformed my life. For me, the two pillars of the inner grove meditation and breath work have increasingly developed a well of healing, soothing inner spaciousness, and silence from which I draw as I face an uncertain and seemingly intractably polarized outer world. Each night, I light the candles on my altars. I pull a soft alpaca cloak around me and turn off the bright lights and noise of the outer world. I sit in front of the shrine to the gods, the candlelight flickering against the statues of Cernunnos and Elen of the Ways, the soft glow reaching across the smooth curves of the horse vertebrae in Epona's place. I become mindful of my breathing, my chest rising and falling. I lengthen its rhythm—four seconds, seven seconds, ten seconds. In, pause. Out, pause. My thoughts flow me as if I am sitting in a stream, their cold tendrils swirling around my mind until they pass. In, pause. Out, pause. My body grows roots into the earth beneath me, and its solid comfort supports my spine, a bridge between earth and sky. Above me, the night sky fills with stars, their ancient light blessing me with a connection to all that is—now and in the past. In, pause. Out, pause. The everyday thoughts recede, and I am in the familiar deep forest, the icy stream winding its way through the trees, the ground springy with pine needles. The white horse comes to me, and I am carried away from the chaos and cacophony of the outer world, of mundane life. I am carried home, to peace.

The generation and maintenance of peace is supported and shared in Druid groves through ritual. A couple dozen Southern and Northern California Druids gathered in a local campground at about a mile high in elevation, under the pines. Around the central campfire, we began our Lughnasadh rite. Influenced by the Gorsedd Cymru, one Druid from Wales stepped toward the fire. Pulling a sheathed sword out and holding it aloft, he partially unsheathed the blade and called: "Is there peace?" The rest of us shouted back "Peace!" He clanged the sword back fully in its sheath. Three times he called to us; three times we answered. We declared peace among ourselves before we gave peace to the rest of the world by giving peace to the quarters.

Druid groups, of course, are not without their conflicts. Conflict exists just as it does for every human group. The centrality of peace-making in Druidry does not entirely prevent Druid groups from fission or falling apart, but it generates a commitment to mutual care and self-work when relationships become difficult. Putting peace at the center is different from the pervasive centrality of forgiveness in the Christo-centric mainstream culture. Peace is not merely about the relationship between two people. It is also about discerning the needs of the entire group and realizing when to step back, when to be solitary, when to fission a new group from an old one, and when to return to a person or group after peace has been regained.

The relationships with fellow grove members have been close, much more so than I ever experienced when I belonged to churches. This is partially because Druid groups are small, most often only a handful to a couple dozen members. Meeting at people's homes generates a familiarity and friendship that is different from those developed in larger religious communities that meet at public locations. The cooperation and reciprocity necessary to sustain a Druid group over time, in which a significant number of people must volunteer to host, cook, set up, clean up, and act as ritualists, is significant as there are no paid clergy to do it for anyone. This tends to generate closeness, but it can also cause the development of conflict and hurt, as people may feel they contribute more than others or as members of the grove have different opinions about ritual or other matters. There is no authoritative figure and no hierarchy, which means that differences and hurts must be resolved through patience and discernment.

In my own experience, both in my own responses to conflict and in observing the responses of others, peace-making as a central value often resulted in retreat for renewal and splitting of groups as the primary actions taken when conflict could not be easily and quickly resolved. The concern for a harmonious flow has meant I have occasionally advocated for splitting away in cases of repeated hurt and retreated to being temporarily solitary in cases of my own depletion or hurt so that I could recharge before re-engagement. Rather than facing such times as failure, viewing them through the lens of inevitability (it is part of human social life to have conflict and occasional hurt) and peace-making (maintaining peace while engaged in recharging and discernment) allowed me to enter periods of solitary practice while also remaining part of a wider community—through my actions, even while alone, I was supporting grove community.

The commitment to peace is at the heart of the way Druids conceptualize their spiritual work in the wider world, a work that begins in the individual and is affirmed by Druids collectively. In nearly all the OBOD Druid rituals I have attended, Druids affirm their commitment to peace—and to love—by joining together in the Druid's Vow:

We swear by peace and love to stand
Heart to heart and hand in hand
Mark, o spirits, and hear us now
Confirming this, our sacred vow

(Order of Bards, Ovates, and Druids Book of Ritual)

The simple action, usually performed in a circle while holding hands, is an outward expression of inward disciplined commitment. It is easy to say we will stand with an open heart and outstretched hand to others. It is hard to maintain it over years of mutual spiritual work. It is even easier to say we will stand in peace and love, but even harder to live peace and love in the world.

Druids come together in ritual to work the magic of mindfulness and presence, and to bring to their own lives and the world healing and a bountiful harvest of loving community. Ritual sustains us in the everyday work of living out our spiritual work—of loving widely and deeply, of developing keen awareness of our impact, of aligning our impact with peace-making bit by bit. Mindfulness and a solid, centered sense of inner peace offers a presence that is rare and powerful. Everyone knows when they are in the presence of someone who is fully at ease in the moment, fully attentive and aware. To me, this is how the inward peace I cultivate as a Druid ripples outward into the world. Whether I am riding a horse or counseling a student, I am drawing from my Druidic practice to offer a quiet, fully present beingness. If I can capture a little bit of the love and peace I feel in nature's responsive presence to me and share that with others, I am one step closer to actualizing a love for all existences.

CHAPTER 11

The Foundation for Divine Connection

Loving Others

FIGURE 9 *Loving.*

I sat in meditation in front of my shrine cabinet. Brigid's candle was lit and the goddess of well and flame, forge and pen, was invited to draw near to me. I felt stuck in my life. My creativity had waned after years of overwork and pandemic anxiety, and my usual boundless energy had evaporated. I did not know what was wrong, but I knew I did not feel quite right. I opened to

Brigid: What made me so resistant? What was at the core of this struggle? Her wisdom came quickly and gently: "You are afraid to care too much. You are afraid to love too much." And with these words, grief swept over me as I recognized the depth of my exhaustion in the face of the ongoing pandemic, an ever-present threat to vulnerable loved ones and disruption in my otherwise happy life. I had lost so much, and my apathy protected me from more loss. But in this protection was also a seawall holding back an ocean of love.

To love is to suffer; to love is to grieve—nothing is permanent, but love follows its object long after the object has transformed and moved on. Life is a temporary performance, a fleeting series of moments linked together in connection and love. Each precious and fragile connection I had was thrown into sharp relief during a pandemic that threatened so many I loved. The pandemic was only one window of time in my life that this had occurred: sometimes with other humans, sometimes with my pets, sometimes with places and the earth as a whole. Connection is a source of wholeness but giving ourselves over to love makes us very vulnerable, because life's ever-transformative process necessarily involves loss. Even when we do our best to care for the lives around us, life is a recycling program, and inevitably we will no longer be connected to the forms we once knew so well.

Last year, my oldest (and first) horse turned thirty years old—the horse equivalent of a human in their mid-to-late eighties. The last two years with him has been a gradual erosion of his vitality as that recycling program comes nearer to claiming his body. Each week I assess his quality of life: Does he still seem happy? Can he manage his basic functions as a horse? Is he in imminent risk? I have attuned myself to this relationship for half my life and my love is both emotion and action. I know that I cannot have him with me in his current form forever. Yet I also know that in loving him so deeply, for so many years, I will also be transformed when his spirit breaks free from his body. Neither of us will ever be the same again. Such is the vulnerability of entangling ourselves in relationship.

I curry his slightly too-long freckled hair, an effect of a pituitary tumor common in elderly horses that causes them to grow a fluffy coat. When he was younger, bright white-grey before the auburn speckles began to emerge, he did not enjoy people fussing over him. He was always kind, but proud and a little aloof. Age has brought with it a revelry in the little joys of his life: being brushed, little walks to visit the farm animals on the ranch, and almost always extra molasses cookies delicately inhaled off my palm. He leans into me when I pull his face close to mine, kissing his velvet-soft nose. As much as he is increasingly limited, he also seems content. I will give him as much of this quiet contentment as I can, and when he cannot enjoy it any longer, I will help him break free to gallop to the Summerlands. This is love: the feeling of wanting to hang on to another forever, but the willingness to do what another needs and what is right.

To love as a Druid is to open oneself to an exchange: to allow oneself to be fully known and to commit to knowing another. Whether an individual, a species, a place, or the earth itself—love begins with seeking an understanding of the other and a right balance of our own needs with the other's needs. It is simple and yet challenging, as it requires commitment to the transformative process of connection. It is this commitment to each being—each existence—that is at the foundation of loving the divine. I am learning how to love divinity through all the intricacies of loving my horses, the mulberry tree in the backyard, the mountains that dominate the horizon in front of my home, my spouse, my students. Each of these relationships asks me to be vulnerable, to be open to learning and changing, to enact reciprocity. Each relationship is an embodiment of an aspect of the divine process relating to itself. If we open to it fully, our lives become enriched with a multitude of perspectives and experiences. The process of connection is one not only of positive feelings but also of sharing in the difficulties of others' lives—and of unfathomably complex process of becoming and being that is the divine whole. The relational, connected goal state is not to make us more comfortable but rather to help us develop into people who are more wise and more able to act in harmony with other beings.

This way of loving alters every relationship one has, demanding that we reflect on both our inward thoughts and feelings and our outward actions related to those with whom we are in relationship. Rather than loving an ideal of who we want them to be, we are asked to open to knowing them as they are—and then to find right relationship from this foundation of deep listening. This does not mean that we have no desires or needs of our own, but in an ecocentric orientation to life, we are equals with other beings, worthy of the same consideration—not more or less. I am committed to knowing and loving myself as much as I am committed to knowing and loving others. It is the same process of listening and cultivating awareness, empathizing, introspectively reflecting, discerning right relationship, and committing to appropriate action regardless of whether I am loving myself, another human, an incarnate other-than-human, or a disincarnate other-than-human.

Such love is revolutionary because it offers us a pathway toward healthy connections with others—relationships that avoid common pitfalls of being myopically focused on idealistic expectations, selfishly inconsiderate, or dangerously self-sacrificial. When we commit to a process of loving based on gathering information and thoughtfully considering right action, we will still fail at perfect relationships, but we advance incrementally toward healthy and happy ones. Over time, working on loving others and myself in this way has transformed my relationships—not only in a general sense but in my individual relationships as well. When the orientation was on divine love first, with the assumption that it would somehow infiltrate into my everyday lived experience, I too often either held onto hope for those around me to be an ideal version of themselves or I sacrificed myself beyond sustainability until I seethed with resentment. Over time, as I entered my second long-term relationship (with my now-wife), I cultivated an awareness of these extremes and used the Druid's Prayer as a middle way—a point of balance.

Instead of loving what I wished her to be, I worked on understanding who she was, then asked myself what loving this beautifully imperfect being should be. Likewise, rather than trying to give what I could not freely offer, I practiced reflecting on my emotions and considering what balancing loving her with loving myself meant for my choices in action. We are human, so our relationship has ebbs and flows, easy and more difficult times. But as I have strengthened my capacity to love in a way that puts relationships with others first and that rests relationships on commitments to learning, forging understanding, and thoughtfully considering and committing to right action, my marriage with her became more thoughtful, more spiritually deep, and more real.

Still, even in the best and dearest of our relationships, grief is the companion of love—and failure is the companion of effort. Relationships are challenging and ever-changing, and to expect otherwise is to embrace a delusion about who we collectively are as a species. This is perhaps even more so when we consider the complex web of all the hundreds—even thousands—of relationships we are in. The needs of various beings do not necessarily merge well together; deciphering what is right and just in our attempts to accommodate these diverse needs and limitations is not easy and sometimes feels impossible. The more acutely we attune ourselves to enacting the relational complexity of love, the more we find we must grapple with both grief and failure.

Failure

To love as a Druid is to witness the grief of the earth as much as its joy. In the modern developed world, life has arguably never been easier as a human being. We have an abundance of liberties and rights, including an entire world of ideas at our literal fingertips. We have appliances to make our lives easier, effective transportation and telecommunication technology to keep us connected more readily than ever before, and spacious and comfortable climate-controlled homes. Modern medicine helps us avoid the deaths so many of our ancestors had. Yet all of this has come at a steep cost to the earth. Our comfort is tied to an unsustainable economy, and other species pay the price for our convenience.

Druidry cultivates understanding and knowledge as a foundational spiritual act. Much of this work is centered on ecology, so we come to understand the necessity of the entirety of intact ecosystems and the processes behind their functioning. We come to know the needs, locations, and behaviors of individual species and the ways they are impacted by human use and management of the earth. In the Anthropocene, the rightness we are taught to know and to love—an order of things that sustains all species, including us—has been upended in an unquenched growth necessary for our current global economy to maintain itself.

The grief we feel is both personal and ecological, for individuals and for the integrity of entire processes. In one OBOD lesson, I was asked to write about my memories of individual trees from my childhood. What came tumbling out of me was a eulogy, and I wept with grief for the individual trees I had loved and lost and for the incessant march forward of suburban development through the stands of trees I had grown up with:

You ask about my childhood tree-friends
The ones that hold my memory
The ones whose memories I hold
And all I can do is gently cry
Few of them have survived humans
Over the course of my relatively short life

Great, enormous trunk with a spiral staircase
Holding a little seat made of branches
That wove themselves together just for me
So I could haul homework, books, snacks
Up into my friend's embrace
Every afternoon, in rain and wind and sun

I cried when I had to leave him
He'd sheltered me for seven years
But in the divorce, he was sold along with the house
Years later when I tried to visit
I saw that the new owners
Had slaughtered every tree on the land

I didn't become so attached
To individual trees after that
But it didn't protect me from grief
As humans dismissed their right to life
As suburban progress slowly devoured
The rural expanse of my childhood

The wild fields and chicken ranches
Were bulldozed into flat, tidy lots
Sometime in my adolescence
And almost no one seemed to miss
The sounds of roosters
After all, the concrete was a sign of progress

Where there were fragrant orange blossoms
And smudge pots in winter
There are hundreds of cookie-cutter houses
And a golf course
I seemed to be the only one who sobbed
As the little field mice sought haven in my old house

The other twenty-something couples I knew
Rejoiced in the increase in house values
And new shopping centers
And an influx of cash to pay for better schools
I didn't know how to explain how much it hurt
To feel hundreds of trees dying at once

To be honest
Remembering the trees who I have loved
Is an exercise in grief and isolation
It reminds me that it seems
Most humans can't hear their wisdom or their pain
Whereas I have never been able to silence them

In spiritual practice devoted to developing empathy, understanding of the worth of all beings, and a love of right action—of just action—we come to love the earth and all existences deeply, and in loving it, we realize its inherent goodness and value. Because the earth is so stressed by our own species, and especially because of the lifestyle of the developed world—the home of most Druids—loving is painful. Love is paired with grief—a grief arising not only from loss but also from harm. This is perhaps the most difficult part of my Druidry: a commitment to witness and reflect on my grief, including the grief arising from the harm my own life does to my beloved earth.

The longer we practice, the deeper we love and the more we know. The deeper we love and the more we know, the more we are aware of the costs to the earth of our own lives. As animists and pantheists, we have strong emotions about harm to other beings and places. A combination of our ecocentric ethical values of mutual care and sustainability, combined with this emotional attachment to nature, produces a high degree of motivation to enact relationships of reciprocity. However, most of us live in economic systems that make it difficult—nearly impossible—to become sustainable (at least not without enormous sacrifices, not only of comfort but also of familial relationships with others who may not share our values). Because of this paradox, Druids are stuck between strong motivation and effective action, and it hurts. In the nearly two decades I have been a Druid, my grief has been constant. Druidry took my inherent empathy and concern for the environment I had since childhood and honed it into a daily religious practice. My feelings toward my own lifestyle have ranged from mild frustration to near-depression. Even as I have done research professionally on environmental projects and taught students environmental justice and sustainability, I have also been quite unhappy with finding a path forward toward greater sustainability in my own life.

At various points, I have contemplated alternatives to the single-family household so common in Southern California. But these alternatives have proven impossible to procure. Co-housing is nearly non-existent. Building codes prevented some of my original ideas for housing design that was affordable and sustainable. In so many metropolitan areas, housing affordability, even for the middle class, is an incredible challenge. Each time we bought single-family homes, we first tried to locate multiple-family dwellings and friends who might want to form a small communal living situation. Each time, the timing and needs of the people who could be involved and the housing market did not align. I hope to soon return to conceptualizing greater sustainability where I am now, but four years have passed as we handled family medical needs and a pandemic that overtook all other priorities. Such are the challenges with living in the contemporary United States.

I have seen, in my virtual and real-world travels in Druidic contexts, rare but viable possibilities: permaculture small farms, tiny off-grid homes, and small-scale communal living spaces. I have participated in a number of conversations with other Druids at various gatherings about future possibilities of communal land and what Druidic community might look like if it were to become more like a Buddhist sangha than a church of the backyard. The conversations have been inspiring, hopeful, and beautiful. The reality has been that most Druids I know have, at least for the present, resigned themselves to working middle-class jobs and supporting single-family households. In a spirituality in which we are allowed to be limited and flawed without divine judgment, and which provides us with ethical values without extensive specific demands, I do not feel fear or shame associated with my rather ordinary American lifestyle. But I do feel grief. Because I live in a relational world and feel the pain of the earth. The earth's pain is my pain. And I cannot quite find a way to extricate myself from causing more of it.

In my studies of Druids, and in my personal network of them, I find I am not alone. Most of us do things to become sustainable and to demonstrate the love we have for the earth. But most of us also know it is not enough. The economic constraints and processes of the United States ensure that each of us consumes orders of magnitude more than is our fair share of the earth. Some action is, indeed, better than no action. However, our moderate actions will not be enough for the processes of climate change, pollution, and Anthropocene extinction to stop. And therein lies the paradox of Druidry: it teaches us to love more broadly and relate more deeply—but we do so in a sociocultural system that makes enacting these inner changes very difficult.

Love is an action verb in Druidry. It is not a state of being so much as a state of doing. It is in our work toward justice, toward rightness that we connect loving others with loving the Divine. We serve the gods through serving the earth and her creatures. Living out this type of love is difficult, and I often fail at it. Or more aptly, I recognize I succeed, with effort, at living out this type of love in small ways, but I struggle to enact it in big ways. My Druidic practice and values have allowed me to cultivate hospitality and mostly being able to be fully present for my students, friends, and family. I am generally able to show compassion and care for others, human and other-than-human alike. I am mostly able to embody my core values that guide how I relate to other humans. But I struggle to enact core values that guide how I relate to plants, animals, and places.

During the first summer of the pandemic, like many people, I turned my focus to my relatively new-to-me yard. I fenced in a small portion to become a vegetable garden, with the intention to improve the soil and simultaneously provide a more sustainable option for our fresh produce than the boxes we had delivered so that we could avoid the exposure risk of the grocery store. A friend came over, helping me build mounds of compost-enriched soil and fill the raised beds. We sweated in the hot early summer sun, dirt streaking our faces and arms, shoveling the bags and bags of compost and soil into tidy garden beds and planting the little organic seeds. Then I watched the ageless miracle as the tiny seeds sent up their first sprouts and leaves in the days that followed. I think every child in the 1980s planted seeds in cups as a school project, and the joy in watching new life emerge never waned for me.

But the joy was cut short. No sooner did each fledgling food source send forth their cotyledons than they were immediately devoured by ravenous ground squirrels. I rapidly realized that a family of the cute little creatures had made themselves a mansion underneath my art shed, immediately flanking my new garden. My first attempt to turn the tide of their destruction was to provide offerings to appease their hunger—scraps of vegetables and fruits from the house were deposited at one of their doors. They ate all the scraps. They also ate every sprout that dared to break ground. I wrestled with a large roll of chicken wire, clipping its metal strands until my hands ached, fashioning little cages over my plants. For a week or two, this worked. But as soon as the plants exited the cages, they were consumed. After a couple of weeks, the squirrels wised up and also learned how to peel back a tiny bit of the cage, just big enough for them to gain entry to the smorgasbord I was so graciously providing.

I bought predator urine. They did not care. I bought some natural spray made of peppermint, which they supposedly would not like. My entire garden smelled like a delicious mojito, but they did not care. I bought a rather expensive fake hawk, which was purported to scare away squirrels. They hid for a few hours, then tested some squirrel's theory that the hawk was not as it seemed. Rapidly, they learned the hawk was a fake and by the next morning, they had tipped him over to confirm their victory. They ate every single plant that grew that year, and after a few months of these incessant battles, I lost the war. I would never put out poison and I could not bring myself to trap them. Even the humane traps could not split up what was otherwise a very merry and increasingly fat squirrel family. The garden reverted to wood chips and stray weeds; I have not yet returned to attempting productivity again. Perhaps a new garden design this year or the next will be more successful. For their part, the squirrels are raising the third generation of their family under my art shed and seem quite pleased to eat all the mulberries and cherries they can manage to gobble up from our trees.

Even when I can put aside the demands of capitalist overculture, it can be challenging to sort out the various needs and limitations of many different beings in nature in order to decipher what right action is. I continued to get produce delivery since my garden fed the squirrels. In a larger picture of cost and benefit, I can justify plans to trap the squirrels and exterminate or relocate them in order to improve the sustainability of my household's food source. At the same time, in a very immediate sense, the squirrels are individual beings with spirits who are simply trying to survive. And I struggle to deny them that, even if that denial is necessary to produce more sustainable outcomes overall. For so many other, more complex choices, I find I am limited by finances, time, skills, and others' needs. I am not alone in this. It is very difficult to live sustainably in an unsustainable society.

This constant dissonance between ideals and reality sometimes produces in me a certain exhaustion, particularly when I am not only spiritually and emotionally connected to the earth, but also have a professional focus on climate change, sustainability, and environmental injustice. The discord between my capabilities and what I know is ideal, as well as the feeling as though my work is like bailing water using a small bucket from a large sinking boat, can combine to create despair. I find that I have to engage in spiritual practice to recharge and reframe this feeling so that I do not sink into what so many Americans feel: apathy. While Druidry attunes me more acutely to the suffering of other beings, it also engages me in the joy of being alive and in relationship with other beings. This salve is not a panacea, but it lessens the pain of the wounds I carry in seeking to be both truthful with myself about my limitations and failures, and simultaneously cultivating deep empathy for all beings.

Hope

Crystal Blanton, a social worker, Pagan author, and friend of mine, once told me that I had to have courage to hope. I have carried that with me for years now. When the grief from loving deeply and broadly feels as if it is too much for me to bear, and I begin to become fatigued and feel as though nothing I do matters, I return to hope as a choice. I ask myself what hope looks like, the same way that I ask myself what love looks like. These become action verbs rather than emotional states. I forgive myself for feeling grief, despair, and apathy—reminding myself that hope is a courageous choice reframes it as a challenge that I can try to meet, fail at, and then try again.

Druidic practice helps me to choose hope. When I walk mindfully on the earth, when I sit under the shade of a tree and open myself to its spirit, when I light a candle in my shrine cabinet at the end of the night and then enter contemplative prayer, I open myself to the joy of connection and its renewing power. While maintaining a relational and empathic worldview connects me to the earth's suffering, it also connects me to its beauty and a feeling of belonging to a precious Something More. Meditation centers me, cultivates an inner peace, and helps me to be aware of building despair so that I can address it. Engaging in creative pursuits provides me a way to express my emotions and envision a better future. Devotional work with the gods reorients me to the virtues I am cultivating and offers a symbolic and spiritual way to address limitations I have in what I can accomplish through action.

The morning after I cried out to Brigid, I tidied the shrine, my act of love for the gods. There is not much I can give them except time—even an offering of excellent whisky is not much, but my time is something I cannot reclaim. When I give it freely, it is an expression of my love for them. I wiped each statue with a soft cloth, picked up the remnants of matches that had lit their candles, rearranged stones and bones into new beautiful shapes. It seems like a simple series of actions disconnected from changing my own life and changing the world, but as I closed the doors to the shrine cabinet, I felt as if I had stepped out of a soothing, healing bath in a mountain stream— refreshed, renewed, reconstituted. I had hope again. I had inspiration again. I felt reconnected to the goodness of existence, of earth, of the divine mystery of which we are all a part. I was ready to try again.

This is the spiral process in Druidry, a process that never ends, as it is one of sustained effort toward a different way of living: we seek to come into awareness and understanding of ourselves and the beings around us, we seek to support right action and justice, we try—and fail—and try again, and in so doing, we cultivate love. This love is in the ways we relate to other beings, not only in the big ways but also (and perhaps especially) in the small and everyday ways. In trying and failing, we have opportunities to ask for assistance and support, to connect to human and other-than-human beings who can nurture that courage to hope that is so important to sustained loving action. Love is not the cause of right relationship but rather its result. We can then transcend our fluctuating emotions and instead focus on commitments we have made. This approach of love-as-process has allowed me to forgive those who have hurt me, including forgiving my own past self. It is a pathway toward reconciliation and change, toward letting go of our separation from one another and all the parts of ourselves, to create a more integrated and whole world.

The Druidic work of inspired creativity and intuitive knowing helps me to create visions of the life I aspire to build and the world I hope to contribute to collectively shaping. I can return to these visions to remind myself of the possibility of what might be when the reality of what is threatens to crush my persistence in finding a way toward a more harmonious life. One vision I return to as a source of hope is a visionary dream I had when I was about ten years old. As is common in these journey-dreams, I entered the dream through a portal—a round mouth of a cave. On the other side, I found an adult version of myself sitting in a small canoe. In the middle of a small mountain lake, the dark water lapped peacefully against the edges of my boat. The wind rustled the autumn golden leaves of aspens and swirled them into the water, carrying my blonde curls with it. I looked out toward the shore where a little village of rough-hewn wood and cob houses formed a distant strand. No sooner than I did this and think of being there, then I lifted out of the canoe, shape-shifting into a water bird. Spreading my wings wide, I caught the wind, soaring to the shore. Gently, as I came into land on the dirt path winding among the houses, I became once again my adult human form, human feet landing on packed earth and wings tucking invisibly into smooth skin.

I was drawn to a building I knew was a dining hall. How I knew, I did not fully know. My mind was split: the child me who struggled to comprehend this world and the adult me who knew it intimately. I walked along the dirt path toward the largest of the buildings, which was still diminutive. My simple chocolate woven shift dress and cream apron swished along with my strides, my leather boots treading steadfastly toward my destination. The houses I passed were small, simple, and quaint. Kitchen gardens in raised beds provided a riot of ripe vegetables and fruit trees were laden with autumn gifts. Colorful but messy bouquets of flowers peeped out of window boxes. Other shifts and robes in muted colors hung drying on lines in the crisp but comfortable air. I came to the great double wood doors of the dining hall and hauled one heavy door open. Inside, a merry small community was feasting on dinner, chatting amiably on bench-style seats at long tables. Children ran freely between tables. There was a deep peace and fulfillment that permeated the crowd, and something more: gratitude. The sense of harmony, of belonging, and of gratitude for this precious life was so palpable that I remember it more than thirty years later as if I am back again among these compatriots tonight.

It may be fanciful to think of a world so different from the rushed, disconnected, materialist one I occupy. But we will never create a different world without first imagining one. The magic of transforming our consciousness and way of life requires inspiration—not only practical but also emotional. Cultivating visions of a future world and a future self that embedded in our emotional reality helps us to hold on to it, to return to it, and to work toward it coming to fruition. The off-grid cob houses, bioregenerative and permaculture small farms, and even historical sites I have toured have given me more crystalized and pragmatic variations of my childhood dream-vision. As I do my best to balance my vision for my household with my wife's vision, my vision for my life with my career's demands, my vision for economy with my nation's options, I hold on to the vision of a society built on a relational worldview. I sit at my shrine and breathe in gratitude, breathe out despair. I breathe in peace, breathe out anxiety. I breathe in forgiveness, breathe out apathy. And then I make one small step forward. I make one small commitment I have not made before. And another. And another. My Druidry deepens and I come a little closer to living it out as my entire way of life, and in so doing, fulfilling my commitment to loving wholly—with all of me, toward all beings. And indeed, through this life's work, I come to love the Divine Mystery of which we are all a part, and all goodness.

CHAPTER 12

The Third Spiral

The Druid in the World

Gently within the greater circle of humankind, may I radiate peace.
– DRUID'S PEACE PRAYER FROM THE ORDER OF BARDS, OVATES, AND DRUIDS

In the chapter on Druid community, I explored how we can understand community in a very broad context within a Druidic relational worldview—across time and also including the other-than-human world. In this last chapter, I will discuss how Druids understand themselves within the overcultural context and how they are building themselves individually and collectively as a countercultural movement in opposition to anthropocentric and materialist norms. Cultural modeling and Druidry-as-culture help articulate how Druids develop, transmit, and maintain cognitive models for domains of religion. Many Druids understand themselves as self-consciously generating a new way of living, seeking to contribute to a future of humanity that is more peaceful, more just, and more sustainable:

> I don't want us to be the parasites we are and hurt Mother Gaia. It's not just this belief system makes me feel good. It's a connection to social action. I use the strength this gives me and I use it for social action, for social change. (Fiona McMillan)

> I've always had the philosophy, and it might be from Girl Scouts, leave it better than you found it. I bring that into Druidry. I feel like I should be doing something, and it's more environmental, but social justice and equality too. I feel like we should be active. (Anon)

For many Druids, particularly those who are actively engaged in Druidic groups, either face to face or online, there is a collective effort to share in order to learn, and to build knowledge and skills that afford greater opportunities to enact Druid values in the world—that is, to make a difference. In this, they function as communities or landscapes of practice.

Communities of practice are social groups who regularly engage with one another around a problem or issue to learn from one another and collectively build useful practices (Wegner 1998). Communities of practice have three structural elements: activities people do together; things in common people care about; and ways of thinking and acting that are developed as a collective effort (Wegner 1998). If we think of cultural modeling as a description of the process by which individuals construct their understanding of themselves, the world, and their options and simultaneously by which collective patterns emerge that can be understood as culture—that is, the mutual emergence process of culture and cognition—a community of practice is like a purpose-driven social group engaging self-consciously in that process. Just as cognition is a social, relational process in cultural modeling theory, so too is learning in a community of practice. Through this purpose-driven engagement, people involved in a community of practice observe one another to build a system of actions to take and contexts in which to take those actions (Pyrko et al. 2017). Because the boundaries of a community of practice are epistemic rather than organizational—based on learning and constructing meaning and selfhood—they are constantly negotiated. Druidry functions in this way. Druids are drawn to it for two primary reasons: they have anomalous experiences they wish to understand and those experiences have generated an empathy for and commitment to the earth. That is, their anomalous experiences have caused them to intuit that nature is sentient and powerful, and this generates a desire to better understand how to show nature respect, reverence, and reciprocity. Druidry is a social group that affords a "home" for this learning process.

There are different levels of practice that have been observed and theorized in social learning models (Pyrko et al. 2019). Druidry itself is not a community of practice, as the term is generally applied to local groups within which people connect and engage to negotiate local practice. Local, face-to-face Druid groves or seed groups function in this way, but Druidry as a whole is global. As such, it is more appropriate to describe Druidry as a landscape of practice, containing all local communities who identify with a common effort to build a body of knowledge. In between these two levels are situated conversations Druids have through texts, both through books and the internet—this would be a network of practice, connecting but not engaging those in it, transcending local contexts. Alternatively, Druidry could be described as a "social learning space," which lacks requirements for shared competence and longevity (Wenger and Wenger-Trayner 2020). Social learning spaces draw people together who participate with one another in a learning process driven by a desire to make a difference and offer a space in which people can share their uncertainties, build knowledge, and translate knowledge into action (Wenger and Wenger-Trayner 2020). Some Druids certainly practice in communities of practice (all the Druids I interviewed have practiced in local groves and seed groups), but many are solitary, whether by choice or by lack of access to a local face-to-face group. However, even self-described solitary "hedge Druids" generally read books and blogs and often participate in online groups, sharing ideas, experiences, and source materials. While Druids are generally loosely and flatly organized as communities of peers, like many Pagans (Berger et al. 2003: 201), they also operate in a social learning space that is uniquely Druidic.

These social learning spaces are generally constructed without authoritative leadership, purposefully drawing Druids together as communities of equals. Every Druid is their own priest, as Elizabeth Boerner describes: "Everyone is the priest. Ritual is a group effort and it's not like you're just sitting there and watching someone perform. You're participating." Druidry mirrors other flatly organized purpose-driven knowledge-oriented groups, often best suited in organizations that work collaboratively and creatively, such as in technology and academic research. (Not surprisingly, many Druids have occupations in industries that also operate in this way—and at times, there are open conversations about drawing from such occupational environments to inform how Druidic communities are structured.) Likewise, Druids view the development of Druidry itself as a collaborative and highly individual activity, drawing from a wide range of sources of inspiration—human and other-than-human—and none of these sources are viewed as authoritative:

> My understanding of Druidry is there is a collection of similar ideas about helping the land, helping the world, the types and names of spirits we interact with in a similar way, but the focus appears to be individual connection and individual action that then gets shared in groups and communities. Hierarchical controlling of the masses is diametrically opposed to what Druidry is. When we gathering together, we are all sharing stories, but no one is telling anyone that how they are doing it is wrong. (Rev. Monika Kojote)

Druidry has both bureaucratic (or more aptly, organizational—as it is not bureaucratic in a Weberian sense) and charismatic voices (e.g., many of the Druidic authors), but none are viewed as leaders (Weber 1946). Ultimately, Druids do not have trust in an authority (see Lincoln 1994 for an extensive discussion on religious authority) outside of themselves, and even then, they position the self as fallible and changeable. Rev. Kirk Thomas, a leader in ADF, explained: "Our founder made one absolute rule and that was rule that the Archdruid is fallible. The archdruid is no special person, he can fuck up just like anyone else." Druidry is, therefore, primarily imagistic rather than doctrinal (Lewis 2004), which is generally true of people who are without a centralized authoritative religious system. Grounded in Harvey Whitehouse's (2000) theory of divergent modes of religiosity, while the doctrinal mode is based on repetition, instruction, and semantic memory, the imagistic mode is based on performance and episodic memory following high emotional impact in ritual. Druidry is a community that seeks to support practitioners in forging a more relational, peaceful, sustainable world, and it does so through offering ritual practices that facilitate powerful spiritual experiences and thoughtful dialogues about their meaning (both through training individual capacity to do so through meditation and through collective capacity to do so through respectful sharing without seeking conformity or consensus).

The history of contemporary Druidry is like other revitalization movements (Wallace 1956), but without a central charismatic figure—it was instead a spiritual movement coterminous with social movements. However, it was and is critical of the overculture, seeking to forge a relational and ecocentric way of life in a largely materialist and androcentric world. Druidry is, like neo-Paganism as a whole, countercultural in nature (Magliocco 2004). New religious movements operate at both individual and social cognitive levels, arising as a response to unsatisfying religious ideas and practices—which can be assuaged through conversion at an individual level or through the development of new religions at the collective level (Tremlin 2005). Arguably, at the heart of contemporary Druidry going back to the Revival period is a baseline assumption that what went wrong for humanity was its disconnect to other-than-human nature, and what is needed are practices that center relationships to other-than-human nature in ways that bring us back into the wholeness of ourselves and correct the sufferings and dysfunctions we have developed as a species (see Metzner 1995 on the psychopathology of the current Western human-nature relationship). Both Druidry and other forms of Paganisms, notably contemporary witchcraft, originate during the Romantic period (Hutton 1999) and were heavily influenced over time by environmentalism and new age spirituality (Clifton 2006).

The boundaries between Druidry as sociocultural movement and as religion are vague and fuzzy, as they are in the case of many contemporary nature-centered spiritual movements (Selberg 2015: 90). Romanticism in the context of Industrialization and the Enlightenment (and with the birth of anthropology, folklore, and neo-Paganism—Magliocco 2004) formed the bedrock of the "Druid Revival"—the earliest phase of the contemporary movement. After the Second World War, Druidry was increasingly informed within a plural and global context during the rise of the environmental, women's rights, and gay rights movements and by the critique of wilderness and preservationist movements. Druidry today is increasingly shaped as a response to climate despair and impending ecological collapse within a context of globalized communication networks via the internet (Rountree 2017). Throughout this time, since its earliest formation in the eighteenth century, there has been an interwoven history of Paganisms and Druidry (Cooper 2010).

While Druidry and witchcraft (particularly Wicca) were developed in a process of mutual influence, unlike witchcraft, Druids generally do not maintain persecution narratives (Magliocco 2004; Pike 2001). This is likely to be because while Druids view themselves as part of social change movements more broadly that may be countercultural in nature, they also tend to view themselves as occupying roles that are vocational rather than prophetic—to position themselves as functioning within society as inspired advisors rather than outside of it. Several Druids in interviews mentioned this was key to why they felt Druidry was right for them in ways that witchcraft or Wicca was not—they did not feel the persecution narrative promoted a psychologically healthy life and many of them did not want to recreate the Christian persecution narrative, which created an experience of the world that generated fear, separation from others, and dysfunctional relationship. Druidry, therefore, is a shared learning space or landscape of practice not only in a functional sense but also in a goal-oriented sense. Communities of practice have primarily been conceptually applied to occupational or hobby skill-building groups, and Druids have often positioned themselves more as reviving a role than a religion. Animist and polytheist religion attentive to pastoral cycles was the pervasive norm of the cultures contemporary Druids draw from as inspiration; Druids were specific occupational roles within those cultures:

> My religion is this animistic, polytheist religion I don't have a name for. A Druid is a role I fill. My elevator speech for Druidry is that a Druid is a story-teller and a keeper of lore. A Druid is a seer and keeper of wisdom. And a Druid is a priest of nature and the gods of nature. So it's doing things in those three realms. (John Beckett)

Iolo Morganwg's (Edward Williams's) work envisioned Druids as "wise and knowledgeable magicians and poets, keepers of an oral tradition that stretched uninterrupted into antiquity," which began the conflation of Druids and Celtic peoples (Magliocco 2004: 36). Over time, the conflation of the two has partially eroded, but the inspiration for Druidry-as-role has not:

> In my own research, my feeling is that Druids in the Indo-European context, is a class. They're the intelligentsia of the Celtic world. They're not just mystics, seers, and magic-workers. We use [Druid] to mean natural philosopher, mystic seer for ourselves, recognizing there are other types of Druids. (Murtagh anDoile)

In this way, Druids are similar to the contemporary neoshamans that view themselves as therapeutic, spiritual, and cultural practitioners in the West (Selberg 2015: 91). However, US Druids generally view themselves under a wider role than shamans do, sometimes encompassing their professional occupations alongside their spiritual identities—particularly as healers (nurses, doctors, herbalists, therapists) and as teachers and keepers of lore (teachers, professors, academic researchers, engineers).

Druids are on a deeply individual spiritual journey, but the journey is often tied to a sense of vocational service to the earth. Druidry offers a landscape of practice that essentially works to develop productive and effective ways to engage in relationship with the other-than-human. Druidry offers a social learning space in which to develop, test, discuss, debate, and refine concepts, approaches, and skills that support a countercultural relational movement. As Rev. Monika Kojote articulated:

> Wisdom and learning and seeking out information is the number one things of all Druid practices. It's interesting because it's not information seeking in order to control, but to be in partnership. So many Druid practices I engage with are about being in best partnership with myself, what my limitations and boundaries are, so I can be in good partnership with the environment around me. And this is in direct opposition to the way the United States socialized us and raised us.

Druidry is a religious subculture arising from a landscape of practice, formed by people whose spiritual experiences pushed them to seek community and meaning outside of the United States' overcultural norms. Often self-consciously borrowing from artistic, philosophical, scientific, academic, and social movements, it provides support for two revolutionary actions: to prioritize self-development within supportive community without seeking conformity or consensus and to develop and maintain practical and spiritual knowledge that aligns human beings in right relationship with the earth. How to accomplish that right relationship is one of the most challenging, yet arguably most significant, questions with which Druids grapple.

Relational Knowing

Most animist religions are situated within traditional ecological knowledge systems (TEK) that were developed and maintained by indigenous people over time through observation, experimentation, and critical reflection. Religion, science, and often magic blend together into systems to help people live sustainably in the context of a local ecosystem. Local ecological knowledge (LEK) systems were developed and maintained by non-indigenous people, generally over short time frames (hundreds rather than thousands of years). In both cases, these types of knowledge systems are grounded in experiential learning and everyday practices—critical elements include localization and emotional engagement (Nazarea 2006). These ways of knowing, developed in relationships with other-than-human beings and places, are not designed the same way as globalized (Western) science—they are inherently intuitive, affective, and flexible. TEK and LEK afford ways of learning that empower each individual to find their own unique pathway to knowing ("coming into knowing"), grounded in mentorship and "kincentric" learning and living, which promotes five particular values: it is mindful of values and worldview, personal, embodied and sensory, situated in time and place, and relational (Beckwith et al. 2017: 420). TEK and LEK forge mutual respect and care, and though often spiritual or religious, such systems are the equivalent of sciences (UNEP 1998; Anderson 1996).

TEK and LEK, in their integration of embodied knowledge, sensory awareness, and attentiveness to place, yield a way of moving through the world that has been called a variety of things by various theorists: habitus (Bourdieu 1980); prehensions and affordances (Ellen 1993); and dwelling and enskillment (Ingold 2000). Cultural modelers would posit these as cultural models that are preattentive, but no less learned through interactions than those of our attentive, consciously selected models of the world around us and ourselves in it. TEK systems that are religious in nature have been extensively ethnographically documented in a variety of economic and social contexts (see, for example, Nelson 1983; Basso 1996; Faust 1998; Lansing 2007). Druidry holds some characteristics in common with TEK and LEK: it is based on experiential learning (Goulet 1998; Reo 2011); recognizes ecosystem complexity while offering simpler solutions for conservation (Berkes and Berkes 2009; Gadgil et al. 1993); addresses diverse variables qualitatively and maintains knowledge in folklore (Berkes and Berkes 2009; Kimmerer 2002); and is spiritual rather than merely objective, valuing ecocentric reciprocity (Kimmerer 2002). However, unlike TEK and LEK, Druidry is not (as a whole) localized or directly engaged in long-term observations of ecosystems (Gadgil et al. 1993; Kimmerer 2002). Druidry may encourage individual Druids to localize their observations, knowledge, and practices, but it functions as a landscape of practice—with generalized approaches and frameworks—rather than as a community of practice, grounded in place.

As found in many TEK systems, Druids have similar broad assumptions, such as the inseparability of the natural world from a conceptualized "supernatural" world and viewing other-than-human beings as persons and agents. However, TEK systems also have elaborate mythology and cosmology grounded in place, as well as ritual practices and taboos that govern how these assumptions articulate with everyday life choices. The lack of localization in Druidry outside the individual can make it difficult to yield the outcomes in actions that TEK and LEK generally achieve. This is because TEK and LEK tend to unite two different motivating mechanisms: *why to be sustainable* (emotion) and *how to be sustainable* (knowledge). Sustainability is difficult to achieve in the United States because our dominant Western science tends to purposefully remove affect and produce specialists rather than cognitive devices that provide salient wisdom for the general public, both of which are exactly opposite to how TEK functions (Anderson

1996). TEK systems, through integrating religion and art with science, help us overcome our cognitive and affective constraints (the things our brains are not good at), such as passing on the costs of production, discounting future needs and effects, feeling apathetic in the face of large-scale problems, and resisting change (Anderson 2014: 20–3). TEK may not always be most accurate, but it tends to be honed over the course of many generations to be highly useful at compelling people to adopt sustainable behavior attuned to localized challenges—which means that integrating the best qualities of Western science and TEK, while difficult, may be the most hopeful as we increasingly face global ecological crisis (Anderson 1996, 2010, 2014; Efird 2017; Gadgil et al. 1993; Gagnon and Berteaux 2009; Moeller et al. 2004).

In such relational epistemologies, the observer is responsive to diverse and changing "other" over time, which permits a greater flexibility in developing complex ideas than materialist science. Rather than having, acquiring, applying, and refining representations of objects in the world (objectivism), relational epistemology develops skills to be in relationship with others, to heighten awareness of the environment, and to maintain a sense of relatedness with others (Bird David 1999). Druidry does not entirely radically depart from Western dualism of self and environment (e.g., when we compare to Tim Ingold's essays in *Being Alive* [2011]), but it does transcend materialism. Similar to holding direct personal spiritual experience and skepticism simultaneously, it tends to hold relational spirituality and Western scientific empiricism simultaneously. Druidry provides a framework to integrate (rather than view as competitive) the relational worldview of animism, the personal experiential process of folk science, and Western science (as a positivist and empirical orientation of relating to a material world, grounded in formal education—as described by Pierotti and Wildcat 2000; Gadgil et al. 1993; Cox 2000). For example, AODA and OBOD both encourage or require reading literature in botany and/or ecology, but also do so for divination systems such as ogham. In this way, it offers one way out of the Eurocentrism of Western science that has privileged the distancing of the human from the other-than-human/natural world, and that has unjustly focused on knowledge and applications for Western advancement at the expense of others (Harding 1994).

Druidry offers a framework for attempting to build or revive LEK—to integrate knowing through tradition and folklore, inspiration and spiritual insight, contemporary scholarly expertise, and experience and experimentation. Druids are encouraged to study mythology, history, and folklore, but rather than attempting to reconstruct pre-Christian religions (as many Celtic Reconstructionists seek to do), the goal is to use such studies to develop a religion our spirituality for the here and now. In this, Druidry does demonstrate heritagization, "processes of cultural production by which cultural or natural elements are selected and reworked for new social uses" (Selberg 2015: 99), but largely through reinterpretation for contemporary practices, contexts, and challenges. As one Druid leader explained:

I've been working out how the ancients did religion and why, and I wrote a book about it. And it seems to me that it's about reciprocity. I give so that you may give. It's how we deal with friends and family. We give love and attention and things to them, and we expect to get that back. And that's pretty much how the ancients looked at it. They would make their offerings. They would give stuff, and in return they expected good stuff back—like protection, that was a big one. Maybe a successful life. Sacrifice isn't about giving until it hurts. Sacrifice is a ritual trope, which is an entire ritual of giving offerings. ADF consciously practices this relationship with the spirits. (Rev. Kirk Thomas)

Reinterpretations and new creative elements are shaped through spiritual processes of inspiration and insight. These are essentially forms of religious epiphanies, particularly in the form of a pluralist model, in which people experience the same ultimate reality but never in its fullness directly, and in the form of a relationship model, in which people do not assume there is an ultimate reality and instead focus on the experience itself (Kellenberger 2017). In both of these models, skepticism about the capacity to understand an ultimate reality (or even its existence) is completely permissible and expected. In this way, unverified personal gnosis is given both meaning and softened in its significance, permitting Druidic subculture to arise organically through sharing without the necessity of coming to orthodoxy or orthopraxy.

These spiritual and folkloric pathways toward knowing are paired with engaging in learning from experts (often scholarly experts) and a personal process of experiential and experimental learning. Druidic orders and online discussion groups encourage reading about local ecology, botany, and biology—including in urban systems, if that is where one lives. At the same time, Druids are offered (and even required to participate in) practices that build embodied knowledge through personal experience and experimentation in the natural world: "AODA's argument is that if you don't have knowledge and direct experience with the living earth, you can't have deep relationship. You can't build deep Druidry without knowledge. You can take courses, you can read books, but you need to apply that knowledge in the woods" (Dana O'Driscoll). Through my own survey research, I found that many Druids (like me) attended nature workshops in local groups (53 percent), attended workshops on nature and sustainability when they are offered at Druid gatherings (72 percent), and discuss sustainability and the environment in a significant portion of their conversations with other Druids (85 percent report they discuss this in one-third of their conversations or more). Gatherings I have been to have included workshops on permaculture, wildcrafting, plant identification, sustainability, back to the land movements, folk science, and herbalism, often integrating and utilizing scholarly experts (who also happen to be Druid) in the facilitation of spiritual and scientific knowledge (Kirner 2015). This knowing through personal spiritual-science integrative learning experiences builds habitus in the Maussian sense, in which the body is shaped by repetitive interactive experience and comes to quite literally embody knowledge—to see and hear and smell what was once difficult to perceive, to enact through muscle memory what was once challenging to do. Integration of forms of knowing is found in multiple Druidic practices, including visualization meditation, movement (walking, hiking, postures and poses, yoga, Tai Chi), body awareness (breathing meditation, relaxation), sensory engagement (cultivating observational awareness), and energy work (gestalts of feeling around specific others and the self, communicated to the self intuitively through color, texture, light, and sound). Druids typically keep journals about these experiences and their learning process over time, and Druid orders often provide structured reflection points in which Druids assess and summarize what they have learned and developed for review by a mentor or tutor. In some cases, Druids are required to include in these practices and reflections specific actions they took to become more sustainable and reciprocal in their relationship with the earth.

Spirit Experience and Relational Ethics

There are many examples of indigenous religions maintaining transmission of TEK and supporting biodiversity conservation (Berkes 1999; Byers et al. 2001; Ramakrishnan et al. 1998; Sponsel et al. 1998); anthropomorphism (or assumptions of personhood) leading to conservation indicators (Chan 2012); and sacred places being used to maintain both cultural heritage and biodiversity (Sponsel 2017). These systems articulate moral codes governing interactions between humans and other-than-humans through ritual, taboo, and other religious and social practices (see, for example, the extensive review of the impact of taboo on conservation of habitat and species by Colding and Folke [2001] and the discussion of religious principles and precepts articulating relationships between humans and between humans and nature in the Inuit Qaujimajatuqangit by Wenzel [2004]). Essentially, humans need emotion with their knowledge if they are to choose behaviors that serve the long-term interests of the ecosystem and social group, rather than those that help themselves in a more immediate way. Kay Milton's work (2002) explored how the conventional Western overcultural view that emotion and rationality are somehow oppositional is actually incorrect; rather, emotion makes rationality possible by giving it direction. She argues that viewing nature as filled with persons may arise from human experience of nature itself rather than due to innate cognitive processes—not with a supernatural or spirit world, but with other-than-humans who are very much like human persons (intelligent animals) and by extension—other less human-like nature (plants, storms, mountains). Learning directly from experience of other-than-human nature, apart from culture and innate cognition, is fully possible for humans as animals in nature. Because we share common cognition and we live in the same world—the same earth—we can come to common knowledge, such as the personhood of nature. In this way, Druidic commonalities are shaped not only by interactions between Druids (or even between Druids and human-created materials many of them access) but also by interactions between Druids and the natural world.

While orthodox beliefs exist in some religions, even in those religions, more intuitive vernacular beliefs exist, which represent the easier-to-grasp concepts, such as anthropomorphic gods. Whitehouse calls these religious beliefs that are more intuitive "cognitively optimal" (2004: 189). These are the concepts that are easiest to process and remember, that command our attention, and that can be understood without any special training. Anthropomorphism is cognitively optimal. This is Theory of Mind and agency detection at work. Ritualization is also cognitively optimal. Religion that includes these features is easy to develop, maintain, and transmit—much easier than Western materialist science. Druidry, like other decentralized nature-centered religions, functions in cognitively optimal ways and therefore does not require centralized authority or doctrine to continue developing and to be transmitted to others.

The experience of personhood—and, by extension, spirit experience— is not merely a byproduct of cognition adapted to social complexity. Perceiving persons in nature are cross-culturally common because it works. There are evolutionary benefits (sustainability) with very little cost. While Western science treats nature as materialist (the impersonal view) and this arguably does not impede knowledge acquisition (even if it makes it less memorable and less easily transmissible), it impedes emotional motivation to conserve nature. Animist religions, on the other hand, posit nature filled with persons as intentional agents. This produces emotional motivation to act with obligatory mutual care. Spirit experience develops two significant aspects of sustainable environmental management systems in traditional societies: respect (Levinas's concept of the "infinitely important other" because "our whole lives are constructed through interaction with them") and sustainability (do not take too much) (Anderson 2014: 78). Both are necessary to put the needs of other-than-human nature before our immediate desires and perceived needs. The lack of respect in this way is why Western scientific bases of sustainability do not work.

Humans arguably have an affinity for nature that aids in a desire to conserve it (Kellert and Wilson 1995). However, enculturation into how to do so and social support for required behaviors are also necessary (Milton 2002). Secular approaches to environmental problems are often insufficient to produce consistent, meaningful action. While religion is not necessarily adaptive for sustainability, it can be (Sponsel 2017). While anthropocentric ecological ethics define sustainability and conservation through the lens of maintaining resources for future human generations (Curry 2011), Druidic ethics are animist and ecocentric—valuing the earth, ecosystems, and other-than-human beings as intrinsically worthy of care. Druids offered:

> I believe that the world is a relational world and that everything affects everything. So if I harm somebody, I'm putting harm into the world. So my ethics are based on that. I think you could say this is a Druid concept. (Kat Reeves)

> Do no harm is probably is where I would start from, and how to prevent someone else being harmed when I witness it is equally important. Helping or offering to help someone to reconnect with that can make such a difference, such an impact. This grand experiment of separation. I think it's coming to a conclusion, but it's going to get real ugly before we let it go. But I want to be remembered as the person who holds that spot, holds that threshold, like you don't have to cross this. You can stay connected. And you are loved. You are love, embodied. So do no harm. (Anon)

> If I look at my life prior to Druidry, I was a completely different person. I was a typical American consumer and in the 17+ years [since] I've totally changed my life. If I'm going to be a Druid, I have to honor these principles. . . . As an animist, all things have spirit. It's helped me come to my sense of being in the world. It's about relationship and connection. (Dana O'Driscoll)

> I like to introduce myself and give an offering—always biodegradable—and say, "I'm here to connect, to pick up trash (my favorite offering), and get to know what life is like in this area." I am a big fan of interacting with spirits of a place that are tied to that place. What are they concerned with? What brings them joy? How do I move safely in this safe? Many nature spirits—not all—but many look at humans as an entire species that is fucking shit up. I go in with that ambassador idea. I'm not better than other humans, but I'm trying to provide a balance. (Rev. Monika Kojote)

Such ecocentrism may be necessary for future sustainability, both pragmatically and ethically (Washington et al. 2017). Druidry offers virtues and values that are contextual, rather than specific ethical codes. This is similar to other religious contextual ethics systems, such as those found in Taoism, in which ethics is grounded in the actor's self-awareness and self-development (Weed 2011: 111). Druidry is, then, not particularly unique in the way its ethics works, but rather is countercultural in its United States' overcultural context. Based on survey research, motivation to enact core values of sustainability is very high; 72 percent of Druids reported their spiritual practices enhanced their personal commitment to sustainability. This affirms Milton's work (2002) that found positive experiences in nature yield emotional connection to it, which motivates environmental activism. It also supports Bron Taylor's (2010) assertion that new religious movements that sacralize nature produce greater commitment and connection to the natural world.

Why Relational Spirituality (Alone) Is Insufficient

Yet spirit experience, personhood of nature, and respect are insufficient to produce sustainability (Pungetti et al. 2012). Druidry is a spiritual ecological movement, but it is also a (largely disorganized) revival of folk traditions and knowledge. It is an attempt to correct the disconnect the Western industrialized world has wrought—not only from nature but from one another and from ourselves. Still, it has its limitations and these are tied to its differences from indigenous animist systems and from ancient Celtic societies. While Druidry has integrated a number of approaches that are hallmarks of TEK (including knowledge of ecology, nature-centered religious practices, and relational philosophy) (Turner et al. 2000), Druidry is not traditional or local, and it has no comprehensive ethical codes or social sanctions.

Deep ecology suggested that we do not need moral rules when we have identification with nature—when we expand our sense of self to include other beings. That expands empathy and gives us the motivation or inclination to act morally without rules (Naess 1985, 1988, 1989). In deep ecology, the fundamental problem at the root of the ecological crisis is separation. If we can shift the worldview to holism, behavioral change will follow (Wu 2019). This identification, as Milton (2002) explains, can mean a variety of different things: nature is similar to me (Naess 1988); nature is me (Livingston 1981; Macy 1987); nature is a part of me (Naess 1989); or I am a part of nature (Seed 1985). It can also mean ontological identification (realizing that we share common experience) or cosmological identification (realizing we belong to one singular reality or process) (Fox 1995). Druid identification with nature has elements of all of these forms of identification, some from scientific ecological tenets and others as spiritual interpretations. Yet despite environmentalism and many of these forms of identification becoming mainstream in the United States, not much has changed in consumption habits (Coeckelbergh 2017). While identification can generate a sense of nature as sacred and as worthy of conservation, it cannot—without TEK or LEK and its attendant moral codes—link motivation to collective patterns of sustainable behavior. That is, it can motivate people individually (and collectively), but it doesn't adequately chart a path forward from a materialist consumer culture or an anthropocentric transcendent one to the collective patterns of long-term sustainability we observe in indigenous animisms and TEK systems. We need emotional connection, knowledge, *and* social support to revolutionize behavior.

In my survey of Druids (and other Pagans) studying their views about and experiences in nature, their motivations toward sustainability, and their behavioral choices at the household level, Druids' household ecological footprints were not appreciably different from the US average. However, this does not mean Druids are not sincerely motivated toward conservation and sustainability. Rather, the overculture makes this very difficult, providing little supportive structure for sustainable behavior and offering conflicting cultural values. Douglas Ezzy (2007) noted that there were limitations in witchcraft to producing environmental sustainability due to a focus on self-development. I would argue that even in the absence of spiritual consumerism (which seems less prevalent in Druidry than in the population sample Ezzy studied), individualism is a key problem for US Druids to fully enact sustainable behavior. There are no clear Western science models of sustainability (problematized as a concept by Gene Anderson [2010]). There are also no clear, consistent Druidic models for sustainable action; in fact, only 14 percent of texts I analyzed discussed ethics at all. Émile Durkheim (1947) theorized that religious ritual provides collectivist motivation for conforming to the social order. In ethnoecological studies, this was supported by the groundbreaking work of Roy Rappaport in 1968 and later Anderson's extensive discussions in 1996, 2010, and 2014, all of which pointed toward linkages between religious ritual and sustainability. So why are Druidic relational ontology, epistemology, and ethics insufficient to generate significantly divergent behavior when it comes to sustainability? The key comes in a gap between affect, motivation, and action. Cultural models can govern all three, but they function independently both as cognitive processes and as cultural phenomena. If one is lacking, behavioral change is not likely.

Aaron Smith's (2014) work proposed a model of religion that included a number of different components, but it insufficiently addressed a gap between religious ritual action and religious morality because it described one of the components of religion as rules or doctrine "through which every thought is filtered and every behaviour is measured" (Smith 2014: 219). Smith's assumptions were that rules were governed by experts, learned early in life and combined with empathy, and yielded innate moral assumptions and collectively moral behavior (2014: 28–9), but these assumptions are heavily Christo-centric. As I have described previously, many indigenous religions do not have authoritative experts or doctrine, yet they still have collectively moral behavior. We can widen Smith's basic conceptualization of religion as interrelated cultural models by addressing religion in the same way we would other subcultures—differentiating between cultural models of emotion, expression, and action (Kronenfeld 2008). Cultural models are not rules or doctrine, but rather loosely organized and situationally contextualized, providing guides for articulating shared values in specific situations (Kronenfeld 2008: 209). Druids arguably share cultural models for ritual action, affect, and motivation, but not sustainable action (i.e., how to articulate relational ethics from values to expectations for behavior). As one Druid elaborated:

> With the environment, it's so hard, because there are all these discussions. Should Druids be vegetarian? Vegan? All organic? And people have their own physical and financial situation, and your locale is what it is. So I don't think that [Druidry] would be the big push but being out there for things that are more sustainable. (Anon)

Shared values or principles and shared cultural models for action differ in their specificity, in the level of guidance they give a practitioner. For example, the concept of *ahimsa* (nonviolence toward other living things) is held in common in Hinduism, Buddhism, and Jainism, but cultural models for actions that express *ahimsa* differ. Many Buddhists are vegetarian; Jains extend this to many other food taboos, as well as actions such as wearing masks and filtering water to avoid harm to microorganisms. In indigenous animisms, there are strong fusions of models for ritual action and ethnoecological norms about how to interact with the other-than-human world that integrate animist worldview with both religious and practical action. The Druid rejection of conformity to religious rules within the context of global religion (the emphasis on individualism and countercultural orientation) removes both elements of the traditional ethnoecological-religious complex: collectively held place-based (localized) knowledge and collectively held rules for behavior. This creates a "trap" in the gap between motivation and action.

Without a distinctive Druid cultural model for sustainable action and relational ethical behavior, the individuals instantiate shared values (which are broad and vague) through mainstream models of action. While there is a concerted effort at political and magical environmental action (that was noted in my survey research, and supports Sarah Pike's 2019 work), there is no model for moving forward into personal practical action, either in an immediate sense or in addressing ecological crisis and potential future collapse. Instead, as David Kronenfeld's work on cultural models offered, "partially different people avail themselves of different cultural models as models for their own behavior" (2008: 211). Druids all feel motivated to take actions that are sustainable, but in the absence of uniquely Druidic models for those actions, they each select their own model from the overculture. One Druid, Elizabeth Boerner, reflected, "I remember we used to talk about activism in our group and I think we finally couldn't make up our minds on something we wanted to do, so we all did something different."

There is a range of cultural models for sustainable actions in American overculture, but most of the available models integrate with mainstream models of self and economy—that is, individualist selfhood that is not processual or relational combined with capitalist consumerism. These cultural models afford Druids a capacity to avoid excessive cognitive dissonance. Cognitive dissonance occurs when there is conflict between internal attitudes and external behavior (Festinger 1957). Druids are not simply variable in their choices to fulfill religious obligations to nature through sustainability and conservation. They are variable within similar contexts of socioeconomic limitations and available overcultural models for action. In general, there is a human propensity to low-cost actions that fulfill a social obligation, such as occasional political action rather than daily household action (e.g., see Wagner-Tsukamoto and Tadajewski 2006; Tadajewski and Wagner-Tsukamoto 2006). This means that while high motivation to be sustainable is necessary for sustainable behavior, it is not sufficient on its own to produce sustainability. Without sufficient knowledge in how to do so, and without sufficient social support or structures making action possible, people tend to select available low-cost actions that resolve cognitive dissonance between values and behaviors.

Cultural models exist within a motivational hierarchy; some carry motivational force (they function as goals) and some carry specific actions that channel motivation into behavior (D'Andrade 1995). We can think of cultural models as occupying at least three levels: master motives are shared values (such as the Druidic love for other-than-human beings), which are articulated into behavior through middle-range models (household sustainability, for example), and then into lower-range models for specific actions (selecting household cleaners). Articulation of all three levels is flexible and therefore produces behavioral variability in a social group (situational variability; D'Andrade 1995: 232). The current challenge for Druidry is that it lacks middle-range motivational models that articulate lower-range models with master motives, yielding high situational variability among Druids.

Both social and cognitive processes govern the decision-making process that produces situational variability. Authoritative people can marginalize some models or synthesize models (Strauss and Quinn 1997: 213) to reduce conflict. Without social processes to reduce conflict, people internalize conflicting models and have to reconcile them at the individual level. They can respond by choosing one model over another; unconsciously selecting parts of models and integrating them; unconsciously compromising between competing models; feeling ambivalent without a workable compromise; compartmentalizing conflicting models so they seem disconnected or are activated in different situations (Strauss and Quinn 1997: 213–14). Generally, people seek to reduce conflict between models in ways that produce positive emotions. Behaviors that produce positive emotions are reinforced over time (Strauss and Quinn 1997: 103). Druids seek to feel positively both in fulfilling their Druidic obligations and values and also in performing other aspects of their identity (related to American overculture, such as in their profession or social relationships). Druidry is a marginalized religion and so Druids must individually reconcile Druidic relational experiences, beliefs, and motivations with those of a materialist anthropocentric consumerist overculture. The individualist model of the self reconciles the two, as it is upheld by both the Druidic subculture and the US overculture. This means individual discretion and choice is paramount (Holland and Kipnis 1994; Strauss 2000, 2002 describe the individualist vs collectivist self models and how the former impacts Americans despite being not fully representative of the reality of selfhood). In my own experience and in discussing the challenges of enacting Druidic ethical values with other Druids, unconscious integration of disparate models, compromise, ambivalence, and compartmentalization are all present in Druidic articulation of conflicting models.

When I review my own and other Druids' choices, there are patterns we can conceptualize as behavioral traps we fall into that are difficult to escape due to their pervasiveness in the overculture (including in US environmentalism). First, there is the green consumption (market environmentalism) trap. Green consumption includes two different ways to reduce internal conflict: an unconscious combination of models of individual consumption choice with sustainability (actions that are sometimes financially costly but socially easy, such as buying solar panels, electric cars, energy efficient appliances, or recycled products) and/or compromise, such as making up for frequent flying by planting trees or reducing meat consumption (effectively working trade-offs in a carbon budget, but still not reaching any significant headway in reducing carbon emissions overall). Second, there is the loving the wilderness into harm trap, which involves compartmentalization of cultural models. In this case, there is a disconnection between individual choices and political and magical activism for sustainability or conservation. For example, Druid gatherings are carbon costly, involving many people flying and driving to remote locations for several days of ritual and workshops. This can produce an ironic paradox: Druids gather to conduct ritual in social groups that kindles powerful spiritual experiences of our relationship to the natural world and to share knowledge through relational frameworks for knowing, but in doing so, we simultaneously contribute to climate change. This paradox is not unique to Druids. It has been noted, for example, in studies that found that loving nature could result in the least-optimal household locations for impact on biodiversity (Peterson et al. 2008). Emotional connection can lead to environmental activism without sustainable action (e.g., see the Root-Bernstein et al. 2013 study on anthropomorphism being unpredictable for its utility for conservation). Essentially, environmentalists' love for nature can result in greater harm to nature when not mediated through collective models for action that meet human needs for social belonging and relational connection while mitigating environmental costs.

Even when we know better, it does not mean we can do better. We live in an overculture and economic structure that makes substantial behavioral change toward sustainability very difficult. We can call this a combination of the time and resources trap and the conflicting goods trap. Pagans in general are limited in the ways they are articulated in market-based societies, as goods and services for sale, rather than as religions supported in more stable and traditional ways. Because Druid groups and orders are relatively small and lack the structure and resources of more established organized religions (which have often accumulated resources over longer periods of time), individual Druids are generally responsible for purchasing books and other materials, travel to gatherings, and their own ritual objects and clothing. In the United States, the self as both worker and as Druid is dependent on generating income and consuming goods and services related to one's identity. Druids may be uncomfortable or unhappy about this, but may also lack the resources or capacity to avoid it:

> I have great reverence for combatting climate change and sustainability, [but] I go to the grocery store and I buy food all in plastic wrap and I'm appalled. We need activism. I'm doing my back yard in restorative gardening. I talk about it, but I'm not pushing people, like you have to do this . . . sometimes your job, which you need to support yourself, is just too much and too all-consuming, and it sucks the life out of you. As a society, it's gone that way. I don't know how to change that. (Elizabeth Boerner)

Druids widely recognize that it is very difficult to extricate themselves from the broader society of which they are a part. Personal relationships, particularly spouses and children, can make it even more difficult to enact household choices that demand more discomfort or inconvenience. Not only does the lack of time and resources limit available choices, Druids often find themselves (as I do) trying to balance the differing values, experiences, needs, and expectations within their families or households. Being loving to one's family members (and honoring their differences) while also fulfilling obligations to love nature can be challenging to reconcile:

> Trying to live better is probably the hardest part of Druidry. It's easy to develop yourself. Trying to expand that to what you do for other people or the environment is a much harder task. And I don't have as many answers as I would like to. When I first joined OBOD, it was what I can do on a personal basis. I've managed some of that, but I compromise all the time for my husband. I'm not a sufficiently social person to push other people. I'm just trying to live right for myself, but also seeing that that's not enough. But I don't have an answer yet. (Dawn)

I am not sure any Druids do have an answer yet. How much can we ask others to sacrifice for our values? How much can we ask of ourselves?

Reflecting on the limitations of Druidry (and even environmental anthropology) in terms of how I instantiate it in my own life was one of the most difficult parts of writing this book. I had to acknowledge that despite my training and middle-class career and income, I struggle and generally fail at sustainability. I have done the low-cost behaviors that I can to meet my sense of obligation to the nature spirits. I have done some higher-cost behaviors, but never consistently. My own actions have tended toward those that have low social cost—or even net social benefits (such as purchasing green products); low emotional cost—not requiring me to navigate complexities in relationships in households; low financial cost—not giving up jobs or lifestyles that are inherently unsustainable; and low time cost—writing a government representative or donating to an environmental nonprofit. I recognize my primary offering to the earth is primarily through teaching environmental justice to my students through my profession—as anthropologist, not as Druid. However, as many of us in environmental research have recognized, the environmental cost for me to live this profession is fairly high. Low-cost behaviors allow me (and other Druids) to perform relational values and obligations through materialist and consumerist actions, signal commitment to nature without confronting the necessity of dismantling capitalism and consumerism in order to forge a sustainable life and society.

The structural and cultural barriers to a truly relational lifestyle—to relational ethics in action—would require significantly stronger community in terms of models for action and in terms of practical and social support. It is not that no one does this, but it is rare because it is so difficult. An inner resistance to making changes that one is otherwise motivated to make has been noted outside of Druidry in convenience oriented cultures (e.g., Steg 2008; Hurd 2006; Gambini 2006). Despite advances in a relational spiritual movement, we still need to move farther along from a surface conservation ethic toward a deep conservation ethic, which would include the forms of learning and emotion that cause us to significantly and strongly prioritize saving every species (Wilson 1984: 138). Druids are trying to do so, but still need to address the gaps between affect, motivation, and action that insufficiently support practitioners in fully living out the relational values they have.

The Hope of Druidic Culture

In Edward O. Wilson's (1984) highly influential work *Biophilia*, he suggested that the conservation ethic would depend on two apparently conflicting (but in actuality, complementary) goals: personal freedom and environmental stewardship. Druidry is a religious subculture that attempts to provide pathways to both. Druidry has all the elements human ecologist Gene Anderson noted as necessary to save the environment: caring, factual, and pragmatic learning (especially about long-term processes), valuing cultural diversity and a sense of unity as an ecological whole (2014: 18–19). In many ways, Druidry has been building a successful ecocentric spiritual subculture for several hundred years. Small and often invisible in the United States, it nevertheless has grown and sustained itself, offering a pathway to deconstructing dualism and locating the self as inextricably bound in relationships of reciprocity with the earth. As a relatively new religious movement, and one that is loosely organized through non-authoritative facilitators and information marketplaces, it has organically developed cultural models for affect and motivation in ways very similar to any nonreligious subculture. Where it has yet to build collective models are in linking motivation to compelling specific pragmatic (everyday) actions.

Yet for a young new religious movement, it is making strides toward integrating environmental action and nature-centered spiritual experience. Druids in the survey reported religious practices that included planting trees, becoming vegan, voting, and protesting environmentally damaging projects. Fifty-nine percent of Druids engaged in at least one environmental protection action a year, 55 percent participated in local environmental restoration actions, and 49 percent participated in environmental education. There is significance in the spiritual practices, too—of rewriting our collective cultural story away from a "march of progress" at the expense and exploitation of others (Uhl 2004: 230), because such stories shape our ways of thought. Rather than focusing on commodification of "ecosystem services" and other still self-serving values, Druidry tells a story that is about the worth and value of all beings, and therefore justice, too, is for all beings (running parallel to Veronica Strang's 2017 environmental anthropological essay on human-no-human relations). The new story Druidry tells is one that aspires to sustainability—and even more so, to reciprocity, to respect, to mutuality. It just has not yet been fully developed.

It is not surprising, then, that environmentalists use Druidry to find a spiritual home for renewal and a space for the spiritual grief of connection in a climate disaster world. When we avoid the dissociation that many Westerners have with nature (Metzner 1995), we encounter a great deal of grief in the choice to continually remain connected to and aware of other-than-human nature. Pike (2019) had noted long-standing overlaps between Paganism and environmental activism, including facilitating processing the suffering of witnessing other beings' suffering, such as those of trees. Some Druids in the survey explained that they were environmentalists first—sometimes activists, sometimes scientists—and it was their environmentalism that drove them to find a spiritual home that would support and align with their environmentalism. While some are still struggling with enacting their values, Druids are aware of structural limitations to sustainability, even if their cultural models for action drawn from the overculture are not always fully consciously selected. This is evident in a high degree of political environmental activism among Druids and in conversations among Druids related to household-level sustainability that arise in many discussion forums, social media posts, grove meetings, and large gatherings.

While there is a challenge for generating new specific norms for behavior and attendant norm compliance, because new norms will compete against already existing norms and goals (Conte et al. 2014: 90), Druidry as a movement is not doomed to failure any more than any new religious movement is. Druids are forging creative responses to the challenges they face, both in terms of a consumerist capitalist overculture and a climate crisis world. Druids are providing a cultural construction that moves beyond humanism—beyond the emphasis on humanity that both science and Christianity (and most world religions) have affirmed. They are attempting to forge a middle way between individualism and collectivism, so that autonomy is upheld but an alternative is offered to the inhumane overculture. The Druidic emphasis on learning from one another and honoring diversity in human culture and worldview helps overcome basic roadblocks to conservation and sustainability, which are disunity among those who would work for it—through racism, ethnocentrism, and gender and class division—to pit people against one another who could otherwise work together (Anderson 2010: 23). The emphasis on mutual respect, deep listening, and ultimately—on peace-making and justice—is inherently foundational to the hope and promise of sustainability as a Druidic value and goal.

What Druids have yet to develop is the social organization to support as-yet-to-be-created specific models for sustainable action. Without these two components, it is much more difficult for individuals to break free from performing consumerism but endorsing sustainability. However, this work of developing a collectivist self and social support, contrary to occasional fears expressed by Druids, does not mean that Druidry must become organized in the same ways that Christianities are, around an authoritative text or leadership body. Already, the organic way that Druids have developed religious cultural models is continuing toward specific models for integrating religious ritual action, motivation and affect, and sustainable behavior that is within individual or household control. This development is fully possible and already happening through the processes inherent in a community of practice. For example, my own interest in understanding my own and others' successes and challenges with enacting ecocentric relational ethics more fully drove my own academic work (Kirner 2015) exploring Druidic revivals of folk botanical knowledge and the limitations of its success. In turn, and unbeknownst to me until conducting interviews for this book, this influenced the Grand Archdruid of AODA, Dana O'Driscoll, to write her own recently published book (and companion journal) integrating ritual and sustainable actions in the Wheel of the Year framework (2021). This was, in fact, precisely a book I had wanted for my own Druidic practice. This is the nature of community of practice and how shared models are developed in Druid community.

Over time, such work in community of practice has the hope to produce memory that is, like in the case of LEK/TEK, both historical and mythic, which is a key part of biodiversity conservation along with local knowledge. Such memory is sensory rather than archival and "challenges rather than surrenders to the purposeful straightening and organized forgetting imposed by modernity" (Nazarea 2006: 328). This form of memory links to ecological memory, which is what allows ecosystems to rebuild after large-scale disturbances, including both within-patch memory ("biological legacies" that are focal points for regeneration) and outside-reserve memory (biodiversity reserves and fallowed land) (Nazarea 2006). Ecological and human memory can integrate in the form of living or working memories used to reconstruct traditions and in the form of cultural borrowing or reconstruction (or re-imagination) based on past resources (as ADF permits through rules of cultural borrowing). Druidry is developing a religious culture to thrive in the context of climate crisis and severe cultural memory disruption (from the pre-materialist and pre-Christian Western past). Druids "mobilize an imaginary relation to the past for fundamentally different conceptions to the present" to address "cognitive and ethical void arising from irreparable loss" (Boutin et al. 2005: 8). The goal of such memory work is to unite aesthetics, emotion, and imagination—and an alternative to the capitalist consumerist and materialist globalized loss of biodiversity and cultural diversity at the heart of unsustainability and despair (Nazarea 2006). Dana O'Driscoll's work echoes what can be learned by cross-cultural studies of environmental ethics that work: minimize waste (use everything efficiently) and diversify use (incentivizing ecosystem health rather than monocropping) (Anderson 2010: 39).

A prime problem in the Western overcultural orientation toward nature is the disarticulation of solutions from place (Sullivan 2017). Druids are actively trying to rearticulate solutions with place through relational orientations; while they share global, broad, general values and concepts, they are encouraged to localize knowledge, practices, and actions. As both interview and survey data demonstrated, they do this through restorative gardening and wildcrafting, local environmental activism, planting trees and groves, and composting. This shows promise for meeting the needs to move forward from Leopold's land ethic toward an ethics of how to care for an unstable world—we no longer inhabit a world of stable ecosystems we can conserve, but rather a world of unstable ecosystems we must actively restore (Anderson 2010: 171). Movements such as Druidry, combining an awareness of environmental crisis at a global scale with localized practice, have the potential for making us more resilient (Berkes 2006). Yet what is apparent is that Druidry, while providing some support for countercultural ecocentric efforts, needs a more robust social support for people to make deeper ecocentric commitments to one another. In both practical and psychological ways, change is most sustainable when it is social and not individual—when we feel a sense of accountability, achievement, and mutual action. This means that we must consider, as we increasingly face the grief of climate crisis, reframing our individualist ethos to become more firmly and fully ecocentric. We can look for examples in indigenous animist religions within egalitarian political contexts to offer models for small-scale communities without a leader in power. This is the challenge: not only to return to practical, experiential, and localized knowledge but to also do the psychological work to heal from our hierarchical and anthropocentric overculture enough to creatively develop an alternative rather than merely react against it. Druids are aware of this challenge, and attempting to work toward meeting it:

> I don't know how to put it into a word, but whatever is the opposite of individualization. That I'm this island and I can do what I want, and I have the right and the freedom to do what I want. And not being aware of consequences. So it's "we" instead of "I." The "us together" is important as a value. The grove. The connections with each other. (Kat Reeves)

Druidry is a religious culture of reconnection, of mutually emergent process, of falling back in love with life—and in developing the capacity to face the grief that comes with loving life in a time of global ecological crisis.

Druids initially seek out a spirituality that speaks to their anomalous (often mystical) experiences, environmental concerns, and desire for freedom in developing their own beliefs and practices. Often stumbling upon Druidry through books or the internet, they become intrigued by the resonance other Druids' expressions of their spiritual paths have with their own. Even if they are solitary, they partake in practices—through accessing texts and conversations Druids share—that kindle more spiritual experiences and affirm a relational ontology, epistemology, and ethics. Druidry becomes a description of *who they are* and *what they do*—that is, not only a religion (in a broad sense) but also a role they take in society—re-enchanting, re-connecting, and re-membering in order to reunite humans with their wild souls and their integration with (and as) nature. Not quite traditional or local ecological knowledge system, but more than global religion, Druids form a community of practice centered on cultivating wisdom, justice, love, and reciprocity with all existences. Druids hope for and work toward a positive impact, however small, on the earth. Together, they try to affirm the courage to hope, and while there are still critical gaps in the structures and models necessary to fully support collective action to become more sustainable, the foundation of emotion and motivation has been laid. And this is no small feat, as "human beings make sacrifices for what they love, not for what they regard as merely a rational means to a material end" (Anderson 1996: 72). The day I finished editing this book, driving back from my horses in a beautiful Southern California winter day right at Imbolc—brilliant blue sky, emerald hills taking on a golden luster in the early evening sun—a red-tailed hawk wheeled suddenly in front of my car, tipping its wings sideways to show me a wide expanse of feathers before it flew away. And I thought this was fitting—the ending is a beginning. Druidry is young and growing, carrying the dreams we collectively share for healing our trauma of disconnection from the earth. As Brigid inspires our crafts and heals our wounds, her flame sparking our own inner fire of insight and creativity, her well restoring us—so too do Druids commit themselves once more to the dreams they hope will come to full fruition in time. The earth wakes up from winter, the promise of the harvest already beginning to germinate deep in the soil, pushing down roots. We, too, stretch as we wake up from our long slumber, ground our wild souls, and reach toward that future light.

BIBLIOGRAPHY

Abram, D. (1990), "The Perceptual Implications of Gaia," in A. H. Badiner (ed.), *Dharma Gaia: A Harvest of Essays in Buddhism and Ecology*, 75–92, Berkeley, CA: Parallax Press.

Adler, M. (1979) (Reprint 1996), *Drawing Down the Moon*, New York: Penguin.

Anderson, E. N. (1996), *Ecologies of the Heart: Emotion, Belief, and the Environment*, Oxford: Oxford University Press.

Anderson, E. N. (2010), *The Pursuit of Ecotopia: Lessons from Indigenous and Traditional Societies for the Human Ecology of Our Modern World*, Santa Barbara, CA: Praeger.

Anderson, E. N. (2014), *Caring for Place: Ecology, Ideology, and Emotion in Traditional Landscape Management*, Walnut Creek, CA: Left Coast Press.

Anderson, L. (2006), "Analytic Autoethnography," *Journal of Contemporary Ethnography*, 35 (4): 373–95.

Apffel-Marglin, F. (2019), "The Spiritual Politics of Bio-Cultural Regeneration," in A. K. Giri (ed.), *Practical Spirituality and Human Development: Creative Experiments for Alternative Futures*, 403–22, London: Palgrave Macmillan.

Asad, T. (1993), *Genealogies of Religion: Discipline and Reasons of Power in Christianity and Islam*, Baltimore, MD: Johns Hopkins University Press.

Atran, S. (2002), *In Gods We Trust: The Evolutionary Landscape of Religion*, Oxford: Oxford University Press.

Atran, S., D. L. Medin, and N. O. Ross (2005), "The Cultural Mind: Environmental Decision-Making and Cultural Modeling Within and Across Populations," *Psychological Review*, 112 (4): 744–76.

Bang, M., D. L. Medin, and S. Atran (2007), "Cultural Mosaics and Mental Models of Nature," *PNAS*, 104 (35): 13868–74.

Barrett, J. (2004), *Why Would Anyone Believe in God?*, Walnut Creek, CA: AltaMira.

Barrett, J. (2007), "Gods," in H. Whitehouse and J. Laidlaw (eds.), *Religion, Anthropology, and Cognitive Science*, 37–62, Durham, NC: Carolina Academic Press.

Barrett, J. (2011), *Cognitive Science, Religion, and Theology: From Human Minds to Divine Minds*, West Conshohochen, PA: Tempelton Press.

Basso, K. (1996), *Wisdom Sits in Places: Language and Landscape among the Western Apache*, Albuquerque, NM: University of New Mexico Press.

Bateson, G. (1972), *Steps to an Ecology of Mind*, Chicago, IL: University of Chicago Press.

Beckwith, B. R., T. Halber, and N. J. Turner (2017), "'You Have to *Do* It': Creating Agency for Environmental Sustainability through Experiential Education, Transformative Learning, and Kincentricity," in H. Kopnina and E. Shoreman-Ouimet (eds.), *Routledge Handbook of Environmental Anthropology*, 412–27, New York: Routledge.

Behar, R. (1997), *The Vulnerable Observer*, Boston, MA: Beacon Press.

Bennardo, G. and V. C. De Munck (2014), *Cultural Models: Genesis, Methods, and Experiences*, New York: Oxford University Press.

Bengtsson, J., P. Angelstam, T. Elmqvist, U. Emanuelsson, C. Folke, M. Ihse, F. Moberg, and M. Nystrom (2003), "Reserves, Resilience and Dynamic Landscapes," *Ambio*, 32 (6): 389–96.

Benvenuti, A. (2014), *Spirit Unleashed: Reimagining Human-Animal Relations*, Eugene, OR: Cascade Books.

Benvenuti, A. and E. Davenport (2011), "The New Archaic: A Neurophenomenological Approach to Religious Ways of Knowing," in B. M. Stafford (ed.), *A Field Guide to a New Meta-Field: Bridging the Humanities-Neurosciences Divide*, 204–38, Chicago, IL: University of Chicago Press.

Berger, H. (1998), *A Community of Witches, Contemporary Neo-Paganism and Witchcraft in the United States*, Columbia, SC: University of South Carolina Press.

Berger, H. and D. Ezzy (2007), *Teenage Witches*, London: Rutgers University Press.

Berger, H. A., E. A. Leach, and L. S. Shaffer (2003), *Voices from the Pagan Census: A National Survey of Witches and Neo-Pagans in the United States*, Columbia, SC: University of South Carolina Press.

Berkes, F. (1999), *Sacred Ecology: Traditional Ecological Knowledge and Resource Management*, Philadelphia, PA: Taylor and Francis.

Berkes, F. (2006), "Knowledge, Learning, and the Evolution of Conservation Practice for Social-Ecological System Resilience," *Human Ecology*, 34 (4): 479–94.

Berkes, M. K. and F. Berkes (2009), "Ecological Complexity, Fuzzy Logic, and Holism in Indigenous Knowledge," *Futures*, 41 (1): 6–12.

Best, S. (2018), "'Bone-Knowing' and the Matrix of Belief: The Ritual and Everyday Significance of Material Environments in Scotland's Contemporary Pagan Witchcraft," MA diss., Department of Social Anthropology, University of St Andrews, St Andrews.

Bielo, J. S. (2015), *Anthropology of Religion: The Basics*, 1st ed. New York: Routledge.

Billig, M. (2013), *Learn to Write Badly: How to Succeed in the Social Sciences*, New York: Cambridge University Press.

Bird-David, N. (1999), "'Animism' Revisited: Personhood, Environment, and Relational Epistemology," *Current Anthropology*, 40 (S1): S67–91.

Blackburn, T. C., K. Anderson, and E. J. Lehman (1993), *Before the Wilderness: Environmental Management by Native Californians*, Menlo Park, CA: Ballena Press.

Blain, J., D. Ezzy, and G. Harvey, eds. (2004), *Researching Paganisms*, Walnut Creek, CA: AltaMira Press.

Blain, J. and R. J. Wallis (2004), "Sacred Sites, Contested Rites/Rights: Contemporary Pagan Engagements with the Past," *Journal of Material Culture*, 9 (3): 237–61.

Bochner, A. and C. Ellis (2016), *Evocative Autoethnography: Writing Lives and Telling Stories*, London: Routledge.

Bochner, A. P. (2001), "Narrative's Virtues," *Qualitative Inquiry*, 7 (2): 131–57.

Bochner, A. P. and C. Ellis (1992), "Personal Narrative as a Social Approach to Interpersonal Communication," *Communication Theory*, 2 (2): 165–72.

Bourdieu, P. (1980), *The Logic of Practice*, Stanford, CA: Stanford University Press.

Bourguignon, E. (1973), *Religion, Altered States of Consciousness and Social Change*, Columbus, OH: The Ohio State University Press.

Boutin, A., A. G. Hargreaves, R. Leushuis, and L. J. Walters (2005), "Introduction," *Journal of European Studies*, 31 (1): 5–9.

Boyer, P. (2001), *Religion Explained: The Evolutionary Origins of Religious Thought*, New York: Basic Books.

Boyer, P. (2003), "Religious Thought and Behavior as By-products of Brain Function," *Trends in Cognitive Sciences*, 7: 119–24.

Boyer, P. and S. Walker (2000), "Intuitive Ontology and Cultural Input in the Acquisition of Religious Concepts," in K. S. Rosengren, C. N. Johnson, and P. L. Harris (eds.), *Imagining the Impossible: Magical, Scientific, and Religious Thinking in Children*, 130–56, Cambridge: Cambridge University Press.

Byers, Bruce A., Robert N. Cunliffe, and Andrew T. Hudak (2001), "Linking the Conservation of Culture and Nature: A Case Study of Sacred Forests in Zimbabwe," *Human Ecology*, 29: 187–218.

Callicott, J. B. and M. P. Nelson, eds. (1998), *The Great New Wilderness Debate: An Expansive Collection of Writings Defining Wilderness from John Muir to Gary Snyder*, Athens: University of Georgia Press.

Chan, A. (2012), "Anthropomorphism as a Conservation Tool," *Biodiversity and Conservation*, 21 (7): 1889–92.

Chang, H. (2016), *Autoethnography as Method*, London: Taylor and Francis.

Clark, A. and D. J. Chalmers (2010), "The Extended Mind," in R. Menary (ed.), *The Extended Mind*, 27–42, Cambridge, MA: MIT Press.

Clarke, P. B. and P. Byrne (1993), *Religion Defined and Explained*, New York: St. Martin's Press.

Clifton, C. S. (2006), *Her Hidden Children: The Rise of Wicca and Paganism in America*, Lanham, MD: AltaMira Press.

Coeckelbergh, M. (2017), "Beyond 'Nature': Towards More Engaged and Care-Full Ways of Relating to the Environment," in H. Kopnina and E. Shoreman-Ouimet (eds.), *Routledge Handbook of Environmental Anthropology*, 105–16, New York: Routledge.

Colding, J. and C. Folke (2001), "Social Taboos: 'Invisible' Systems of Local Resource Management and Biological Conservation," *Ecological Applications*, 11 (2): 584–600.

Conquergood, D. (1991), "Rethinking Ethnography: Towards a Critical Cultural Politics," *Communication Monographs*, 58: 179–94.

Conte, R., G. Andrighetto, and M. Campenni (2014), *Minding Norms: Mechanisms and Dynamics of Social Order in Agent Societies*, New York: Oxford University Press.

Cooper, M. (2011), *Contemporary Druidry: A Historical and Ethnographic Study*, Salt Lake City, UT: Sacred Tribes Press.

Cox, P. (2000), "Will Tribal Knowledge Survive the Millennium?," *Science*, 287 (5450): 44–5.

Creswell, J. (1998), *Qualitative Inquiry and Research Design: Choosing among Five Traditions*, Thousand Oaks, CA: Sage.

Csikszentmihalyi, M. (1990), *Flow: The Psychology of Optimal Experience*, New York: Harper and Row.

Curry, P. (2011), *Ecological Ethics: An Introduction*, Cambridge: Polity Press.

D'Andrade, R. (1995), *The Development of Cognitive Anthropology*, Cambridge: Cambridge University Press.

D'Andrade, R. G. and C. Strauss, eds. (1992), *Human Motives and Cultural Models*, Cambridge: Cambridge University Press.

Day, M. (2005), "Rethinking Naturalness: Modes of Religiosity and Religion in the Round," in H. Whitehouse and R. N. McCauley (eds.), *Mind and Religion: Psychological and Cognitive Foundations of Religiosity*, 85–108, Walnut Creek, CA: AltaMira Press.

Denzin, N. K. (1989), *Interpretive Biography*, Newbury Park, CA: Sage.

Derrida, J. (1978), *Writing and Difference*, trans. A. Bass, Chicago, IL: University of Chicago Press.

Descola, P. (2013), *Beyond Nature and Culture*, trans. J. Lloyd, Chicago, IL: University of Chicago Press.

Devereux, P., J. Steele, and D. Kubrin (1989), *Earthmind*, New York: Harper & Row.

Droogers, A. (1996), "Methodological Ludism: Beyond Religionism and Reductionism," in A. van Harskamp (ed.), *Conflicts in Social Science*, 44–67, London: Routledge.

Durkheim, E. (1947), *The Elementary Forms of the Religious Life: A Study in Religious Sociology*, New York City: Free Press.

Durkheim, E., S. A. Solovay, J. H. Mueller, and G. E. G. Catlin (1938), *The Rules of Sociological Method*, Chicago, IL: The University of Chicago Press.

Efird, R. (2017), "Perceiving Nature's Personhood: Anthropological Enhancements to Environmental Education," in H. Kopnina and E. Shoreman-Ouimet (eds.), *Routledge Handbook of Environmental Anthropology*, 441–51, New York: Routledge.

Eliade, M. (1964), *Shamanism: Archaic Techniques of Ecstasy*, Princeton, NJ: Princeton University Press.

Ellen, R. (1993), *The Cultural Relations of Classification: An Analysis of Nuaulu Animal Categories from Central Seram*, Cambridge: Cambridge University Press.

Ellis, C. (2007), "Telling Secrets, Revealing Lives: Relational Ethics in Research with Intimate Others," *Qualitative Inquiry*, 13 (1): 3–29.

Ellis, C., T. E. Adams, and A. P. Bochner (2011), "Autoethnography: An Overview," *Forum: Qualitative Social Research*, 12 (1).

Ellis, C. and A. P. Bochner (2000), "Autoethnography, Personal Narrative, Reflexivity," in N. K. Denzin and Y. S. Lincoln (eds.), *Handbook of Qualitative Research*, 2nd ed., 733–68, Thousand Oaks, CA: Sage.

Engelke, M. (2007), *A Problem of Presence: Beyond Scripture in an African Church*, Berkeley, CA: University of California Press.

Erikson, E. H. (1994), *Identity and the Life Cycle*, New York: W. W. Norton.

Escobar, A. (1999), "After Nature: Steps to an Antiessentialist Political Ecology," *Current Anthropology*, 40 (1): 1–30.

Evans, H. (1989), *Alternate States of Consciousness*, Wellingborough: Thorson's Publishing.

Ezzy, D. (2004), "Religious Ethnography: Practicing the Witch's Craft," in J. Blain, D. Ezzy, and G. Harvey (eds.), *Researching Paganisms: Religious Experiences and Academic Methodologies*, 113–28, Walnut Creek, CA: AltaMira Press.

Ezzy, D. (2006), "White Witches and Black Magic: Ethics and Consumerism in Contemporary Witchcraft," *Journal of Contemporary Religion*, 21 (1): 15–31.

Ezzy, D. (2007), "Popular Witchcraft and Environmentalism," *The Pomegranate*, 8 (1): 29–57.

Faivre, A. (1994), *Access to Western Esotericism*, Albany, NY: SUNY Press.

Faust, B. B. (1998), *Mexican Rural Development and the Plumed Serpent : Technology and Maya Cosmology in the Tropical Forest of Campeche, Mexico*, Westport, CT: Bergin & Garvey.

Festinger, L. (1957), *A Theory of Cognitive Dissonance*, Stanford, CA: Stanford University Press.

Fisher, W. K. (1985), "The Narrative Paradigm: In the Beginning," *Journal of Communication*, 35 (4): 74–89.

Fisher, W. R. (1984), "Narration as Human Communication Paradigm: The Case of Public Moral Argument," *Communication Monographs*, 51 (1): 1–22.

Fox, W. (1995), *Toward a Transpersonal Ecology: Developing New Foundations for Enviromentalism*, New York: State University of New York Press.

Frake, C. O. (1980), *Language and Cultural Description*, Stanford: Stanford University Press.

Gadgil, M., F. Berkes, and C. Folke (1993), "Indigenous Knowledge for Biodiversity Conservation," *Ambio*, 22 (2/3): 151–6.

Gagnon, C. A. and D. Berteaux (2009), "Integrating Traditional Ecological Knowledge and Ecological Science: A Question of Scale," *Ecology and Society*, 14 (2): 19.

Gambini, B. (2006), "Cultural Assumptions against Sustainability: An International Survey," *Journal of Geography in Higher Education*, 30 (2): 263–79.

Geertz, C. (1988), *Works and Lives: The Anthropologist as Author*, Palo Alto, CA: Stanford University Press.

Gibson, J. J. (1966), *The Senses Considered as Perceptual Systems*, Boston, MA: Houghton Mifflin.

Gibson, J. J. (1979), *The Ecological Approach to Visual Perception*, Boston, MA: Houghton Mifflin.

Gill, S. and J. Clammer (2019), "Multidimensional Mysticism," in A. K. Giri (ed.), *Practical Spirituality and Human Development: Creative Experiments for Alternative Futures*, 17–38, London: Palgrave Macmillan.

Glendinning, C. (1995), "Technology, Trauma, and the Wild," in T. Roszak, M. Gomes, and A. Kanner (eds.), *Ecopsychology: Restoring the Earth, Healing the Mind*, 41–54, Berkeley, CA: Counterpoint.

Gokhale, Y., N. A. Pala, A. K. Negi, J. A. Bhat, and N. P. Todaria (2011), "Sacred Landscapes as Repositories of Biodiversity: A Case Study from the Hariyali Devi Sacred Landscape, Uttarakhand," *International Journal of Conservation Science*, 2 (1): 37–44.

Goulet, J. (1998), *Ways of Knowing: Experience, Knowledge, and Power among the Dene Tha*, Lincoln, NE: University of Nebraska Press.

Greenway, R. (1995), "The Wilderness Effect and Ecopsychology," in T. Roszak, M. Gomes, and A. Kanner (eds.), *Ecopsychology: Restoring the Earth, Healing the Mind*, 122–35, Berkeley, CA: Counterpoint.

Greenwood, S. (2009), *The Anthropology of Magic*, London: Bloomsbury.

Grindal, B. (1983), "Into the Heart of Sisala Experience: Witnessing Death Divination," *Journal of Anthropological Research*, 39 (1): 60–80.

Guthrie, S. (1993), *Faces in the Clouds: A New Theory of Religion*, Oxford: Oxford University Press.

Guthrie, S. E. (2007), "Anthropology and Anthropomorphism in Religion," in H. Whitehouse and J. Laidlaw (eds.), *Religion, Anthropology, and Cognitive Science*, 37–62, Durham, NC: Carolina Academic Press.

Harding, S. (1994), "Is Science Multicultural?: Challenges, Resources, Opportunities, Uncertainties," *Configurations*, 2 (2): 301–30.

Harner, M. (1990), *The Way of the Shaman*, San Francisco, CA: Harper and Row.

Harper, S. (1995), "The Way of Wilderness," in T. Roszak, M. Gomes, and A. Kanner (eds.), *Ecopsychology: Restoring the Earth, Healing the Mind*, 183–200, Berkeley, CA: Counterpoint.

Harrington, M. (2000), "'Conversion' to Wicca?," *Diskus* 6.

Harrington, M. (2002), "The Long Journey Home: A Study of the Conversion Profiles of 35 Wiccan Men," *REVER Revista de Estudos Da Religiao*, 2: 18–50.

Harris, P. and K. Corriveau (2014), "Learning from Testimony about Religion and Science," in E. Robinson and S. Einav (eds.), *Trust and Skepticism: Children's Selective Learning from Testimony*, 28–41, New York: Psychology Press.

Harvey, G. (1999), "Coming Home and Coming Out Pagan But Not Converting," in C. Lamb and M. D. Bryant (eds.), *Religious Conversion: Contemporary Practices and Controversies*, 233–46, London: Cassell.

Harvey, G. (2005), *Animism: Respecting the Living World*, Columbia, SC: Columbia University Press.

Henare, A., M. Holbraad, and S. Wastell (2007), "Introduction: Thinking through Things," in A. Henare, M. Hobraad, and S. Wastell (eds.), *Thinking Through Things: Theorizing Artefacts Ethnographically*, 1–31, New York: Routledge.

Henkel, H. (2005), "Between Belief and Unbelief Lies the Performance of Salāt: Meaning and Efficacy of a Muslim Ritual," *The Journal of the Royal Anthropological Institute*, 11 (3): 487–507.

Henry, J. (1997), *The Scientific Revolution and the Origins of Modern Science*, Basingstoke: Macmillan.

Holland, D. and A. Kipnis (1994), "Metaphors for Embarrassment and Stories of Exposure: The Not-So-Egocentric Self in American Culture," *Ethos*, 22 (3): 316–42.

Holland, D. and N. Quinn, eds. (1987), *Cultural Models in Language and Thought*, Cambridge: Cambridge University Press.

Hufford, D. (1995), "Beings Without Bodies: An Experience-Centered Theory of the Belief in Spirits," in B. Walker (ed.), *Out of the Ordinary: Folklore and the Supernatural*, 11–45, Logan, UT: Utah State University Press.

Hurd, B. H. (2006), "Water Conservation and Residential Landscapes: Household Preferences, Household Choices," *Journal of Agricultural and Resource Economics*, 31 (2): 173–92.

Hutton, R. (1999), *The Triumph of the Moon: A History of Modern Pagan Witchcraft*, New York: Columbia University Press.

Hutton, R. (2009), *Blood and Mistletoe: The History of the Druids in Britain*, New Haven, CT: Yale University Press.

Ingold, T. (2000), *The Perception of the Environment: Essays on Livelihood, Dwelling and Skill*, London: Routledge.

Ingold, T. (2011), *Being Alive: Essays on Movement, Knowledge and Description*, London: Routledge.

James, W. (1902), *Varieties of Religious Experience: A Study in Human Nature*, New York: Penguin.

James, W. (1950), *Principles of Psychology*, New York: Dover.

Johnston, L. F. (2013), *Religion and Sustainability: Social Movements and the Politics of the Environment*, Sheffield: Equinox.

Jung, C. G. (1970), *C.G. Jung: Psychological Reflections: A New Anthology of His Writings, 1905–1961*, Princeton, NJ: Princeton University Press.

Kehoe, A. (2000), *Shamans and Religion: An Anthropological Exploration in Critical Thinking*, Prospect Heights, IL: Waveland.

Kellenberger, J. (2017), *Religious Epiphanies across Traditions and Cultures*, London: Palgrave Macmillan.

Kellert, S. R. and E. O. Wilson, eds. (1995), *The Biophilia Hypothesis*, Washington, DC: Island Press.

Kimmerer, R. W. (2000), "Native Knowledge for Native Ecosystems," *Journal of Forestry*, 98: 4–9.

Kimmerer, R. W. (2002), "Weaving Traditional Ecological Knowledge into Biological Education: A Call to Action," *Bioscience*, 52 (5): 432–8.

Kimmerer, R. W. (2013), *Braiding Sweetgrass : Indigenous Wisdom, Scientific Knowledge and the Teachings of Plants*, Minneapolis: Milkweed Editions.

Kirner, K. D. (2015), "Pursuing the Salmon of Wisdom: The Sacred in Folk Botanical Knowledge Revival among Modern Druids," *Journal for the Study of Religion, Nature, and Culture*, 9 (4): 448–82.

Kirner, K. D. (2017), "Cognition and Cultural Modeling," in H. Kopnina and E. Shoreman-Ouimet (eds.), *Routledge Handbook of Environmental Anthropology*, 428–40, London: Routledge.

Kirsch, T. (2004), "Restagin the Will to Believe: Religious Pluralism, Anti-Syncretism, and the Problem of Belief," *American Anthropologist*, 106 (4): 699–709.

Kopnina, H. N. (2012), "The Lorax Complex: Deep Ecology, Ecocentrism and Exclusion," *Journal of Integrative Environmental Sciences* (9) 4: 234–54.

Kronenfeld, D. B. (2008), *Culture, Society, and Cognition: Collective Goals, Values, Action, and Knowledge*, Berlin: Walter de Gruyter.

LaChapelle, D. (1988), *Sacred Land, Sacred Sex : Rapture of the Deep : Concerning Deep Ecology and Celebrating Life*, Silverton, CO: Finn Hill Arts.

Laidlaw, J. (2016), "A Well-Disposed Social Anthropologist's Problems with the 'Cognitive Science of Religion'," *Anthropology of This Century*, 16.

Lansing, J. S. (2007), *Priests and Programmers: Technologies of Power in the Engineered Landscape of Bali*, Princeton, NJ: Princeton University Press.

Le Guin, U. (1985), *The Language of the Night: Essays on Fantasy and Science Fiction*, New York: Berkeley Books.

Le Guin, U. (1986), "The Mother Tongue," *Bryn Mawr Alumnae Bulletin*, Summer: 3–4.

Lee, D. (1993), "Religious Perspective in Anthropology," in A. C. Lehmann and J. E. Myers (eds.), *Magic, Witchcraft, and Religion: An Anthropological Study of the Supernatural*, 3rd ed., 10–17, Palo Alto, CA: Mayfield.

Leopold, A. (1949), *A Sand County Almanac*, New York: Oxford University Press.

Levinas, E. (1969), *Totality and Infinity*, trans. A. Lingis, Pittsburg, PA: Duquesne University Press.

Lévy-Bruhl, L. (1926), *How Natives Think*, trans. L. A. Claire, New York: Knopf.

Lévy-Bruhl, L. (1949/1975), *The Notebooks on Primitive Mentality*, trans. P. Riviere, New York: Harper & Row.

Lewis, G. (2004), "Religious Doctrine or Experience: A Matter of Seeing, Learning, or Doing," in H. Whitehouse and J. Laidlaw (eds.), *Ritual and Memory: Toward a Comparative Anthropology of Religion*, 155–72, Walnut Creek, CA: AltaMira Press.

Lewis, J. R. (2015), "New Age Medicine Men versus New Age *Noaidi*: Same Neoshamanism, Different Sociopolitical Situation," in S. E Kraft, T. Fonneland, and J. R. Lewis (eds.), *Nordic Neoshamanisms*, 127–40, New York: Palgrave Macmillan.

Lincoln, B. (1994), *Authority: Construction and Corrosion*, Chicago, IL: University of Chicago Press.

Livingston, J. (1981), *The Fallacy of Wildlife Conservation*, Toronto: McClelland and Stewart.

Luhrmann, T. M. (1989), *Persuasions of the Witch's Craft: Ritual Magic in Contemporary England*, Cambridge, MA: Harvard University Press.

Luhrmann, T. M. (2022), *How God Becomes Real: Kindling the Presence of Invisible Others*, Princeton, NJ and Oxford: Princeton University Press.

Lynch, G. (2010), "Object Theory: Towards an Intersubjective, Mediated, and Dynamic Theory of Religion," in D. Morgan (ed.), *Religion and Material Culture: The Matter of Belief*, 40–54, London: Routledge.

Lyotard, J. (1984), *The Postmodern Condition: A Report on Knowledge*, trans. G. Bennington and B. Massumi, Minneapolis, MN: University of Minnesota Press.

Macy, J. (1987), "Faith and Ecology," *Resurgence*, July–August: 18–21.

Maffi, L., ed. (2001), *On Bio-Cultural Diversity: Linking Language, Knowledge, and the Environment*, Washington and London: Smithsonian Institute Press.

Maffi, L. (2005), "Linguistic, Cultural, and Biological Diversity," *Annual Review of Anthropology*, 34: 599–617.

Magliocco, S. (1996), "Ritual Is My Chosen Art Form: The Creation of Ritual as Folk Art among Contemporary Pagans," in J. R. Lewis (ed.), *Magical Religions and Modern Witchcraft*, 93–120, Albany, NY: State University of New York Press.

Magliocco, S. (2004), *Witching Culture: Folklore and Neo-Paganism in America*, Philadelphia, PA: University of Pennsylvania Press.

Magliocco, S. (2018), "Reconnecting to Everything: Fairies in Contemporary Paganism," in M. Ostling (ed.), *Fairies, Demons, and Nature Spirits: 'Small Gods' at the Margins of Christendom*, 325–48, London: Palgrave Macmillan.

Mair, J. (2013), "Cultures of Belief," *Anthropological Theory*, 12 (4): 448–66.

Malafouris, L. (2013), *How Things Shape the Mind: A Theory of Material Engagement*, Cambridge, MA: MIT Press.

Malinowski, B. (1954), *Magic, Science, and Religion*, New York: Doubleday.

Marcus, G. E. and M. M. J. Fisher (1986), *Anthropology as Cultural Critique: An Experimental Moment in the Human Sciences*, Chicago, IL: University of Chicago Press.

Maslow, A. H. (1964), *Religions, Values, and Peak-Experiences*, Columbus, OH: Ohio State University Press.

Maslow, A. H. (1970), "Psychological Data and Value Theory," in A. Maslow (ed.), *New Knowledge of Human Values*, Gateway edition, Chicago, IL: Henry Regnery.

Mauss, M. (1972), *A General Theory of Magic*, trans. R. Brain, New York: W. W. Norton.

Mayer, G. (2008), "The Figure of the Shaman as a Modern Myth: Some Reflections on the Attractiveness of Shamanism in Modern Societies," *The Pomegranate*, 10 (1): 70–103.

Mayer, G. and R. Grunder (2010), "Coming Home or Drifting Away—Magic Practice in the 21st Century," *Journal of Contemporary Religion*, 25 (3): 395–418.

McDaniel, J. (2011), "Introduction: Spiritual Body, Spiritual Senses, Past and Present," in T. Cattoi and J. McDaniel (eds.), *Perceiving the Divine through the Human Body: Mystical Sensuality*, 1–16, New York: Palgrave MacMillan.

McDaniel, J. (2018), *Lost Ecstasy: Its Decline and Transformation in Religion*, Cham, Switzerland: Springer Nature.

Metzner, R. (1995), "The Psychopathology of the Human-Nature Relationship," in T. Roszak, M. Gomes, and A. Kanner (eds.), *Ecopsychology: Restoring the Earth, Healing the Mind*, 55–67, Berkeley, CA: Counterpoint.

Milton, K. (2002), *Loving Nature: Towards an Ecology of Emotion*, London and New York: Routledge.

Moeller, H., F. Berkes, P. O'Brian Lyver, and M. Kislalioglu (2004), "Combining Science and Traditional Ecological Knowledge: Monitoring Populations for Co-Management," *Ecology and Society*, 9 (3): 2.

Morgan, D. (2010), "Introduction: The Matter of Belief," in D. Morgan (ed.), *Religion and Material Culture: The Matter of Belief*, 1–18, London: Routledge.

Motz, M. (1998), "The Practice of Belief," *Journal of American Folklore*, 111 (441): 339–55.

Naess, A. (1985), "Identification as a Source of Deep Ecological Attitudes," in M. Tobias (ed.), *Deep Ecology*, San Diego, CA: Avant Books.

Naess, A. (1988), "Self-Realization: An Ecological Approach to Being in the World," in J. Seed, J. Macy, P. Fleming, and A. Naess (eds.), *Thinking Like a Mountain: Towards a Council of All Beings*, Philadelphia, PA: New Society Publishers.

Naess, A. (1989), *Ecology, Community, and Lifestyle: Outline of an Ecosophy*, trans. and ed. D. Rothenberg, Cambridge: Cambridge University Press.

Nazarea, V. D. (2006), "Local Knowledge and Memory in Biodiversity Conservation," *Annual Review of Anthropology*, 35: 317–35.

Needham, R. (1972), *Belief, Language, and Experience*, Chicago, IL: University of Chicago Press.

Neisser, U. (1976), *Cognition and Reality: Principles and Implications of Cognitive Psychology*, New York: WH Freeman and Company.

Neisser, U. (1988), "Five Kinds of Self-knowledge," *Philosophical Psychology*, 1 (1): 35–59.

Nelson, R. (1983), *Make Prayers to the Raven: A Koyukon View of the Northern Forest*, Chicago, IL: University of Chicago Press.

Newberg, A. and E. D'Aquili (2001), *Why God Won't Go Away: Brain Science and the Biology of Belief*, New York: Ballantine Books.

Nisbett, Richard E. (2003), *The Geography of Thought*, New York: Simon and Schuster.

O'Driscoll, Dana (2021), *Sacred Actions: Living the Wheel of the Year through Earth-Centered Sustainable Practices.* Atglen, PA: Red Feather Mind, Body, Spirit.

Order of Bards, Ovates, and Druids (n.d.), *Book of Ritual.*

Order of Bards, Ovates, and Druids (n.d.), "Peacemaking in Druidry." Available online: https://druidry.org/get-involved/peacemaking-in-druidry (accessed May 14, 2023).

Order of Bards, Ovates, and Druids (n.d.), "The Use of Ritual in Druidry." Available online: https://druidry.org/druid-way/teaching-and-practice/use-ritual-druidry (accessed May 14, 2023).

Orion, L. (1995), *Never Again the Burning Times: Paganism Revived*, Prospect Heights, IL: Waveland Press.

Paden, W. (1988), *Religious Worlds: The Comparative Study of Religion*, Boston, MA: Beacon Press.

Pargament, K. I. (2002), "Religious Methods of Coping: Resources for the Conservation and Transformation of Significance," in E. Shafranske (ed.), *Religion and the Practice of Clinical Psychology*, Washington, DC: American Psychological Association.

Pearson, J. (2002), "'Going Native in Reverse': The Insider as Researcher in British Wicca," in E. Arweck and M. D. Stringer (eds), *Theorizing Faith: The Insider/ Outsider Problem in the Study of Ritual*, 97–113, Birmingham: University of Birmingham Press.

Peters, L. and D. Prince-Williams (1980), "Toward an Experiential Analysis of Shamanism," *American Ethnologist*, 7 (3): 397–418.

Peterson, M. N., X. Chen, and J. Liu (2008), "Household Location Choices: Implications for Biodiversity Conservation," *Conservation Biology*, 22 (4): 912–21.

Pierotti, R. and D. Wildcat (2000), "Traditional Ecological Knowledge: The Third Alternative (Commentary)," *Ecological Applications*, 10 (5): 1333–40.

Pike, S. M. (1996), "Rationalizing the Margins: A Review of Legitimation and Ethnographic Practice in Scholarly Research on Neo-Paganism," in J. R. Lewis (ed.), *Magical Religion and Modern Witchcraft*, 353–72, Albany, NY: State University of New York Press.

Pike, S. M. (2001), *Earthly Bodies, Magical Selves: Contemporary Pagans and the Search for Community*, Berkeley, CA: University of California Press.

Pike, S. M. (2019), "'Wild Nature' and the Lure of the Past: The Legacy of Romanticism among Young Pagan Environmentalists," in S. Feraro and E. D. White (eds.), *Magic and Witchery in the Modern West: Celebrating the Twentieth Anniversary of 'The Triumph of the Moon*, 131–52, Cham, Switzerland: Springer Nature.

Posey, D. A., ed. (1999), *Cultural and Spiritual Values of Bio-Diversity*, London: UNEP Smithsonian Institute Press.

Poulos, C. N. (2021), *Essentials of Autoethnography*, Washington, DC: American Psychological Association.

Pungetti, G., G. Oviedo, and D. Hooke, eds. (2012), *Sacred Species and Sites: Advances in Bioculture Conservation*, New York: Cambridge University Press.

Pyrko, I., V. Dörfler, and C. Eden (2017), "Thinking Together: What Makes Communities of Practice Work?," *Human Relations*, 70 (4): 389–409.

Pyrko, I., V. Dörfler, and C. Eden (2019), "Communities of Practice in Landscapes of Practice," *Management Learning*, 50 (4): 482–99.

Pyysiäinen, I. (2005), "Religious Conversion and Modes of Religiosity," in H. Whitehouse and R. N. McCauley, *Mind and Religion: Psychological and Cognitive Foundations of Religiosity*, 149–66, Walnut Creek, CA: AltaMira Press.

Ramakrishnan, P. S., K. G. Saxena, and U. M. Chandrashekara, eds. (1998), *Conserving the Sacred for Biodiversity Management*, Enfield, NH: Science.

Rappaport, R. A. (1968), *Pigs for the Ancestors; Ritual in the Ecology of a New Guinea People*, New Haven, CT: Yale University Press.

Reid, S. (1996), "As I do Will, So Mote It Be: Magic as Metaphor in Neo-Pagan Witchcraft," in J. R. Lewis (ed.), *Magical Religion and Modern Witchcraft*, 141–67, Albany, NY: State University of New York Press.

Reo, N. J. (2011), "The Importance of Belief Systems in Traditional Ecological Knowledge Initiatives," *International Indigenous Policy Journal*, 2 (4): 8–.

Richardson, L. (2005), "Writing: A Method of Inquiry," in N. K. Denzin and Y. S. Lincoln (eds.), *Handbook of Qualitative Research*, 2nd ed., 959–78, Newbury Park, CA: Sage.

Rizutto, A. M. (1979), *The Birth of the Living God*, Chicago, IL: University of Chicago Press.

Robertson, A. F. (1996), "The Development of Meaning: Ontogeny and Culture," *Journal of Royal Anthropological Institute*, 2: 591–610.

Ronai, C. R. (1995), "Multiple Reflections of Child Sex Abuse: An Argument for a Layered Account," *Journal of Contemporary Ethnography*, 23 (4): 395–426.

Root-Bernstein, M., L. Douglas, A. Smith, and D. Veríssimo (2013), "Anthropomorphized Species as Tools for Conservation: Utility Beyond Prosocial, Intelligent and Suffering Species," *Biodiversity and Conservation*, 22 (8): 1577–89.

Rorty, R. (1982), *Consequences of Pragmatism (Essays 1972–1980)*, Minneapolis, MN: University of Minnesota Press.

Rosaldo, R. (1989), *Culture and Truth: The Remaking of Social Analysis*, Boston: Beacon Press.

Roszak, T. (1993a), "Awakening the Ecological Unconscious," *In Context*, 34 (Winter). Available online: https://www.context.org/iclib/ic34/roszak/ (accessed January 8, 2022).

Roszak, T. (1993b), *The Voice of the Earth: An Exploration of Ecopsychology*, New York: Touchstone.

Roszak, T. (1995), "Where Psyche Meets Gaia," in T. Roszak, M. Gomes, and A. Kanner (eds.), *Ecopsychology: Restoring the Earth, Healing the Mind*, 1–20, Berkeley, CA: Counterpoint.

Rountree, K. (2012), "Neo-Paganism, Animism, and Kinship with Nature," *Journal of Contemporary Religion*, 27 (2): 305–20.

Rountree, K. (2017), "Introduction: 'We Are the Weavers, We Are the Web': Cosmopolitan Entanglements in Modern Paganism," in K. Rountree (ed.), *Cosmopolitanism, Nationalism, and Modern Paganism*, 1–20, New York: Palgrave Macmillan.

Samuel, G. (1990), *Mind, Body and Culture: Anthropology and the Biological Interface*, Cambridge: Cambridge University Press.

Schutz, A. (1962), "Common-Sense and Scientific Interpretation of Human Action," in *Collected Papers of Alfred Schutz*, vol. 1, 3–47, The Hague, the Netherlands: Martinus Nijhoff.

Seed, J. (2007/1985), "Anthropocentrism," in B. Devall and G. Sessions (eds.), *Deep Ecology: Living as if Nature Mattered*, 243–7, Layton, UT: Gibbs M. Smith.

Selberg, T. (2015), "Shamanism—A Spiritual Heritage?: The Significance of the Past in Shamanic Discourses," in S. E Kraft, T. Fonneland, and J. R. Lewis (eds), *Nordic Neoshamanisms*, 89–102, New York: Palgrave Macmillan.

Sewall, L. (1995), "The Skill of Ecological Perception," in T. Roszak, M. Gomes, and A. Kanner (eds.), *Ecopsychology: Restoring the Earth, Healing the Mind*, 201–15, Berkeley, CA: Counterpoint.

Shepard, P. (1982), *Nature and Madness*, San Francisco, CA: Sierra Club Books.

Shweder, R. A. (1991), *Thinking through Culture: Expeditions in Cultural Psychology*, Cambridge, MA: Harvard University Press.

Shweder, R. A. (2012), "Anthropology's Disenchantment with the Cognitive Revolution," *Topics in Cognitive Science*, 4: 354–61.

Sidky, H. (2017), *The Origins of Shamanism, Spirit Beliefs, and Religiosity: A Cognitive Anthropological Perspective*, London: Rowman & Littlefield.

Siikala, A. (1982), "The Siberian Shaman's Technique of Ecstasy," in N. Holm (ed.), *Religious Ecstasy*, 103–21, Stockholm: Scripta Instituti Donnerianna Aboensis XI.

Singler, B. (n.d.), "A Discussion of Conversion through the Example of Modern Pagan Witchcraft," 1–14. Available online: https://www.academia.edu/5068352 /A_Discussion_of_Conversion_through_the_Example_of_Modern_Pagan _Witchcraft (accessed February 19, 2023).

Smith, David M. (1998), "An Athapaskan Way of Knowing: Chipewyan Ontology," *American Ethnologist*, 25 (3): 412–32.

Smith, A. C. T. (2014), *Thinking about Religion: Extending the Cognitive Science of Religion*, New York: Palgrave Macmillan.

Sørensen, J. (2007), *A Cognitive Theory of Magic*, Lanham, MD: AltaMira Press.

Sponsel, L. (2012), *Spiritual Ecology: A Quiet Revolution*, Santa Barbara, CA: Praeger.

Sponsel, L. (2017), "Spiritual Ecology, Sacred Places, and Biodiversity Conservation," in H. Kopnina and E. Shoreman-Ouimet (eds.), *Routledge Handbook of Environmental Anthropology*, 132–43, New York: Routledge.

Sponsel, Leslie E., Poranee Natadecha-Sponsel, Nukul Ruttnadakul, and Somporn Juntadach (1998), "Sacred and/or Secular Approaches to Biodiversity Conservation in Thailand," *Worldviews: Environment, Culture, and Religion*, 2: 155–67.

Steg, Linda (2008), "Promoting Household Energy Conservation," *Energy Policy*, 36 (12): 4449–53.

Stephen, M. (1995), *A'asia's Gifts: A Study in Magic and the Self*, Berkeley, CA: University of California Press.

Strang, V. (2017), "Justice for All: Inconvenient Truths and Reconciliation in Human-Non-Human Relations," in H. Kopnina and E. Shoreman-Ouimet (eds.), *Routledge Handbook of Environmental Anthropology*, 259–75, New York: Routledge.

Strauss, C. (2000), "The Cultural Concept and the Individualism-Collectivism Debate: Dominant and Alternative Attributions for Class in the United

States," in L. P. Nucci, G. B. Saxe, and E. Turiel (eds.), *Culture, Thought, and Development*, 85–114, Mahwah, NJ: Lawrence Erlbaum Associates.

Strauss, C. (2002), "Not-So-Rugged Individualists: US American's Conflict Ideas about Poverty," in F. F. Piven, J. Acker, M. Hallock, and S. Morgen (eds.), *Work, Welfare, and Politics: Confronting Poverty in the Wake of Welfare Reform*, 55–69, Eugene, OR: Oregon State University Press.

Strauss, C. and N. Quinn (1997), *A Cognitive Theory of Cultural Meaning*, Cambridge: Cambridge University Press.

Sullivan, S. (2017), "What's Ontology Got to Do with It? On the Knowledge of Nature and the Nature of Knowledge in Environmental Anthropology," in H. Kopnina and E. Shoreman-Ouimet (eds.), *Routledge Handbook of Environmental Anthropology*, 155–69, New York: Routledge.

Tadajewski, M. and S. Wagner-Tsukamoto (2006), "Anthropology and Consumer Research: Qualitative Insights into Green Consumer Behavior," *Qualitative Market Research*, 9 (1): 8–25.

Tambiah, S. (1991), *Magic, Science, Religion, and the Scope of Rationality*, Cambridge: Cambridge University Press.

Tart, C., ed. (1969), *Altered States of Consciousness: A Book of Readings*, San Francisco, CA: Harper.

Taves, A. and E. Asprem (2016), "Experience as Event: Event Cognition and the Study of (Religious) Experiences," *Religion, Brain & Behavior*, 7 (1): 43–62.

Taylor, B. (2010), *Dark Green Religion: Nature, Spirituality, and the Planetary Future*, Berkeley, CA: University of California Press.

Tellegen, A. and G. Atkinson (1974), "Openness to Absorbing and Self-Altering Experiences ('Absorption'), a Trait Related to Hypnotic Susceptibility," *Journal of Abnormal Psychology*, 83 (3): 268–77.

Tremlin, T. (2005), "Divergent Religion: A Dual-Process Model of Religious Thought, Behavior, and Morphology," in H. Whitehouse and R. N. McCauley (eds.), *Mind and Religion: Psychological and Cognitive Foundations of Religiosity*, 69–84, Walnut Creek, CA: AltaMira Press.

Turner, N. J., M. B. Ignace, and R. Ignace (2000), "Traditional Ecological Knowledge and Wisdom of Aboriginal Peoples in British Columbia," *Ecological Applications*, 10 (5): 1275–87.

Turner, V. W. (1995), *The Ritual Process: Structure and Anti-Structure*, New York: Aldine de Gruyter.

Tylor, E. B. (1970), *Religion in Primitive Culture*, Gloucester, MA: P. Smith.

Uhl, C. (2004), *Developing Ecological Consciousness: Path to a Sustainable World*, Lanham, MD: Rowman & Littlefield.

UNEP United Nations Environment Programme (1998), *Report of the Fourth Meeting of the Parties to the Convention on Biodiversity*, Nairobi, Kenya: United Nations Environment Programme, UNEP/CBD/COP/4/27.

Unsworth, S. J. (2012), "Anthropology in the Cognitive Sciences: The Value of Diversity," *Topics in Cognitive Science*, 4: 429–36.

Vaitl, D. and U. Ott (2005), "Altered States of Consciousness Induced by Psychophysiological Techniques," *History of Political Thought*, 3 (1): 9–30.

Van der Veer, P. (2014), *The Modern Spirit of Asia: The Spiritual and the Secular in China and India*, Princeton, NJ: Princeton University Press.

Van Gennep, A. (1909), *The Rites of Passage*, London: Routledge.

Van Leeuwen, N. (2014), "Religious Credence Is Not Factual Belief," *Cognition*, 133 (3): 698–715.

Versluis, A. (2007), *Magic and Mysticism: An Introduction to Western Esotericism*, Plymouth: Roman and Littlefield.

Vitebsky, P. (2010), "Shamanism," in P. Moro and J. Myers (eds.), *Magic, Witchcraft, and Religion: A Reader in the Anthropology of Religion*, 150–7, New York: McGraw-Hill.

Viveiros de Castro, E. (1998), "Cosmological Deixis and Amerindian Perspectivism," *Journal of the Royal Anthropological Institute*, 4 (3): 469–88.

Viveiros de Castro, E. (2011), "Zeno and the Art of Anthropology: Of Lies, Beliefs, Paradoxes, and Other Truths," *Common Knowledge*, 17 (1): 128–45.

Wagner-Tsukamoto, S. and M. Tadajewski (2006), "Cognitive Anthropology and the Problem-Solving Behaviour of Green Consumers," *Journal of Consumer Behaviour*, 5: 235–44.

Wallace, A. (1956), "Revitalization Movements," *American Anthropologist*, 58 (2): 264–81.

Walsh, R. (1995), "Phenomenological Mapping: A Method for Describing and Comparing States of Consciousness," *The Journal of Transpersonal Psychology*, 27 (1): 25–56.

Wanless, C. (2019), *The Religious and Social Significance of Individualized Religion: Practice Communities and Networks of Transmission in Hebden Bridge*, Ann Arbor, MI: ProQuest Dissertations Publishing.

Washington, H., B. Taylor, H. N. Kopnina, P. Cryer, and J. J. Piccolo (2017), "Why Ecocentrism is the Key Pathway to Sustainability," *Ecological Citizen*, 1 (1): 35–41.

Weber, M. (1946), *From Max Weber: Essays in Sociology*, trans. H. H. Gerth and C. W. Mills, Oxford: Oxford University Press.

Weed, L. E. (2011), "Daoist Mysticism: Embodiment, Eudaimonia, and Flow," in T. Cattoi and J. McDaniel (eds.), *Perceiving the Divine through the Human Body: Mystical Sensuality*, 105–20, New York: Palgrave MacMillan.

Wenger, E. (1998), *Communities of Practice: Learning, Meaning and Identity*, Cambridge: Cambridge University Press.

Wenger, E. and B. Wenger-Trayner (2020), *Learning to Make a Difference: Value Creation in Social Learning Spaces*, Cambridge: Cambridge University Press.

Wenzel, G. W. (2004), "From TEK to IQ: Inuit Qaujimajatuqangit and Inuit Cultural Ecology," *Arctic Anthropology*, 41 (2): 238–50.

White, L. A. (2021), *World Druidry: A Globalizing Path of Nature Spirituality*, self-published.

Whitehouse, H. (2000), *Arguments and Icons: Divergent Modes of Religiosity*, Oxford: Oxford University Press.

Whitehouse, H. (2004), "Toward a Comparative Anthropology of Religion," in H. Whitehouse and J. Laidlaw (eds.), *Ritual and Memory: Toward a Comparative Anthropology of Religion*, 187–205, Walnut Creek, CA: AltaMira Press.

Whitehouse, H. and J. Laidlaw (2007), *Religion, Anthropology, and Cognitive Science*, Durham, NC: Carolina Academic Press.

Wilson, E. O. (1984), *Biophilia: The Human Bond with Other Species*, Cambridge, MA: Harvard University Press.

Winkelman, M. (2014), "Evolutionary Views of Etheogenic Consciousness," in J. H. Ellens (ed.), *Seeking the Sacred with Psychoactive Substances: Chemical Paths to Spirituality and God*, 34–64, Santa Barbara, CA: Praeger.

Wise, A. (2002), *Awakening the Mind: A Guide to Mastering the Power of Your Brain Waves*, New York: Tarcher/Putnam.

Woolley, J. (2018), "Practical Magic: The Political Economy of British Paganism, From Religious Affiliation toward Popular Enchantment," *Implicit Religion*, 21 (2): 180–201.

Wu, S. (2019), "Ecological Holism: Arne Naess's Gestalt Ontology and Merleau-Ponty's Bodily-Flesh Phenomenology," in A. K. Giri (ed.), *Practical Spirituality and Human Development: Creative Experiments for Alternative Futures*, 437–54, London: Palgrave Macmillan.

Wullf, D. (2014), "Mystical Experience," in E. Cardeña, S. Lynn, and S. Krippner (eds.), *Varieties of Anomalous Experience: Examining the Scientific Evidence*, 397–440, Washington, DC: American Psychological Association.

York, M. (2010), "Idolatry, Ecology, and the Sacred as Tangible," *The Pomegranate*, 12: 74–93.

Zaleha, B. D. (2017), "Battle of the Ecologies: Deep versus Political: An Investigation into Anthropocentrism in the Social Sciences," in H. Kopnina and E. Shoreman-Ouimet (eds.), *Routledge Handbook of Environmental Anthropology*, 288–301, New York: Routledge.

INDEX

absorption   56, 68, 70, 74
action   73, 100, 112, 115, 117, 119,
    125, 168
  and cultural modeling   139, 195–8,
    201–2
  in Druid community of
    practice   182–4, 187, 203–4
  environmental and
    sustainable   131, 188, 192–8,
    200–3
  right   148, 150, 155–7, 160–3,
    172–9
affect, see emotion
afterlife, see death
agency   74–6, 91, 110, 122–3, 132–4,
    138–9
  detection system   126–7, 142, 192
Alban Arthan   32, 130, 158–9
Alban Eilir   32, 165–6
Alban Elfed   32, 112
Alban Hefin   32, 91, 161–2
American Models of Mind and
    Nature   128–9
ancestors/ancestral   1, 27, 33, 35,
    44–5, 69, 71, 95–105, 119–21,
    124, 132–3, 152, 154, 156, 159,
    162, 164–5
  and gods   132–3
  homeland(s)   19, 22, 97
  mighty dead   101–2
  trauma and healing   21–3, 33, 65,
    98–100, 120–1
Ancient Order of Druids in American
    (AODA)   5, 9, 11, 14, 65, 75,
    86, 120, 126, 148, 156, 189–90,
    202

animal   40, 65, 83–8, 111, 125–7,
    135, 150–1, 153, 160, 164, 171,
    177, 191–2
  soul   30, 57
animism/animist   52, 62, 75–6, 78,
    80, 86, 123–4, 140, 151, 162,
    175, 186, 189, 192–3
  Druidic   124–8, 132, 141, 186,
    193–4
  evolution of   127–8
  indigenous   127–8, 137, 187–8,
    194–6, 204
  new   124
anthropomorphism   191–2, 198
archetypes   29, 108, 116, 131
Ár nDraíocht Féin (ADF)   5, 14, 65,
    71, 120, 148, 184, 190, 203
attentional focus   68, 71
autoethnography   7–12
awen   10, 12, 33, 68, 72–3, 119, 152,
    159

Bardic arts/bards   9–10, 13, 46–9, 63,
    72, 148, 160
belief   2–3, 13, 46, 53, 60–2, 77–80,
    100, 103, 111, 128, 132, 135,
    139, 141–3, 182, 197
  cognitively optimal   192
  in spirits   60, 74, 76, 107–10,
    123–7
Beltane   32, 34, 44–5, 108
biocentrism, see ecocentrism/
    ecocentric
biodiversity conservation   191, 203
biophilia   126, 192, 200
biospheric altruism   123

body   42–3, 47, 68
  positivity   64–5, 68–9
Book of Nature   66

capitalism   134, 178, 200, 203
Celticity   65, 98
Christo-centrism   2, 63, 72–3, 79, 86,
    133, 136, 140, 143, 168, 195
climate change   122, 157, 160, 178,
    185, 189, 201, 203
cognitive
  anthropology   55, 138–42
  attitudes   79
  dissonance   79, 162, 165, 178,
    197
  experiential self-theory (CEST)   78
  science of religion   55
  shift   130
collectivism   128, 198, 202
colonialism   21–2, 54, 65, 96, 98,
    121, 136, 165
community   119–21, 140
  of practice   143, 183–7, 202, 204
consciousness   59, 66, 77–8
  altered states of   40, 51, 53–61, 67,
    70, 72, 78, 88–9, 140, 142
  ecological (forms of)   125–6
  integration   68, 72, 130, 161
  shifting (states of)   33, 52, 68, 78
  theories of   59
  unconscious   55–7, 72, 125, 198
consumerism   135, 163, 195–200,
    202
  green consumption   198
conversion   62–4
countercultural movement   134–5,
    142, 165, 182, 185–7, 193, 196,
    203
creativity/creative   45, 68, 71–2, 110,
    153, 170, 180
  co-creativity/co-creative   11, 114,
    124, 128, 153, 156, 160
cultural
  appropriation   64–5
  modeling/models   139–42, 182,
    188, 195–8
  relativism   77, 128, 142
culture   138–42

dark green religion   125
death   2, 33–7, 43, 78, 99–103, 105,
    113, 116, 119, 125, 130, 162–4
deities, *see* gods
discernment   57, 73, 77, 148, 163,
    168
disenchantment   129
divination   119, 153–4
doctrine   3, 46, 58, 65, 76, 134, 136,
    140, 142, 192, 195
dream   10, 25, 30–2, 35, 39–40, 48,
    51, 106–7, 109, 112, 180–1
Druid(s)
  agnostic   14, 78–9, 109, 124, 134,
    142
  ancient   2, 5, 71, 73, 121
  animist/animism   124, 126–8, 132,
    162
  atheistic   75, 79, 109–10
  choice to become   64, 66
  community   74–5, 90, 96, 101,
    120, 135, 137, 140, 142, 168,
    182
  as counter-cultural
    movement   134–5
  cultural models   195–6, 201, 204
  definition of   4–5
  diversity in   3–4, 12, 14, 64, 66,
    110, 126, 132, 134, 141–2, 190,
    201–2
  ethics   192–200, 203
  ethnoecology   80, 157, 188–9, 195
  festivals (holidays)   31–2
  gathering   112–13, 148, 154, 156,
    160, 167, 176, 190, 198
  group   14, 32, 119, 167–8, 184,
    190
  hedge   5, 13, 184
  history   51–3, 121–2, 185–6
  identity   62, 75, 142
  and internet   185, 190, 204
  and jungian influence on   122,
    126, 130
  leadership   5, 46, 101, 140, 155–6,
    183–5, 201
  literature   13, 66, 109, 118–20,
    142, 155–6, 184, 189, 204
  localization   18–19, 69, 188, 203

magic 20, 122
mentors 9, 62, 73, 191
ontology 122, 127–8, 134
pantheist 109, 132, 175
peace prayer 166
polytheist 5, 14, 52, 75, 109, 111,
124, 131–2, 134, 141, 186
prayer 86, 124, 137, 148, 150,
160, 173
revival period 2, 5, 121, 148, 185
as role 186, 204
rural 123
solitary 2, 5, 13–14, 32, 37, 101,
118–20, 123, 168, 184, 204
study 72–3, 90, 148, 155–7
urban 18, 91–3, 123, 162
vocation 54, 117, 149, 186–7
vow 168–9
as way of life 100, 136, 180–1,
185
and work life 148–9, 184, 187,
199
Druidism (in contrast to Druidry) 4–
5
dualism (and critique of) 50–1, 53,
58, 61, 69, 72, 76, 80, 128–30,
132, 134, 136–8, 189, 201
dwelling and enskillment 188

earth, see nature
ecocentrism/ecocentric 59, 75, 80,
120, 122–3, 139–40, 143, 163,
172, 185, 188, 193, 200–4
ecology/ecological 18, 25, 73, 86,
90–1, 125–6, 150, 173–5
consciousness 125
deep 125, 194
of mind 122
spiritual 137, 141, 194
ecopsychology 63–4, 130
eisteddfod 48, 73, 112
elements 29–32, 108, 116, 119, 154
emotion 188–9, 191–204
empathy 10, 23, 64, 91, 116, 127–8,
150, 160, 162, 175, 178, 183,
194–5
environmentalism/environmental
stewardship 67, 78, 125, 185,
192–4, 196–8, 201

epistemology, see knowing/knowledge
esotericism 51, 53
ethics 10, 51, 126–8, 150, 163,
175–6, 192–6, 200–3
experience
anomalous 57, 61–3, 67, 70,
74–5, 140, 142, 204
from environment 67–9
source hypothesis 61
spiritual 1, 3, 7, 9–14, 50–6,
59–61, 66–7, 72–5, 78–9, 103,
110–11, 120, 125–6, 131–4,
142, 156, 185, 187, 189, 198,
201, 204
extended mind theory 59

fae/faeries 85, 107–10, 113–14, 131,
133–4
Fair Folk, see fae/faeries
faith frame 67, 133
flow state 72
folklore 5, 9, 65, 73, 79, 98, 109,
111, 128, 131, 134, 155, 185,
188–9
free will 114, 134, 136
Gaian spirituality 125
garden/gardening 69, 91–4, 130–1,
135, 147–9, 161–2, 177–8, 180,
199, 203
gods 29, 86, 103, 107–9, 111, 114,
119, 131–4
and animal forms 88, 111
as archetypes 131, 133
Belenus 108–9, 111–12
Brigid 11, 22, 52, 110–12, 159,
170–1, 179, 205
Ceridwen 29, 47, 63
Cernunnos 88, 115–16, 159,
167
co-creation with 114, 133
devotion to 113–17, 179
Elen of the Ways 116, 151, 167
Epona 84, 88, 114, 167
Lugh 32, 159
The Morrigan 44, 106, 113, 159
Tailtiu 32
Great Spirit 86, 107–8, 124
grief 23, 31, 34, 116, 130, 155, 171,
173–5, 178–9, 201

habitus   188, 191
healing   32–3, 41–2, 54, 71, 92,
    99–100, 108, 110, 117, 159–61,
    167, 169, 205
heritagization   189–90
homecoming narrative   62, 140,
    142
hope   178–9

imagination   25–6, 53, 57, 67, 71,
    128, 133–4, 167, 203
Imbolc   32, 110, 204
immanence   70, 79, 132
immigration   96–7
individualism   65–6, 128, 195–6, 198,
    201–3
information processing   78
initiation   31, 36–7, 41, 46–7, 51,
    63–4, 89, 112
interbeing/interconnection   42, 68–70,
    91, 124–6, 172, 179
interpretive drift   74–5

journaling   9, 11, 71, 73, 115, 152,
    191
Jungian
    collective unconscious   125
    influence on Druidry   122, 126,
        130
    shadow   130
justice   148, 150, 157, 160–1, 163,
    165, 174, 177, 201

knowing/knowledge
    and altered states of
        consciousness   60–1
    community of practice for
        building   183–4
    experiential   66, 92, 147–50,
        187–8, 191–2
    importance of   148, 190
    intellectual   150–1, 155
    intuitive/inspired   33, 61, 92,
        150–3, 180
    limitations in   76–9
    and love   172–3, 175–7
    and perception   69, 75
    relational   187–91
    and relationships   128, 163, 172–3

skill-building   72, 148, 182
spiritual   150–1, 155
study for   90, 155–7
ways of   52–3, 60–1, 75–6, 150–5,
    190
wisdom   89, 126, 148, 150, 157,
    165

Law of the Harvest   163
liminality   26–7, 29–33, 46–7, 88,
    104, 119–20
Local Ecological Knowledge
    (LEK)   187–9, 194, 202–3
love   86–7, 148, 150, 157, 160,
    169–73, 175–81
Lughnasadh   32, 167

magic   6, 22, 52–3, 122, 160
    and consciousness   26–7, 30, 33,
        51–2, 77–8, 122
    druid   20, 22, 67, 119, 122
magical/spiritual childhood
    narrative   62–3
material engagement theory   59
materialism   59–60, 136, 180, 189,
    192, 198, 203
meaning-making   68, 73–4, 77, 124,
    134
meditation   67–8, 166–7, 179
    breathing and sitting   41, 57, 119,
        167
    discursive   9, 11, 14, 68, 119, 156
    inner grove   25–6, 37, 41, 88,
        167
    light-body   41, 159
    visualization   9, 25, 41, 57, 68, 70,
        88, 119, 167
memory   11, 25, 75–6, 135, 185,
    202–3
methods/methodological   10–13, 66,
    74, 76–8, 119–20
Mighty Dead   101–2
mind, see consciousness
mindfulness   68–70, 130–1, 169
moral/morality   123, 125, 129, 139
    codes   191, 194–5
motivation   75–6, 160, 175, 188,
    192–201, 204
mutual care   92–4, 125, 167, 188, 192

mysticism 6, 12–13, 35, 40, 50–1, 70, 76–7, 106–7, 112, 115, 132, 134, 204
myth/mythology 31, 73, 98, 113–14, 119, 126, 134, 164, 189
  Arthurian 119
  Finn McCuill 126
  Mabinogion 119
  Taliesin 29–30, 47, 63, 126, 134

nature 69, 86, 124–7, 129–33, 135, 176, 200
  engagement in 68–9
  materialist orientation toward 120, 127, 129, 135
  obligations to 125, 200
  observation of 69, 87, 119
  personhood of 127, 191–2
  regimes 129
  spirits 74, 83–94, 103, 119, 123–4, 133
near death experience 30, 57, 125
neurodivergence 40–1, 103
norms 64, 66, 75, 136, 138, 182, 187, 196, 202
nudity (skyclad) 43–4
nwyfre 61

objectivity (challenges to) 7–8
offerings 27, 85, 110–11, 116, 120, 124, 154, 161–2, 190
Ogham 49, 52, 111, 119, 153–4, 189
ontology 122, 126–8
Order of Bards, Ovates, and Druids (OBOD) 5, 18, 29, 35–6, 46, 62–3, 65, 71, 75, 78, 86, 88–9, 101, 104, 120, 122, 126, 130, 135, 148, 152, 155–6, 160, 165, 168, 174, 189
orthodoxy/orthodoxic 1, 12, 58, 64, 75, 78, 110, 136–7, 140, 190, 192
orthopraxy/orthopraxic 1, 12, 58, 75, 110, 137, 140, 190
other-than-human beings/persons 86, 88–9, 91–3, 121, 126–8
  and transmigration of souls 103, 128
out of body experience 30, 57, 125

participatory consciousness/ participation 51, 53, 55, 77–8, 80, 139–42
peace 165–9
peak experience 61, 72
perception/perceptual 51, 60, 69, 72, 84, 127–8
  and belief 80
  ecological 75
  sensory 30, 69
  shift 74–5, 130
  skill 69
  training 67, 80, 140
persecution narratives 186
personal gnosis 13, 46, 71, 78, 90, 98, 108, 124, 134, 190
personhood 69, 86–7, 91, 93, 122–4, 127, 133, 191–2, 194
place
  ancestral connection to 97
  liminal 26–7, 119
  as persons 18, 121
  sacred 65, 119, 121–3, 129, 131, 191
  thin 26–7, 40, 109
  wild 130–1
play 77–8, 133
poetry 9, 11, 33–4, 46, 48, 71, 73, 107, 120, 148, 152, 160
polytheism 5, 109, 114, 124, 131–2
postmodernism 76–7
prayer 27, 44, 52, 57, 67, 105–6, 111, 114, 159, 162, 166, 179
  Druid's prayer 86, 124, 137, 148, 150, 160, 173
prehensions and affordances 188
present orientation 73, 124, 169
priming 123
psychopathology (in relationship to nature) 63–4, 185

queerness 45–6, 68

reality 58–60, 76–9, 124–5
reciprocity 19, 22–3, 27, 53, 87, 91–2, 108–9, 111, 132, 168, 172, 175, 183, 188, 190, 201, 204
reconstructionism 5, 189
re-enchantment 129, 135

reflection (practice of) 9–10, 12, 68–9, 72–3, 79, 100, 126, 131, 134, 187, 191
reincarnation 29, 34–6, 63, 96, 100, 103, 119, 163
  and pre-death experience 57
  and prior life experience 125
  and transmigration of souls 103
relational
  consciousness 66, 68
  ethics 128, 163, 175–6, 196, 200, 202, 204
  and evolutionary adaptation 127
  experience 57, 67, 75, 126, 197
  knowing 150, 187–91, 204
  ontology 126–8, 163, 204
  personhood 122–3
  self 9, 122
  worldview 75, 122, 127, 140, 143, 148, 150, 179, 181
relationship(s) 86–7, 90, 92, 102, 122–3, 125–6, 128, 132, 151, 172–3, 199
  right (or appropriate) 128, 132, 135, 160, 168, 171–3, 179, 187
religion
  as adaptive 192
  ancient 137, 186
  decentralized 2, 4, 80, 192
  defining 2, 79–80, 100, 135–43
  domains in 139
  as evolutionary byproduct 55, 76
religiosity, modes of 185
religious
  ecstasy 56, 58, 134
  identity 3, 100, 132, 141
revitalization movements 185
rightness, see justice
ritual
  and altered states of consciousness 56, 71, 142
  as art 46, 71
  and attentional focus 71
  and the body 47
  casting circle or sphere 120
  central rite 71, 120
  closing 71, 120
  and the dead 102
  divorce 104–5

dying 101–2
healing 99–100, 158–60
initiation 36–7
justice 160–1
liturgy 46, 71, 166
  and morality 191, 195
objects 71, 121, 199
opening 71, 120, 165
of passage 104
peacemaking 165–7, 201
space 47, 71
taboo 188, 191, 196
Wheel of the Year 31–2, 44, 69, 71, 119, 140, 202
rules of engagement 119

sacralization 73, 88, 91–2, 126, 130, 135, 194
sacredness of material world 121–3, 125, 129, 132
Samhain 32–4, 56, 102, 113, 130, 158
schema/schemata 69, 139–40
science (western) 76, 129, 188–9, 192, 195
self/selfhood 35–7, 40, 50–1, 56
  actualization 61, 161
  deep 11, 57, 130
  development of 55, 61–4, 122, 128, 135, 166–7, 172
  ecological 69
  interpersonal 69
  narrative/story 10–12, 64, 80
  and nature 126, 130, 194
  as process 58–9, 72, 124, 138
  relational 122–4, 172, 194
  transformation of 74, 163–4, 171, 179–80
  trifold 124–5
  wild 11, 14, 57, 61–3, 92, 129–30, 142, 162, 204–5
sexuality 43–6
shamanism/shamanic/shaman 14, 53–4, 76, 186–7
shape-shifting 29, 113, 126, 128, 133, 164, 180
shining ones 106–17
sidhe 60, 131, 133–4, see also fae/ faeries

skepticism   50, 58, 77–80, 125–6,
    142, 189–90
social sanctions   128
soul-journeying, *see* trance
spirit(s)   27, 57–9, 94, 107, 126
    ancestor   95–105, 119–21, 133
    evolutionary benefits of   192
    experience   57–60, 70, 76, 107–8,
        111, 134, 192
    guide   37, 161
    land   123–4, 162
    nature   74, 83–94, 103, 119,
        123–4, 133
    obligations to   91, 94, 126
    of place   18, 20, 22–3, 74, 94, 123
    relationships with   126, 134, 154
    shining ones   104, 106–17
    and theory of mind   126–7
spiritual
    contemplation   10, 68
    development   5, 87, 100–1, 111,
        114–15, 134, 148
    ecstasy (*see* religious, ecstasy)
    experience   1, 3, 7, 9–14, 50–6,
        59–61, 66–7, 72–5, 78–9, 103,
        110–11, 120, 125–6, 131–4,
        142, 156, 185, 187, 189, 198,
        201, 204
    kindling   67, 70, 142, 204
    knowing   150–1
    practice   5, 11, 13, 31, 67–73,
        77, 99, 108, 110–11, 115, 119,
        122–3, 129–31, 155–6, 175,
        178, 193, 201
    seeking   61–2, 75
story-telling   7–9, 71, 201
subject-object relationship   122–3

Summerlands   34–5, 101–3, 164,
    171
supernatural (and critique of)   51, 73,
    132–4, 139, 188, 191
sustainability   80, 91–2, 119, 127–30,
    160, 162–3, 173–82, 188–204
    american cultural models of
        196–8
    challenges to   176, 195–200
synchronicity   6, 68, 73, 156

Taliesin   29–30, 47, 63, 126, 134
text analysis   13, 67, 119–20
theology   5, 58, 132, 136
Theory of Mind   126–7, 142, 192
traditional ecological knowledge
        systems (TEK)   69, 80, 122,
        137, 187–91, 194–6, 202–3
trance   32–4, 41–2, 48, 51, 53–5, 63,
        67, 70–1, 108, 119
transcendence   37, 40, 76, 132
trees   26, 119, 131, 133, 174
    communication with   89–90
    as persons   85–6, 89
truth   78–9

unitary experience   51, 56–7, 61, 75
unverified personal gnosis (UPG), *see*
        personal gnosis

Wheel of the Year   31–2, 44, 69, 71,
        119, 140, 202
whiteness   99, 121
wildness/wilderness   19–20, 129–31
wild soul, *see* self/selfhood, wild
witchcraft   51, 53, 59, 71, 100, 122,
        134, 185–6, 195